Compliments of

BERNHARDT
WEALTH MANAGEMENT

7601 Lewinsville Road, Suite 210
McLean, VA 22102
(703) 356-4380
www.BernhardtWealth.com

Profiles in Success

Inspiration from Executive Leaders in the Washington D.C. Area

Volume 9

By Gordon J. Bernhardt, CPA, PFS, CFP®, AIF®

Copyright 2015 © Gordon J. Bernhardt, CPA, PFS, CFP®, AIF®

ISBN: 978-0-9849572-9-3

All rights reserved. No part of this publication may be reproduced, distributed, or transmitted in any form or by any means without the prior written permission of the publisher, except in the case of brief quotations embodied in critical reviews and certain noncommercial uses permitted by copyright law. For permission requests, or to obtain additional copies of this book for $29.99, contact the publisher below:

Gordon J. Bernhardt, CPA, PFS, CFP®, AIF®
7601 Lewinsville Road, Suite 210
McLean, VA 22102
(703) 356-4380
Toll-free: (888) 356-4380
www.BernhardtWealth.com

First edition – Volume 9

All profits from the sale of this book will be donated to a qualified charity, including but not limited to BEST Kids, Inc. (www.bestkids.org), YouthQuest Foundation (www.youthquestfoundation.org) and Network for Teaching Entrepreneurship (www.nfte.com).

Gordon Bernhardt conducts interviews of business leaders in the Washington D.C. area who come recommended by their peers. The enclosed profiles are a result of these interviews. As a result of these additional insights Mr. Bernhardt has published these case studies. Gordon Bernhardt is President/CEO of Bernhardt Wealth Management, a registered investment adviser with the Securities and Exchange Commission. Registration is mandatory for all persons meeting the definition of investment adviser and does not imply a certain level of skill or training. The business leaders may or may not be clients of Bernhardt Wealth Management. These interviews are independent of investment advisory services and do not imply any endorsement of Gordon Bernhardt or Bernhardt Wealth Management by the business leaders.

This book exists because of all the inspirational individuals who so graciously shared their stories with me. I am thankful for the opportunity to get to know each and every one of you.

To my team at Bernhardt Wealth Management—Tim Koehl, Solon Vlasto, Olivia Dewey, Trent White, Bonnie Armstrong, Kate Brodowski and Emily Burns—I would never have been able to do this without your efforts and support throughout the process.

I am deeply grateful to David Belden, Founder of ExecuVision International, and Peter Schwartz, Host of Executive Leaders D.C. and President of Peter Schwartz & Associates, for your help and encouragement on this project. Thank you.

And lastly, this book would not have been possible without the guidance and creative support of the Impact Communications team.

Contents

1	Foreword	85	Dalena Kanouse
3	Introduction	89	Grace L. Keenan
	Profiles in Success	93	Max Kryzhanovskiy
5	Wanda Alexis Alexander	97	Sylvia Lagerquist
9	Ian Altman	101	Rebecca Linder
13	Joseph Appelbaum	105	Carol J. Loftur-Thun
17	Alex Armour	109	Kimberly "Kymm" McCabe
21	Alex P. Bartholomaus	115	Sean McDermott
25	David Belden	119	Brendan McGinnis
29	Kathleen Benson	123	Carolyn Merek
33	Paul Boudrye	127	Sarah E. Nutter
37	Khari M. Brown	131	Bill Ploskina
41	Paula Calimafde	135	Dan Regard
45	Matt Curry	139	Carlos Rivera
49	Robert Dickman	143	Brian Roberts
53	Cameron Doolittle	147	Anita Samarth
57	Herbert S. Ezrin	151	Karin Schwartz
61	Jon Frederickson	155	Les Smolin
65	Steven Freidkin	159	Hildegarde M. Sylla
69	Wendy Gradison	163	Trenor Williams
73	Tom Guagliardi	*167*	From Gifford to Hickman *by Gloria J. Bernhardt*
77	Bill Jaffe		
81	Sid Jaffe		

Foreword

It is hard to believe that this is the ninth volume of *Profiles in Success*. For me, it is even more amazing to have been included in it. As you will read in this volume, most of these insightful interviews conducted by Gordon Bernhardt reveal that most successful business people did not start out with that as a goal. Many of us fell into the business world because we needed to earn a living. It was only after a lot of trial…and even more error… that we discovered the value of our chosen path.

Nearly every story addresses the deeper meaning behind the struggle towards creating a profitable business. The stories also address the question, "Why would anyone take the risk and accept the challenge of starting a business in the first place?" The answers are as unique as each of the individuals interviewed, and as universal as our individual search for meaning.

As founder of ExecuVision International, I have had the privilege of helping transform over 200 organizations on four continents. I have personally seen the difference that transformation can make in the lives of owners, executives, and employees when every single person is contributing at his or her highest level of ability.

As a former member and current Master Chair at Vistage, I have seen the benefits that an executive peer group, combined with individual coaching, can bring to business owners and CEOs. Gordon's sharing of this collection of stories has a similar effect. Yes, each story is unique, while they all share the common theme of overcoming hardship, enduring dark nights of doubt, risk, failure, perseverance, and finally, some semblance of success.

In today's business world, there is a fundamental question being asked. The question is who are more important, shareholders or stakeholders? Shareholders are the owners of the company. Stakeholders are anyone touched by the organization: owners, employees, customers, vendors, families, the surrounding community, etc. Clearly, the emphasis in this collection of companies is on stakeholders. As you will read, the shareholders often eat last.

And one more thing…when you read these stories, it is fascinating that so many of the subjects do not consider themselves successful. Here is a collection of high-achievers who mostly ignore what has gone before because they are constantly looking for the next challenge, the next opportunity to create something new and different.

What is also special about this edition is the wide range of generations, ages, experience, and variety of businesses. Even with all these differences, there are even more similarities. The people on these pages are similarly driven to achieve. Not driven in a negative, out-of-control way; driven in a considered, dedicated, determined way.

These are disciplined people consistently exercising good judgment and willingness to take risks. These are people accepting that, despite good judgment, not all these risks work out. There is an acceptance that failure is a part of success. The failure is still painful, but for the people in this volume, it was not devastating. It was a necessary part of the process.

In this volume, the ninth in an unending series, you will not meet a Bill Gates, Mark Zuckerberg, or Marissa Mayer. You will meet, instead, enterprising individuals from a wide variety of businesses – technology, retail, consulting, networking, philanthropy, expert testimony, etc. – all the facets of business that make up our world. What you will meet is an exceptional collection of stories about the everyday heroes who drive our economy, create jobs, and provide opportunities for other people to shine.

Enjoy!

David Belden
Founder
ExecuVision International
dbelden@iexecuvision.com

David Belden works with some of the most progressive companies in the world to create organizations where every member has the opportunity to achieve his or her highest potential. Through, *ExecuVision International*, a professional training and coaching firm, he has helped build teams that have exceeded all previous accomplishments while providing fulfilling and satisfying challenges for all participants. He also serves as a Vistage Master Chair, facilitating CEO and executive peer groups. With both ventures he has the opportunity to spend time with the younger generation joining the workforce in whom he has witnessed an eagerness to contribute at their highest ability.

Introduction

"Consult not your fears but your hopes and your dreams. Think not about your frustrations, but about your unfulfilled potential. Concern yourself not with what you tried and failed in, but with what it is still possible for you to do." – Pope John XXIII

There are as many different ways to lead people as there are leaders. The definitions and descriptions of leadership styles can range from rather simple to quite complex. But most often styles can be identified by how a leader relates to others, if and how they access the skills and expertise of others, and how they communicate. Some basic styles of leadership include: autocratic, consultative and democratic, among others such as bureaucratic, coaching or visionary.

There is no one correct style that fits all and typically a leader will need to employ various styles depending upon the situation. With much practice, a good leader is able to recognize when to use one style over another.

For example, an autocratic leader should almost always be the exception to the rule. This style is reserved for extreme emergencies such as during a crisis or when someone's safety is at risk. These types of situations call for quick decisions about what, where, when, why, how things are done, and who will do them. There's not time for collaborative input. While maintaining all decision-making power during such rare circumstances may be necessary and appropriate, an autocratic style on a long-term basis runs the inevitable risk of low morale, reduced productivity and ineffective leadership.

On the other hand, democratic leadership can be applied when there is time to deliberate and come to a consensus in which a majority vote binds the entire group to a final decision. This may work best when there is no need for central coordination – such as self-directed work teams.

Consultative leadership would actually move the team forward better when two or more individuals offer their input based on their unique expertise or experience, but ultimately the leader will assemble the collective contributions into appropriate action. Much like a football quarterback, a consultative leader's job is to direct his team toward the end goal. He calls the plays and must be prepared to change the play if it doesn't appear that it will succeed. Naturally, a consultative leadership style can be most effective when creative problem-solving and planning are involved.

What's the upshot? If you take one cup of democratic leadership, two cups of consultative with a dash of dictatorial "to taste," you will lead based on the need and in a way that advances and inspires those you are leading. Over time you'll have a winning recipe for long-term success with any team in your life.

Consultative

I have found that a consultative style has been particularly effective and essential in my life, not only as a small-business owner, but also an advisor to highly successful individuals and business leaders. In fact it is one of the six core characteristics – the "Six Cs" – that I believe are imperative for a trusted financial advisor to have: character, chemistry, caring, competence, cost-effective and consultative.

You may have discovered that some financial advisors tend to be more transactional than consultative, as they focus mostly on selling you products which they think you "need." However, a consultative advisor prefers to spend time listening to you, getting to know your hopes and your frustrations in order to work together to prepare a portfolio right for your needs.

Being consultative plays a primary role in my ability to build long-term client-advisor relationships. In my practice, that involves even more than working together with clients in an open and honest partnership to meet their goals. Just as importantly, we also work hand-in-hand with our clients' estate planning attorneys, accountants and other financial professionals. Our expansive professional network includes a talented team of trusted advisors who offer specific expertise and objective counsel when necessary.

Notably, our consultative approach isn't limited to professionals. Although many times one spouse functions as the point person when it comes to finances, it's imperative that both partners understand and participate in the management of the family finances. In fact, many of our clients broaden their family's involvement by bringing their children into the planning process. Even very young children can learn something about managing the household finances; and sharing the estate planning process with adult children can be especially fulfilling.

While there's no question that in today's complex environment you may require the expertise and counsel of a range of financial professionals, it's crucial that when you assemble such a team, you designate a quarterback or your personal chief financial officer. In fact, recent research from State Street Global Advisors and the Wharton School at the University of Pennsylvania found that many investors who work with multiple financial advisors without a lead advisor shoulder additional portfolio risk.

How so? Think about it. Without a consultative quarterback to foster communication and coordinate your financial plan, multiple advisors could cloud your financial picture. For example, without communication between advisors, overlapping exposures could create an unintentional overexposure to a single stock or asset class that increases your overall portfolio risk. Or, if you worked with two advisors and one underweighted small cap, while the other over weighted the asset class, you'd have an unintended market neutral exposure. Additionally, over time, your portfolio would be prone to style drift, or a critical need to rebalance might go unmet.

If you work with multiple financial professionals, I highly recommend designating someone to serve as your quarterback or personal chief financial officer who embraces a consultative leadership approach.

This volume of *Profiles in Success* features a diverse mix of executive leaders from our community who exercise just as many different leadership styles. While enjoying their personal stories consider the effectiveness of your own leadership style and what you could learn from these winning individuals.

Gordon J. Bernhardt,
CPA, PFS, CFP®, AIF®
President and Founder
Bernhardt Wealth Management, Inc.
www.BernhardtWealth.com

Since establishing his firm in 1994, Gordon Bernhardt has been focused on providing high-quality service and independent financial advice in order to help his clients make smart decisions about their money. He specializes in addressing the unique needs of successful professionals, entrepreneurs and retirees, as well as women in transition throughout the Washington, D.C. area. Over the years, Gordon has been sought out by numerous media outlets including MSN Money, CNN Money, Kiplinger and The New York Times for his insight into subjects related to personal finance.

Wanda Alexis Alexander

LADY OF THE YEAR

The auditorium filled with applause so thunderous that Wanda Alexander couldn't even hear her name as it was called. Her friend nudged her, and when she looked up, she saw that the high school tenth and eleventh graders were waving at her, the teachers in the bleachers were clapping, and her senior classmates were giving her a standing ovation. By the time she made her way to the podium, the swell of love had brought tears to her eyes.

That year, Wanda had quit the basketball and volleyball teams so she'd have time to work a job at the mall. She had gotten the job so she could afford new clothes, with the ultimate goal of winning Best Dressed when she graduated in June. Everyone voted, including the teachers. Much to Wanda's dismay, the Best Dressed award was given to someone else that night, but much to her surprise, she was given a different honor: Lady of the Year. "At the time, the meaning of the award didn't register for me," she remembers today. "Everyone saw me, except me. But I've grown up into her. I was always that lady; I just didn't know it. Now I get it."

Today, Wanda is the President and CEO of Horizon Consulting, Inc., a mortgage and real estate consulting firm with an expertise in single-family FHA loans, and through that leadership position, she works to empower others to see the good in themselves that might otherwise go overlooked. All those years ago, she never would have identified herself as Lady of the Year, but thanks to the insight imparted to her through classmates and teachers, she has become that lady. "Years ago, I had the great honor of meeting my lifelong hero, Maya Angelou," Wanda says. "She once said, 'There is no greater agony than bearing an untold story inside you.' My life's goal is to empower others to identify those internal stories so they can be told. To me, that's a crucial aspect of leadership."

Horizon was built from the ground up with this vision in mind. Wanda was running a multi-family division for a real estate company in the early 1990s, wielding her powers of negotiation through workouts on defaulted and foreclosed HUD-insured properties. Then, one day in 1993, a coworker, Stephen Coakley, took her out to lunch to ask if she'd go into business with him. "I asked if he was mistaking me for someone who didn't appreciate a check that clears every two weeks," she laughs. "The answer was no, but I was willing to help him."

Suddenly, at the end of 1993, tragedy struck a week before Christmas when three of Wanda's close friends were in a car accident. Two lost their lives, while the third lost 85 percent of the use of her legs. "It woke me up," Wanda avows. "I asked myself, what am I doing with my life? The stress of my job had begun to manifest itself physically, culminating in surgery that same December, and I was beginning to see why people say stress can kill you. Everything culminated in the realization that that wasn't how I wanted to live."

From the time she was a little girl, Wanda knew she'd work hard in life and earn a good living, but she never aspired to own her own company. When she began to explore her options, however, a headhunter told her she had what it took. "She had me sit down and figure out how much money I had earned for my previous company," Wanda recalls. "I had never thought about it that way. She saw things in me I didn't see at the time, and she saw me get excited when my perspective shifted and I realized what was possible."

Wanda ultimately agreed to join forces with Stephen on the condition that she purchases a majority interest in the firm, and that the company move from his basement to real office space. With that, Horizon sublet its first office in Reston, Virginia, and Wanda came on board in September of 1995. Over the next several years, they coined the phrase "high volume workflow management." In an industry where the backroom functions of the Federal Housing Administration (FHA) remain opaque, Wanda brought a nuanced understanding of the FHA single-family and multifamily products.

For years, Horizon's team on-site at HUD's home ownership centers reviewed every FHA loan application in the country to determine whether it got insured or rejected. "I know everyone says not to put all your eggs in one basket, but my plan from the beginning was to touch every single-family loan through our firm, and it's worked beautifully," Wanda affirms. "The diversifying comes with the other services we provide for single-family loans, like auditing and valuation appraisals."

Horizon began as a contractor, but as it brought more and more to the table, Wanda and her team raised themselves to consultants, and have advised on a number of HUD initiatives. Now, they've graduated to trusted advisor status, an honor that speaks directly to the highly conscientious attitude Wanda brings to her work. "I teach my team that every single loan they touch has a history and represents a family," she says. "One loan might represent an elderly couple who wants to live their lives out comfortably while still being able to afford their prescriptions. From the applicants, to the loan processor, to the underwriter, to the broker, so much energy goes into every single file. Every person who has processed a particular loan has impacted it, and my employees are some of the last people to touch it. That's sacred. At Horizon, we understand that we're all connected, and that we're here to serve one another."

Her professional philosophy draws directly from her faith, which took center stage the day her mother passed away from a heart attack when Wanda was 23. "Losing my mother moved the earth from under my feet," she remembers. "I don't believe that anything else has defined me more than that moment."

Wanda had been in graduate school in the months leading up to the unexpected death, but had left her apartment and resigned from her job in March at her mother's urging. Mrs. Alexander had asked Wanda to move home so she could concentrate on her classes full time. Wanda's two older sisters had married and moved away from the family's home in Prince George's County, Maryland. Her younger brother was a senior in college, and her younger sister was fifteen. "I'll never forget the way my sister's voice sounded on the phone when she called to tell me something was wrong with Mom, and that I needed to come to the hospital," Wanda recalls. "It was cloudy that day, but on the way there, I saw the sun come out. I had the sense of a voice saying, 'Your mother is with me.' I knew she was gone, and in that moment, I learned that God was real, and that we're all connected in this way we don't understand."

When her mother disappeared, Wanda stepped into her role without missing a beat, displaying the fearlessness that has been a hallmark of her character from the time she was a little girl. Born in Washington, D.C., Wanda's steadfast commitment to going after what she wanted in life was first demonstrated when she was three years old, playing with her older sisters out front of their apartment on I Street Northeast. Most children got excited when the ice cream man came to the neighborhood, but Wanda's true love was the balloon man. "Whenever I'd see those beautiful colors come into view down the street, I'd go crazy," she laughs. "Then one day, I disappeared. My mom had the entire neighborhood and the police department out looking for me."

Three neighborhoods away, a lady noticed a small girl trailing along behind the balloon man and called the police. Before long, a police car pulled up in front of the Alexander's house with Wanda in the backseat, balloon in hand. "I was fearless—I went after what I wanted, and I got it," she remembers.

It was that same fearlessness that compelled her to start skipping school when she was six years old—not because she was a bad child, but because the classes didn't stimulate her. Her older sisters were in a different wing of the school, and she'd wave at them through the window of their classroom. In first grade, she would convince her friend Gwen to accompany her down the road to a hot dog restaurant with spinning stools. "I never had any money, but I always got a hot dog," she muses. "There were always people looking out for me; I just didn't realize it at the time."

It was that same year that she got caught by her father, whom she idolized. Not wanting to disappoint him, she abandoned her roaming ways and committed to spending her school days at school. Then the family moved to Prince George's County, Maryland, and Wanda watched her all-black classroom transform into an all-white environment. "I had a lot of great experiences there, and I always had the feeling that I needed to prove myself, which was ultimately a good thing," she remarks today. "No one ever had to tell me to do my homework or study, because I wanted to be the best. I would notice the smartest people around me, and I'd focus my attention on them."

Through it all, Wanda dreamed of being in charge. She dreamed of excelling in a professional environment and earning promotions for hard work, someday living in a nice house and traveling the world. But she never framed this dream in terms of leadership, and easily overlooked the instances in her life where her leadership qualities shone through. When she was fourteen, she worked at a daycare, where she and the other interns were responsible for making sure children took naps and had their milk and cookies. Wanda naturally went into leadership mode, dividing the tasks among the interns and directing them as needed to conquer the challenge. Within a week, she was formally put in charge of managing her peers.

Even outside of work environments, she was the organizer at church and Sunday school, and was always trying to be in charge when playing with her siblings and friends. In class, she wasn't afraid to fight for justice, even if it meant standing up to a teacher who was picking on a student unfairly. "My parents always taught us that people see excellence, so we needed to operate in excellence," she remembers. "I never thought about leadership as a gift, and I never saw myself as a natural leader, but looking back, I realize that other people saw those things in me."

As Wanda made her way through high school, the administration had to design a whole new mathematics course curriculum because she was too smart for the classes they offered. She participated in Latin Club and the Yearbook Club, and she graduated a member of the National Honor Society. Neither of her parents had graduated from college, but they raised their children with the understanding that higher education would be an essential part of their future. "I never felt pressure; I just knew it would happen," she says. With that, she enrolled at the University of Maryland, planning to use her brilliance in numbers to earn an accounting degree.

But college, in all its glory, wasn't enough for Wanda. Even as she dove into the experience and relished it for all it had to offer, she was eager to get a leg up in the world through genuine work experience, landing a job first at the Department of Labor and then with the National Corporation for Housing Partnerships (NCHP). "I was living la vida loca—a social butterfly who was traveling to D.C. three days a week for work," she remembers. "I was President of the Sweetheart Club for the Phi Beta Sigma fraternity, earning the nickname 'The Godmother' because I was always there for people to talk to. At the time, I hated that name because it wasn't sexy, but looking back, it was another instance of my true self shining through."

With so much going on in her life, and with the inflated academic ego she had built up in high school, Wanda began picking and choosing which of her classes she would attend based on whether she liked the professor or the subject matter. She shouldn't have been surprised when, as a junior, she received a notice that she'd been kicked out due to academic probation from dropping classes at will but she was. At the advice of her mother, she set up a meeting with the Dean of the Business School, who she'd taken several classes with.

When Wanda walked into the room for the meeting, the Dean said he'd been waiting for her. He was happy to strike a bargain to readmit her to the university, and he posed a question to her that nobody else ever had. "For the first time in my life, someone looked me in the eye and asked me what I loved to do," she remembers. "I realized that I love to connect with people and help them find that 'Aha!' moment for themselves. I believe everybody is born good, without exception, but sometimes, life interferes and prevents them from seeing or feeling or believing that. I had a gift for listening to people to hear what they weren't saying, and to provide leadership to those in need. I had wanted to become an accountant because I was good at numbers, and because I would make a good living that way, but I realized that, at my core, that wasn't my life."

With renewed strength of spirit, Wanda earned her Bachelor of General Studies and began working on her master's, when her mother passed. Amidst the trauma of the loss, she continued her work at NCHP. She had planned to go to law school, but when NCHP created an Asset Management Division, she knew it was the place she needed to be. Though she was just an admin at the time, she approached the Executive VP of the new division, explaining her passion and interest in his work and how she saw it as the wave of the future. Her fearlessness again led her to actively move toward her objectives, and he agreed to take her on.

Despite her success at work, Wanda still had an important lesson to learn in her personal life before she could truly begin to heal from her mother's death. Always in salvation mode, she worked so hard making sure others were taken care of that she lost herself. "Whenever anyone needed anything, I'd jump to the rescue," she recalls. "I'd make sure all the bills were paid, and all the needs were met, but I was abandoning myself. Finally, I realized it was not my responsibility to save people, but to serve them."

From that moment on, Wanda used that breakthrough to fully embrace a life of servant leadership, empowering herself to empower others. Focusing on Horizon's core principles of honesty, integrity, hard work, and professionalism, it's the legacy she shapes every day through her firm, and it's the foundation of Wanda Alexis Alexander, LLC, a new platform through which she did twelve speaking engagements in 2013. "I get absolute and total joy out of creating things and helping others," she avows. "At the end of the day, being a CEO and building a company has allowed me to pursue my true passion, which is serving, training, coaching, and creating with others. We've built Horizon into a company of excellence, and I'm truly proud of the impact my employees and I are able to have on others, and each other."

Horizon was recognized by the Inc. 500, which Wanda certainly counts as an accomplishment, but she was far more humbled when she was named the Loudon County Business Woman of the Year in 2005. "That was amazing because I typically fly under the radar, but a lot of people in my life wrote in to the Loudon County Board of Supervisors and a woman's group to let them know that I was doing good work," she says. "It had a tremendous impact on me, both for the support of my friends and colleagues, and for recognizing my role in how far women have come over the last generation. When I was young, my mother's credit card had my father's name on it. We're so empowered now, and I'm honored to continue fighting for women's empowerment in the workplace." Wanda has also been honored through a Distinguished Alumni Award from the University of Maryland—a powerful testament to her parents' unyielding belief in their children's education.

In advising young people entering the working world today, Wanda reminds us all that, no matter our circumstances or our trials, our lives are on purpose, and our lives matter. It's the belief that compels her employees to see the tremendous meaning and honor in each day of their work, and it's the outlook that has shepherded her through good times and bad.

Above all else, however, Wanda's story is about the power of seeing in others what they can't see in themselves, and in turn trusting that others can see in you what you, yourself, haven't seen yet. If she has been able to dedicate her life to seeing the promise and potential in those around her, it's because her high school class was able to see the depth underneath her carefully-selected outfit. It's because her college classmates were able to see her character based in faith and family, rather than her more mischievous exterior. It's because her parents, teachers, coworkers, and friends didn't always see disobedience and bad behavior, but instead a spirited and fearless young lady who faced the world head on. And it's because Maya Angelou, in their brief meeting, took both her hands, looked her in the eyes, and said, "My God, girl, you're beautiful. I'm not talking about out here—I'm talking about in there."

Ian Altman

The Dynamics of Success

After knocking on three different doors and having three successful experiences, eleven-year-old Ian Altman was feeling elated. His baseball team had given each player a set of raffle tickets to sell that included coupons for $1 off every $2 spent at a popular local pizza place. The prize for most tickets sold was a new bike, and Ian was determined. It was his first attempt at sales, and after being greeted warmly by the first several houses he tried, his confidence was soaring.

When the door of the fourth house opened, he gave his winning smile and began presenting his objectives, when he was abruptly cut off. "We don't want any!" the man in the doorframe grumbled, promptly slamming the door in Ian's face.

Shock and the sting of rejection swept over him in equal parts, and he ran home in tears, swearing off the contest and giving up on his dream of winning the bike. His mother, however, lent some constructive comfort. Pointing out that three of the four attempts had been successful, she asked him to take a step back from the effect to examine the cause. "Why do you think those people didn't buy it?" she asked. "Maybe they don't eat pizza. If they don't, it wouldn't make sense for them."

It was the first time Ian had taken a critical lens to the science and art of sales. He began selling raffle tickets again, but more thoughtfully. Then, several days later, he was walking past the house that had broken his spirit that first day, when he noticed several pizza boxes in their trashcan.

Facing his fear, he marched up to the door and knocked. A woman answered, and he tried a different approach. "I noticed you have pizza boxes outside," he said. "With each raffle ticket you buy to support the baseball league, you get a coupon you can use to get $2 off for each $1 ticket. One of the other neighbors said they'd be a fool not to buy a bunch of them, unless they didn't eat pizza. So how many would you like?"

As the woman handed him a $20 bill to buy a book of twenty tickets, Ian understood that selling is so much more than making an ask and hoping for a positive outcome—it's about tapping into why something matters to a person. "Making that connection was key for me, and it's stuck with me ever since," Ian says today. Now the founder, President, and CEO of Grow My Revenue, LLC, he has built a career out of reconstituting the seller-buyer relationship and re-conceptualizing of what it means to enrich another's life through sales. "I work with people to help them step back and say, 'What's the biggest problem people face that I'm good at solving?'" he explains. "By taking this approach, you never feel like you're selling—you're providing a much-needed service to people. Through a focus on perspective and attitude, we improve the buyer-seller dynamic, leading to real and sustainable success for our clients."

Ian launched Grow My Revenue, a consulting firm specializing in helping clients target and win business by tackling their toughest sales challenges, in 2010. In this capacity, he ensures his clients focus on the right strategic accounts for growth, and that they understand how people make purchasing decisions. He helps clients frame themselves not as salespeople, but as trusted advisors. Many of these tenets are reflected in his first book, published in 2012 and titled *Upside Down Selling: An Integrity-Based Sales Approach to Avoid Being Predictable*. Aimed at helping leaders engage their non-sales employees in the growth of their business, he drew on case studies of companies that doubled their growth rate by pursuing 40 percent fewer opportunities while strengthening their sales team. "Integral to our philosophy is the idea of working smarter, not harder," he points out. "If a client has a great product or service, the key to revenue growth is oftentimes just getting that message out to the right people."

Today, Ian works on strategic growth initiatives with a maximum of six companies per quarter. He aims to impart new skills and evolve clients to a state of independence within two quarters—the general timeframe for results to become evident. Seeing best results in the business/professional services and technology sectors, he notes that the client must be willing to put in the work to change. "It has to be a priority for them," he says. "Adding value is important to me, and if I'm not confident we can achieve results, then I don't want to be involved. The simple lesson is that if you're selling to a market that doesn't see the value in what you do, go sell somewhere else. Helping clients do that is my life's calling, and it's a practice I live by myself."

Thanks to his integrity- and outcomes-based approach to business, Ian is invited to deliver keynote addresses all over the globe. He works with CEO coaching organizations like Vistage International, and with leadership groups like the Entrepreneurs' Organization. He's a seasoned speaker, at home before crowds of 20 or 2,000, and hosts workshops for companies hoping to shorten their sales cycles or shift the focus of their customers from price to value. To supplement these efforts, Ian partners with other highly respected experts to host the Remarkable Growth Experience twice a year, limiting attendance to a hundred people. "We call it an 'experience' instead of calling it an 'event' or 'conference.' Eighty-six percent of attendees report that it's the single best event they've ever attended," he says. "We get emails to secure spots even before we've announced the time or place of the event. It's great that we've been able to team up with the right people and deliver an experience that's so effective."

Effective design and sales was a cornerstone of his childhood growing up in Southern California as the youngest of four. His father ran manufacturing in the garment industry, managing huge factories for companies like White Stag, as well as more refined women's boutique operations. "My mother had the tougher job in raising all of us," he laughs. "On top of that, she volunteered for everything, serving as President of the Homeowners Association and the PTA. I ended up inheriting that gene from her—I always join organizations intending to be a member, but invariably taking on leadership roles."

As a boy, Ian was a natural attention magnet, so much so that he caught the eye of a child talent manager while out to dinner with his family when he was eight years old. When the woman came over and told his parents he would be great as a child actor, Ian thought she meant 'acrobat.' "I thought, how cool will this be!" he laughs. "When we went in for the first interview, I remember thinking, 'Where's the trapeze?'"

Ian soon became a seasoned pro, acting in over fifty commercials for national companies like Mattel Toys and McDonalds, and even winning several parts for television and film. He'd land one gig for every five auditions—an exceptional hit ratio for the industry, but a healthy lesson in hard work and rejection for a young boy. On the days he had to miss school for acting, a tutor was provided on-set to make sure he kept up with his studies. All the while, he played sports and lived a normal childhood in the San Fernando Valley of Los Angeles.

Ian retired from acting at age 15 and invested his time in starting a band during his junior year of high school. They sent demo tapes to studios all over town, and as he was graduating from high school, they received word that one label wanted to have them record some songs in the studio and potentially sign them. "I turned it down, though, because I was heading to college and saw music as a hobby, not a career. Who knows?" he says. "Acting and music were fun, but they weren't what I wanted to do professionally." Rather, Ian wanted to become a doctor. When he started college at UC San Diego, he jumped on the pre-med track but found that he hated chemistry. He asked the guidance counselor how much chemistry he would have to take between then and completing medical school. The counselor said, "All of it." Ian replied, "What other majors do you have?" He graduated with a degree in Quantitative Economics and Decision Science.

Ian wanted to stay involved in baseball in college, but he had torn his rotator cuff, so playing wasn't an option. Taking the opportunity to reconstitute the possible, he teamed up with a physical education teacher at the university who taught umpiring, and who showed Ian that anything is possible—you just have to figure out how to do it. "I learned that the umpire organization in San Diego produces more major league umpires than any other North American association, by a landslide," he says. "I learned how to umpire, which in some ways is about resilience, given that it's a relatively thankless role. But I really enjoyed it, being in college and umpiring Division I college baseball. Because of my age, I had to get approval from both teams before each game, and there I was—umpiring alongside college kids my own age."

Ian was told time and again that he should go pro, but he remained resolutely focused on developing a more stable, long-term profession. The summer after his freshman year, he got a job as an assistant selling microfilm services to law firms. He saw tremendous flaws in the sales approach of his superior, so he sought permission to try again with prospects that had previously said no. He ended up reversing a large number of previous rejections, and by the end of the summer, the CEO named him the Western Area Director.

Ian had achieved a nearly perfect GPA his freshman year, but his focus shifted dramatically as he sought to pragmatically balance academics with his new position. He was fully engaged in classes like Decision Theory, which he saw tremendous value in, but then flippantly dismissive about others like Labor Economics, which seemed to be based on unfounded and nonsensical assumptions.

Oftentimes, he would ace the first midterm and then check out for the rest of the semester, averaging out to a C. "I was audacious enough to ask professors to set up alternate times for me to take tests if I had prior work engagements, like a trade show in Chicago," he recalls. "As if that wasn't a big ask! But there were benefits for the educators as well. They wanted to see if their material actually applied to the real world, so I'd do internships with them and put it into practice in the workplace. Bridging that gap between academia and real world business environments in that way was invaluable."

When Ian finished with school, he continued his professional stint with the same company, helping to design software that could perform character recognition from scanned document images. He was surpassing his performance plan, yet the company itself was faltering, and when the owner said they'd have to reduce his compensation, he decided to leave the company. When a partnering firm from Washington, D.C. heard of the change, they promptly contacted Ian to hire him as a consultant for a trade show, and then brought him in to meet with the CEO for an interview. When Ian laid out his salary demands, the CEO pointed out that that was a lot for someone his age. "When you decided to hire me for the trade show, I'm sure my age never entered the conversation," Ian said boldly. "Either this makes sense, or it doesn't."

The company decided it did, in fact, make sense, and Ian landed the position and the salary he deemed appropriate. He worked there for several years before leaving in 1993 to start his first company, ITM Associates. Focused on applying technology to solve business challenges, the company was fairly novel at the time. Their first client was one of the top pharmaceutical companies in the world, who was looking for ways to speed up FDA approval of new drugs. "All the other firms vying for the project were focused on finding ways to force the FDA to change," Ian explains. "Instead, we asked the company how long it took them to get their own documents to the FDA. It turned out there was considerable lag time on their end as well—about a year. We proposed that the company focus resources to shorten its own review time, providing a basis to convince FDA reviewers that it would make their time more efficient as well."

Ian's approach succeeded in saving the company an average of 23 review days per submission, and at 11 submissions per year, the value added translated to a quarter of a billion dollars in annual savings for the pharmaceutical company. That victory drew the attention of major insurance companies and other new clients, and by 1998, ITM was named a "Fast 50" company in the Washington, D.C. area by Washington Technology. They created a software solution that engendered its own company, and both businesses were sold to an investment banking group, BTI, in 2005. Ian was asked to stay on and run the enterprise, raising the value of the 4 million privately-held outstanding shares from $25 per share to $500 in just over three years. The company grew from $100 million to $2 billion in value and underwent an international expansion to twelve countries, including China and India. "I was flying 175,000 miles a year doing joint ventures all over the world, meeting with the Secretary of State in one country or the Secretary of Interior in another," he remembers. "They were all just clients with a need, from anti-counterfeiting to fraud prevention."

Through it all, his wife, Deborah, was the rock of the family. The two had met seven years out of college, and her pragmatic and grounded approach to life was a perfect balance to his passion for growing businesses. As he flew around the world building a company, she handled the day-to-day of raising their children and keeping the household intact while balancing her career in physical therapy. "She's a source of calm and support for me, and she's amazing with our kids," Ian avows. "She has all the patience in the world and doesn't take things too seriously. I'm really lucky to have her."

Ian remembers fondly the power players he worked with and the incredible individuals he had the opportunity to lead and support, but by 2008, he felt he was no longer building something—just going through the motions. With that, he left the company and assumed the presidency of a country club, allowing him to play golf and spend quality time with his family while doing pro bono consulting work for struggling businesses. He was ultimately named one of the top 21 country club presidents in the world by *Boardroom Magazine* and was hailed for his transformative leadership, but to him, it was more about building something. "My focus was on creating memories for my family and thinking about what I wanted to do next," he recalls. "I didn't want to rush into anything. Then, I realized that, whenever someone came to me with a business challenge, I was inclined to drop whatever I was doing to help them achieve a state of growth. It was what I truly loved to do—things that many people view as challenging, but I view as easy and fun. With that, I started Grow My Revenue and began helping people translate their companies into beacons that truly capture their ideal clients' attention."

In advising young people entering the working world today, Ian highlights the importance pursuing work because it's one's passion, and not due to the pressure of others. "If you thoroughly enjoy your work, it won't feel like work," he says. "Learn from people who do it well, and never do something that doesn't resonate with your own sense of integrity. And, in interviews, ask about the characteristics that make people succeed or fail in the position under consideration, and whether the interviewer thinks you have those skills. That method of engagement is sure to set you apart."

The suggestion, a microcosm of his business and life philosophy as whole, shows how taking the time to redraw the lines of any given situation can transform the dynamics at hand, leading to more genuine connections and more successful outcomes. The idea is a central point in his most recent book, *Same Side Selling: A Radical Approach to Break through Sales Barriers*. By re-conceptualizing of the line between buyer and seller, the approach turns confrontation into cooperation and seats people on the same side of the table, instead of across from one another. "If you push, you create resistance," he says. "If you create interest and then give space, the right people will come to you. In many ways, sales is the purest form of leadership—it's about trusting and respecting people, feeling the energy of a room or organization, communicating it, building consensus, and getting people aligned on a common vision. In business, in family, and in life, so many of the challenges we face can be overcome through an attitude flip, a perspective rotation, and a slight but profound adjustment to the dynamics at work."

Joseph Appelbaum

Windows of Opportunity

Driving his youngest son to college with his older son in the car, Joe Appelbaum looked at the open road outside the car window and spoke to his boys about opportunity. "Work as hard as you can, but not to make me proud," he said. "Make yourselves proud. If you can make yourself proud in everything you do in life, you'll be happy. Look for every opportunity and know it's a window to your own happiness."

Joe realized his own first window of opportunity, quite literally, in windows. He was only twelve years old when his mother approached him with a simple proposal that would change his life. She asked him to wash the double-hung windows of their suburban colonial home in New Jersey for $2 each. As Joe calculated the house's twenty windows, he realized this would earn him $40—not bad for a young boy growing up in the 1970s. Joe quickly accepted his mother's offer.

As he completed the task over the next two days, he got to thinking. "If I made $20 a day and worked six days a week, I could make $120 a week," he recalls now. "But if I hired someone else and paid them half of what I made, I could make $180 a week." With that, Joe started Joe's Window Washing Service, and by the time he was 18, he was making $1,000 a week after expenses. "That experience showed me that I could do anything," he says. "My mother gave me a simple task and I turned it into a business, and an industry. It taught me that there are windows of opportunity everywhere—you just have to be willing to pay attention and take action."

Now the President and founder of Potomac Companies, Inc., an employee benefits consulting practice ranked in the top ten in the mid-Atlantic region, Joe's entrepreneurial spirit and business efforts are defined by this philosophy of continual growth. "I learn something every single day," he says. "I take everything I see and experience and put it back into life and business. I take every opportunity to listen, learn, and apply."

With clients nationwide, Potomac Companies specializes in Helping Employers Manage the Future Cost of Health Care® by establishing, informing, and maintaining employee benefit plans. As this entails human capital costs, their work goes hand in hand with improving the productivity, health, and happiness of a company's employee base. When Potomac Companies was first launched, its work focused on copays and deductibles. Today, that focus has expanded to include the attrition rates and profitability aspects associated with an organization's human capital.

"We're about so much more than just insurance," Joe affirms. "If a client only wants us to manage their benefits and get them the best deal, then we do that. But we really love when a client wants to take full advantage of our expertise to learn how to improve the productivity and happiness factor of their employees. With this in mind, our company is evolving to create and accommodate total engagements with clients. We consult and coach our clients on instituting wellness programs by providing ideas, and helping bring in the right staff and most suitable vendors. Our goal is to control costs and integrate those services and solutions into each client's unique culture to ensure ongoing success."

Joe started in the insurance business on April 1, 1985, and launched Potomac Companies five years later when he realized there was a better way to serve clients. "I didn't want to be operating like a large insurance company," he recalls. "I didn't want to be forced to push a particular product from a particular carrier if it wasn't in the best interest of an individual client or company. We're all different people, and we require different care. I founded Potomac Companies so that I could offer independent, client-centric service that takes the individual needs of each company into account." This fiduciary focus is being cemented as the company changes from a commission-based to a fee-based practice, augmenting its evolution to address broad shifts in the health care space as the Affordable Care Act pushes the national mindset away from crisis management and towards prevention.

Joe's entrepreneurial spirit and the philosophy behind his work were instilled by his parents during his childhood. His father was a partner at a paper company that operated in New York and New Jersey. He would calculate, without computers, how to best slice and dice each massive roll of paper for newspapers, magazines, and publishers. His mother, who went back to work after the children went to school, worked as a paralegal and opened her own store with a friend.

As the oldest of three children, Joe worked a paper route and loved playing sports. He also got involved in local walkathons as a child, raising money for charity. He went into his father's office asking for donations and then went door-to-door along his paper route. In his first year, Joe raised more money than anyone in the state. "As a kid, there was glory in winning anything at all," he laughs, looking back. "But each year, I wanted to do better than the last year, and it felt good knowing it was all going to a good cause." Throughout his teenage years, Joe was the highest-sponsored participant in all of New Jersey, and today, he continues in this lifelong tradition of philanthropy by giving to the Brain Tumor Society and the Leukemia and Lymphoma Society.

Joe was a decent student who truly excelled when the material interested him, but he was far more excited about running his lucrative window washing business. In the summers, he worked six days a week, and if it rained, he'd work an extra day to make up for it. In the winters, he would clear a neighbor's driveway with a snow blower, and in exchange for his labor, he was given free rein to use the machine elsewhere. Anytime a big snowstorm hit New Jersey, Joe was out working from dawn to dusk. It was in those backbreaking days that the steel of his work ethic was forged.

Even with his incredible commitment to entrepreneurialism and fundraising for charity, Joe found time to play music and even considered pursuing it full-time after graduating high school. He dreamed of starting a band, but when his parents said they would either pay for instruments or for college, he decided education was the more pragmatic route. Joe chose college and was admitted to Carnegie Melon. He worked hard his first semester, but a severe case of mononucleosis set him far behind his peers. He ended up transferring to Rutgers University, where he discovered a fresh start and a newfound interest in economics. Still, school felt like a hiatus from his real love—business. "I broke out in hives every time I passed the library," he recalls. "The only thing I was thinking about was *not* being in school. I wanted to be out in the world, doing and building things."

Joe filled this need through Joe's Window Washing Service, which he ran until he was 23. Once he finished college and set his sights on broader horizons, he sold the business to his younger brother, who worked it through his own college career and later sold it to their neighbors. Those neighbors ran it through college as well, eventually moving to California and relocating the business. They continue to operate it today.

As fate would have it, window washing proved to be a window into opportunities beyond Joe's Window Washing Service, and into other industries. One day, Joe happened to wash windows for the Senior Vice President of Russ Berrie and Company, now known as Kid Brands, Inc. The man was so impressed with his accomplishments that he insisted Joe come work for him, marking his first job out of college. "I was selling little stuffed animals and novelty items to pharmacies and toy stores," Joe remembers. "It was the most boring job I ever had, so I aimed higher."

With that, Joe went on to interview for sales positions at 42 different companies, and was offered 40 of those positions over the course of several months. By this time, however, he had learned to be selective. When asked in interviews if he had any questions, Joe developed a short list that he would pose to each employer to gauge whether or not it was the job for him. First, he asked if he would be assigned a territory, and what his base salary would be. He then asked what the top seller was making. Oftentimes, he found he would be restricted to a certain geographic area determined by the employer, and that the highest-paid salespeople were making less than he made in his window washing business. "Most of the companies had specific limits to how much I could succeed, without open-ended possibilities," Joe explains. "I knew those situations weren't right for me. I didn't want any restrictions."

When Joe posed these questions in an interview with Equitable Life Insurance Company, however, it was a different story. His territory would be the entire United States, and the top seller at the company had made $386,000 the previous year. Furthermore, the top seller in all of Equitable Life had made $22 million the previous year. Joe's next question was, "When do I start?"

Joe began his tenure at the company making phone calls. But by his third week on the job, his manager asked him to attend a meeting in his place at the Equitable Life headquarters. In a discussion about the company's large group product, Joe sat amongst the managers that had been working in the business for decades and were at the pinnacle of their careers. "That was another profound window of opportunity, and I was eager to learn," he says. "I absorbed everything that was said that day and the next day, I started calling big businesses and got a meeting with Pepsi to show them our products. I realized that, to some extent, anyone can get an appointment with anybody. I accomplished that without a title or a reputation."

Through this experience, Joe began talking to business owners and realized that, on his own and outside the confines of the company, he would have more leeway to sell products and services that brought the most value to his customers. With the vision of starting a one-stop shop that would have a client's best interests at heart, he started Potomac Companies. Through the past three decades, his clients have remained steadfastly loyal, proclaiming it the best employee benefit brokerage and consulting firm in the area. "I do what I do because it allows me to help people," Joe affirms. "It helps people protect their families, and it's my way of changing peoples' lives for the better."

Joe is perhaps best equipped to change other peoples' lives for the better because his was so profoundly and positively changed in 2004. He was sitting alone at a bar, reading a 401(k) manual and drinking a cosmopolitan. "This beautiful woman in a red leather jacket and black slacks came in with her friend, and it was like I was hit over the head with a sledgehammer," he laughs. "Her name was Pam, and we got married the following year. Since that time, I've been so thankful for the joy in my life. The happiness factor is vital to success, and our marriage is a stable balance to the ups and downs that come with each month." Having grown up exposed to her family's restaurant business, and now with a real estate business of her own, Pam has incredibly intuitive advice when it comes to people and the unforeseen obstacles that are vital to personal and business growth.

Over the years, and with Pam by his side, Joe has grown from a fly-by-the-seat-of-your-pants business owner, with no road map and no mentor, into a seasoned entrepreneur who keeps his team streamlined and energized by focusing on the company's vision. "It used to be that people came in, worked, and got paid, but didn't have a clear trajectory," he recalls. "Now, it's about what we're building together. Everyone knows the collective goals and what they need to do to achieve them. I'm engaged, asking the right questions, and constantly thinking of ways to improve."

In advising young people entering the working world today, Joe emphasizes the importance of relationships. "Knowledge is kept once it's gained, but relationships aren't done deals once they're formed," he says. "They can be lost if you don't nurture them and make them strong. Focus on growing them, as they will enrich you personally and professionally."

He was living and breathing this advice that day he drove his son to college, treating that moment in time as an important rite of passage and an opportunity to strengthen the bonds of family. It's how he approaches all moments—as opportunities to enrich and deepen one's identity and experience—and the key to building character and expertise from moment to moment. "Every opportunity and every interaction you have, every time you learn or get exposed to something new, contains information that you can build on for the future," he says. "Take each nugget and use it somewhere. Embrace it, store it, pull it back out later on, perfect it, and make it your own. That's how you build you."

BERNHARDT
WEALTH MANAGEMENT

Alex Armour

Perseverance to Burn

In the quiet of early morning, as the summer sun inched its way above the horizon, Alex Armour and his grandfather prepared for another day of hard work. As their neighbors slept, the young man and the old man gassed up their mowers and then set off for the hills. The air, thick with fuel and heat, filled their lungs and cloaked their senses as the two worked for hours on end. By the day's close, after the lawns of their small town in Arkansas were manicured to perfection, Alex and his grandfather would take a quick rest before dawn compelled them to start all over again.

For a teenager like Alex, mowing lawns was tough, but the freedom associated with the pocket money he earned was enough incentive to take on the job every summer until he graduated from high school. Fortunately, manual labor was a choice as opposed to a way of life for Alex, a fact which drew an invisible line between himself and his grandfather. Prior to mowing lawns for a living, Alex's grandfather worked a backbreaking job on the railroad, a career ripe with physical hardships that far eclipsed those of landscaping. A father figure and moral anchor to his grandson, he urged Alex to diligently pursue an education so he could avoid the consequences of manual labor. "My grandfather would always say, 'Make sure you get into those books so you don't end up doing the work I have to do,'" Alex remembers.

Now the President and cofounder of Offspring Solutions, a technology consulting firm, Alex has exceeded his grandfather's expectations while continuing to defy the barriers of classism. He credits his ability to persevere, a characteristic he gleaned from his grandfather, as to why he's now so successful and how he was able to start his own business. "Whenever I decide that I want to get something done, it's going to get done, period," Alex affirms. "If I'm 100 percent sure about anything in this universe, it's that I have perseverance to burn."

Offspring Solutions, now almost ten years old, is the product of Alex's desire to create something out of nothing and to bring innovative solutions to government and commercial customers. Originally founded with four employees, the team has now grown to 43 people and has expanded its offices to Virginia and Georgia. Alex credits the rapid development of Offspring Solutions to its group of experienced professionals dedicated to providing premier services in application modernization, data analytics, infrastructure modernization, and project management (PMO) services. From project and program management all the way to predictive analytics, Offspring Solutions has the capabilities to achieve its clients' organizational and business goals.

Currently, due to the company's specialization in analytics, Offspring Solutions primarily serves government agencies like the Department of Health and Human Services and the U.S. Department of Homeland Security. While the company could easily continue to focus its service on the government sector, Alex has grand plans for the future and for the expansion of Offspring Solutions. "I intend to generate half of our revenue from the federal sector and the other half from the commercial sector," he says. "The company just moved into new office spaces, and we're working quite hard to accelerate the growth of our commercial side."

While the expansion of Offspring Solutions will require a great deal of work, Alex is more than prepared to take on the job thanks to his tenacious and enterprising nature. Growing up in a modest small town in Arkansas, he always knew he would have to differentiate himself if he wished to reach great heights. "I leveraged the demanding work of mowing lawns into being better at sports," he recalls. "Once I recognized that my work ethic was higher than most and that I was better than most of my peers athletically, I knew athletics could allow me the opportunity to move on from my small town environment."

Naturally talented at football, Alex was the number two running back in Arkansas his junior year of high school and helped lead his team to many victories, including a 1986 state championship game. "I'll never forget the first touchdown I scored as a running back," he muses. "It's amazing to me that, as a 43-year-old man, I can still remember that moment running down the field as a nine-year-old. Kids have those seminal moments that truly boost their self-confidence, and that was mine." As fate would have it, however, an ankle injury in high school cut his impressive career short. No longer the football star of his church-going and close-knit community, Alex went through a period of angst and confusion about his personal and professional future post-injury. The life altering experience, however, illustrated to him the value and necessity of a college education. While he credits sports as a confidence builder and an excellent crash course in leadership, he would no longer view athletics as a top priority. "Sports could be your way out, but it shouldn't be considered a primary way of life for the vast majority of athletes," he explains. "Today, it's still very difficult for me to operate at a high level when I know someone else is controlling my destiny." It's a lesson Alex also tries to impress on his young son, Amari, a budding football star. "Just this past week, Amari received the highest grade in his class on a fraction test, and it made me exceptionally proud," he remembers. "I said, 'This is worth 500 touchdowns.'"

Shortly after Alex's discontinuation from high school football, the calls from the military academies poured in—a windfall which brought him renewed hope. The academies offered an excellent education, an opportunity to serve the country, and the opportunity to play Division I football. This was a combination Alex couldn't resist. Never one to give up in the face of adversity or shy away from a new adventure, Alex decided to attend the U.S. Air Force Academy. The move not only cemented his desire to get serious about his future, but it also pleased his grandfather and mother, two people who had always championed the pursuit of a post-secondary education. His post-high school plans also allowed him the opportunity to pursue business seriously, a desire he realized a few years after mowing lawns with his grandfather. "At the end of each day, my grandfather would give me my money and then I would think about how many lawns I could mow to make more," Alex says with a chuckle. "Under my picture in my high school yearbook it says, 'I'm going to own my own business. So, I just consider Offspring the logical unfolding of my life.'"

At the academy, Alex hunkered down and made a commitment to earn high marks in all of his classes—a promise which he quickly fulfilled. Even when an extremely arduous Physics course threatened to knock down his grade point average, he was able to avoid the threat due to hard work and persistence. "I decided I wasn't going to be one of those people who lost a letter grade after the Physics final, so I kicked it into high gear and worked really hard," he recalls. "Not only did I receive an A+ in that course, but I ended up as sixth in my class of 300. It was a lesson in doing what others are unwilling to do in order to separate yourself from the pack."

In Alex's fourth year in the Air Force, he decided to apply to the prestigious Air Force Institute of Technology, a decision motivated by his love for learning and his desire to improve his skills as a cost-analyst. As first lieutenant with an impressive military background to boot, he strongly believed he would be accepted into the institute. To his surprise and disappointment, however, one of his supervisors didn't support his matriculation into the program, and he was ultimately rejected. The loss reminded him of his days as a fallen football star and how much he hated to depend on other people to further his career and life. "The camaraderie within the military is something that I still miss," Alex says. "However, my attempt at an advanced career was thwarted, and I didn't think a 20-year military career was the right choice for me and my family."

Rising from the ashes once again and drawing on his extensive perseverance reserves, Alex secured an honorable discharge from the military and later a job with KMPG consulting, a success he credits to his past position as Chief of Financial Management Operations in the Air Force. Alex's wife, Aundrea, also worked at KMPG, an added bonus to an already sweet deal. At the company, he learned a lot about the importance of networking and how essential connections are in the business world. KMPG is also where Alex discovered his passion for technology consulting, a flame which led him to move on to PeopleSoft, a technology consulting firm. After three and a half years at PeopleSoft, when Oracle took over the company's operations, he and three other colleagues decided to create Offspring Solutions. While two of those three colleagues no longer work with Offspring Solutions, the break-up of the original group taught Alex a valuable lesson about collaboration and partnerships. "The shared vision wasn't articulated well between the four of us," he explains. "Now I know that partners must be fully aligned in order to truly be successful. Otherwise, it can be a debacle."

Admittedly, there weren't a lot of stops between the military to the launch of Offspring Solutions, a feat Alex attributes to perseverance and an assuredness of his career goals. "I always tell my kids that the earlier you decide what you want to do and who you want to be, the better," he affirms. "There shouldn't be any doubt in your mind that you can get it done."

The "get it done" attitude is a large piece of Alex's leadership philosophy as President of Offspring Solutions. All about the bottom line and the satisfaction of his clients, he works very hard to instill an honest atmosphere and level playing field at his company. "I'm positive that I don't know everything, but I'm even more positive that you don't know everything," he jokes. "I never want to get into the 'who's smarter than who' scenario. Instead, let's be smarter together. You can't fight the human condition of those that want to be seen as right, even when wrong. So at the end of the day, you just have to rely on fact over opinion. I don't take on the pressures of having to be right all the time. I do take on the pressures of being a collaborative leader, which is not always an easy task." His dedication to avoid petty competition allows him to focus on what truly matters, which is creating new and innovative solutions for the company's clients. "Leaders that dictate from the top down were applauded in the past, but I tend to manage more collaboratively to maximize the talents of my team," Alex affirms. "I never enjoyed anyone dictating to me, so I don't dictate to others unless direction is needed. I am the compass."

Independence and self-preservation are important values to Alex, not only as a leader, but as a father. Paving his way to success with his own hands, he hopes his children will also discover and then relentlessly pursue their own passions at an early age. In particular, Alex's daughter, Ayanna, is someone he tries to motivate despite his own fatherly reservations. A talented singer, she has a distinct and unparalleled love for music and the arts. "I don't have experience in that area, but I don't want to stand in the way," Alex explains. "I'm going to allow her to do whatever she wants to do."

Aundrea, like her husband, also shares the philosophy that all goals and passions should be doggedly pursued until they reach fruition. In fact, she was instrumental to her husband's decision to start his own business. As a strong businesswoman in her own right, complete with an MBA, she was able to assist her husband with operational and financial considerations during the inception of Offspring Solutions. "Aundrea never discouraged me or gave me push back about creating my own business because she understands who I am," Alex avows. "She has been the main stability in my life, and one of the primary reasons for Offspring's current success."

Besides tirelessly supporting one another, Alex and his family have a long history of supporting their local community through SeeBeyond, a foundation he started to help cultivate the lives of disadvantaged young people. "We set up chess classes at our local schools and instituted debate instruction for younger kids," Alex explains. "Our goal is to create opportunities for leadership—opportunities I didn't necessarily have at my school." SeeBeyond is one of Alex's many passions, and he hopes to dedicate his time to the foundation after his career comes to a close and the curtain falls on that particular stage of his life.

To an outsider, managing a foundation like SeeBeyond might appear daunting in the midst of leading a rapidly growing business, but motivating young people to chase after their dreams comes naturally to Alex. With many seasons of wisdom to dispel to grade school students in search of inspiration, his message is clearly sincere. "Be sure to focus on what you really care about, and the money will come," Alex affirms. "There's already so much uncertainty out there, so you might as well do what you love." In addition to passion, he urges young people to put in 110 percent, no matter where their talents or hopes fall. Similarly to his grandfather, he is confident in his belief that hard work and perseverance will pay off in every situation, but he also warns young students to be smart about their career decisions. "Don't be negligent about what the financial rewards will be," he says. "Understand that there are financial consequences to every passion."

While those hazy summer days of mowing lawns are now long gone, Alex still holds the memories of his grandfather and his words of wisdom close to his heart. In his desk drawer at work, one can find his grandfather's birth certificate and railroad card—quiet reminders of his family's journey. While Alex's grandfather lacked a formal education, he was smart enough to know that the future of his grandson wasn't attached to the history that limited his own. To him, watching the success of his grandson was like bearing witness to a rare comet—a force burning through space at incredible speeds that not many people can say they were lucky enough to experience. "After seeing me graduate from college, my grandfather considered himself a true success," Alex remembers. "He was very proud of what I had accomplished and would literally say, 'Alex, you did alright for yourself.'" Having done more than alright, Alex's life has been about creating things—athletic victories, jobs, a business, opportunity, family, hope—that weren't there before. And even after all this, like a comet that passes Earth and continues along a determined trajectory, he still has perseverance left to burn.

BERNHARDT
WEALTH MANAGEMENT

Alex P. Bartholomaus

The Race You're Running

Today, Alex Bartholomaus believes that, if a high level executive in sales or leadership re-thinks their career in terms of what type of distance race they're running, they can take their performance to a new level of success by preparing for it in a new way. "It's about building up your endurance," he says. "One's ability to endure comes from a variety of areas—your awareness of yourself, the help from your support team both at work and outside of work, and the amount of training you put in physically, mentally, emotionally, and professionally. A lot of high-level executives think they're in a sprint, but it's a marathon. Know the race you're running. You may not know where it'll take you in the end, but you'll know how to train for it, and therefore, how to finish it."

Alex is the founder and Managing Partner of People Stretch Solutions, a management consulting firm that focuses on revenue growth, sales development, and leadership teams in the pursuit of excellence. He's keenly aware of the rise and fall of the terrain around high-level executives, the fortitude of their muscles, and the stride that will get them to the finish line. But when the race first started, he couldn't have guessed how long he might be running or what his own unique blend of endurance was made of.

The starting gun came with a diagnosis in 1996. His mother, who had been sick with breast cancer since 1992, was told that the illness had metastasized, and that she didn't have long. Alex had been with the business for two years since graduating from college. His father, a successful entrepreneur, had launched a wine import business called Billington Imports that was doing $3 million in annual sales at the time. Fatigued from running the business all those years and emotionally drained by his wife's illness, he decided to hand the keys to Alex. "I think he named me CEO because he wanted to focus on Mom, and because he knew I had a vision for the future of the business," Alex recalls. "He said it was time to pay off my college loans, so if I messed up, just figure out a solution quickly and learn from it. He really let me run with it."

Driven by a relentless pursuit of excellence and the opportunity to make a difference in the wine industry, Alex took off. He made his fair share of mistakes along the way, but he had great mentors in his grandfather, his father, and the many owners and distributors in the industry who had been won over by his father and wanted to see the business succeed. "Some people took me under their wing," he says. "Others were very skeptical of how young I was. But what I lacked in experience, I was determined to make up for in knowledge. By the time I became CEO, I knew more about wine than most professionals in the sales side of the industry."

Alex's mother passed away in 2000, when his daughter was three months old. "When someone close to you dies, a haze sets in," he explains. "But when it lifts, you're left with perspective. I felt that appreciating every moment of life was the only way to respect those who no longer had the opportunity to live it."

Through the early years of running the business and the haze that set in after his mother's passing, Alex was a fair leader, but a hard one. "I guided myself on principles that seemed logical to me," he remembers. "I didn't ask anyone to do anything I wasn't willing to do. I treated others as I wanted to be treated. I expected everyone to shoot for the stars so they'd land on the moon. But not everyone responds well to that no-nonsense approach."

The business did incredibly well with Alex at the helm, escalating from $3 million to $15 million in annual revenues within eight years. He had gotten an idea of the race he wanted to run, setting his sights on building a $100-million company. "It was all excellence, drive, growth, and endurance," he recounts. "I really wasn't thinking about what it meant for my family. I wasn't fully cognizant of what it was costing me to invest all that time in my professional life."

Alex's race took an abrupt turn, however, with a second earth-shattering diagnosis at the end of 2002: his son, Jack, was severely delayed in speech and development at age two. He was given the label PDD NOS (pervasive developmental disorder not otherwise specified). Alex and his wife, Mary, had a suspicion it could be autism, but it was too early to be sure. Committed to doing everything they could to see that Jack received optimal care and support, Alex and Mary read a great deal about developmental psychology and neuroscience. This education ran parallel to the work Alex was doing in the professional realm to educate himself on psychology and behavioral science after witnessing the performances of several solid employees plummet unexpectedly. As the haze of the loss of his mother was dissipated by the need to be present and active for his son, these parallel lines of study began to converge, leading to the groundbreaking realization that success is about investing in people holistically.

"I had always pursued excellence and demanded it from my employees, but I hadn't realized that excellence can only be achieved if you address a person in his or her totality," he explains. "A person's emotional intelligence, self-awareness, empathy, and ability to self-regulate remain constant at home and at work, and will create systemic problems that span both spheres. Through this intuitive journey, I came to the understanding that we need to pursue both excellence and a holistic approach to get a deeper understanding of why people struggle and why they're successful."

Alex's rigorous academic pursuit revolutionized his perspective of what it means to be the CEO of a growing business, and in the aftermath of that watershed moment in 2003, he found himself with an immense new toolbox. Able to offer uncommon insight that factored in the differences between intrinsic and extrinsic motivation, self-limiting beliefs, and the challenges of picking up emotional cues, he began treating each of his employees not the way he would want to be treated, but the way they, as individuals, each wanted to be treated. Over the next five years, revenues escalated to $37 million annually.

Alex's heightened perceptions of human nature allowed him to pick up on subtle shifts in his home life as well. By August of 2008, he could tell his father wanted to sell the company. And though his wife, Mary, deserved a medal for her patience and perseverance through his long absences from home, he knew his course needed an adjustment to better balance his priorities. "It meant a lot to me to be present in the formative years of my children," he says. Eight months later, the company was sold, with Alex agreeing to stay on an additional year with the acquirer.

Not long after the sale of the company in 2009, Simon Sinek came out with his thought-provoking book, *Start with Why*. It was an introspective period for Alex, and after deeply reflecting on his own values and beliefs, he realized the real reason he gets out of bed each day. "Very simply, I realized I love challenging people to recognize their own bias and limitations, so those roadblocks don't prevent them from getting to the next level of performance," he avows. "I love watching people step up, see things differently, make changes, and make choices. There's always a perceived reason as to why someone can't do something, and I love applying the tools of psychology, behavioral science, neuroscience, and emotional intelligence to surpass those imagined obstacles."

With that, Alex hung the shingle for People Stretch Solutions in 2010 and set to work creating a new ecosystem within his consulting model. With several senior consultants and full-time project managers working with him, the company is now doing almost a million in revenue on an uncommonly lean platform with a high value proposition. Though it focuses on sales and leadership, the team also excels at marketing. The business serves primarily commercial companies that are between $25 million and $500 million in size, with the resources to invest in bringing in capable experts to advise them on how to reach their targets faster. "This is not a lifestyle business," he affirms. "The vision is to create another growth company. And with our phenomenal spheres of influence and board of advisors, we're perfectly situated to realize that goal."

Today, to keep perspective and to remind himself not only of where he's going, but of how far he's come, Alex simply glances down at the watch his wife, Mary, gave him for his 35th birthday. With an understated elegance and uniquely handcrafted movements, the timepiece is a work of art, reminding him of his warm, passionate, aesthetically-minded mother. Understated and classic, it also reminds him of his grandfather, a Chilean farmer who worked till he was 77 and taught Alex good, old-fashioned, salt-of-the-earth values. Unyielding and resilient, it also reminds him of his father, an entrepreneur who cofounded the first wine import company in 1977 before striking out to launch Billington Imports in 1985.

Born in Washington, D.C., Alex and his family lived in Arlington for the first five years of his life and then moved to Annandale, where he savored his public school experience. "After visiting my grandfather in Chile as a child and witnessing extreme poverty and hardship, I was appreciative of everything," he recalls. "I had seen parents literally kill themselves to send their kids to good schools, so I was grateful for the good public schools I had access to here in the U.S. I invested my energy in school and was driven by my competitive nature to be the best."

As a kid, Alex thought he might grow up to work on Wall Street. From the money he scraped together doing odd jobs like shoveling snow or raking leaves, he invested in stocks. "We always had what we needed, but we had to save up for things we wanted," he remembers.

After performing at the highest levels, both academically and athletically, Alex graduated twelfth in his class of 500 and was accepted to the College of William and Mary. His parents agreed to cover tuition and board, but he was responsible for all other expenses—a weight he shouldered with appreciation. The summer after his freshman year, he sold cutlery. "Commission-only work teaches you what sales is really all about," he laughs. "It was a great experience. Then, during my sophomore year, I got a job at a golf course. My father had already given me the best education possible in relationship management, and that work experience truly put those skills to the test." In that capacity, Alex's natural leadership qualities shone through as he pushed his coworkers to hustle and ensured his department ran smoothly. Those leadership skills were honed further while he served as President of his fraternity. "Some of the learning experiences I went through as an early leader were painful at the time, but they all really helped me to evolve."

Graduating college, Alex was in discussions with different companies, including AOL. But ultimately, the 22-year old thought the gateway into the international spirits industry afforded by the family business was a no-brainer. Working to build business relationships across international borders and with diverse groups of people cultivated in him a love of culture and meeting new people. Then, in 1996, the same year he took over running the company, Alex met Mary through mutual friends. "I'm very lucky to have met someone who is such an incredible teammate," he says today. "Though we're very different, our values are perfectly aligned. Cheryl Sandburg's book *Lean In* explains how a woman being successful as an executive climbing the ladder needs a spouse to support them, and I have been lucky to have a very supportive one."

When his mother passed, Alex and his brother, Erik, decided to launch a project through Billington Imports called 2 Brothers Big Tattoo Red, where fifty cents from each bottle sold was donated to cancer or hospice. In seven years, they raised one million dollars for charity. Since then, Alex has worked to better the community through 5k charity runs, pro bono work, and other avenues.

Now, as managing partner at People Stretch Solutions, Alex sees his work as a consultant as a form of alchemy, transforming people's performances into gold, unlocking the perspective and insight that launches paradigm shifts within corporate cultures. "We tend to work with CEOs who are very ambitious and dissatisfied with the status quo, always looking for the road to that next plateau or number," he explains. "Does the problem lie with the team? The CEO? The process? The culture? Oftentimes, the answer is all of the above. That's why a holistic approach is crucial to achieving top performance. Seeds of undoing can be hidden behind a veneer of success. We think people fail because they don't go deep enough to find those seeds. People will avoid the world of psychology because it's very murky and emotionally risky. It's not easy work, but it's incredibly important, and that's a level where we operate very comfortably."

In advising young people entering the working world today, Alex stresses the importance of curiosity and exploration. "People are often curious, but they don't know where to go, so they remain inactive," he explains. "But it's important to explore—both the world around you, and your own personality. Exploring is building endurance. What race do you want to be in? There's only one way to find out—start running."

BERNHARDT
WEALTH MANAGEMENT

David Belden

Step Outside and See

For many, the idea of being an outsider carries negative connotation, implying rejection and loneliness. For David Belden, however, it's sacred. James Dean, a childhood idol of his, is famous for saying, "Include me out." Bob Dylan, another hero, said, "To live outside the law, you must be honest." Jean-Paul Sartre, a French philosopher and World War II prisoner, set himself apart from everyday life to examine and unlock some of its most profound details. "They were all outsiders, taking the time and space to look at their society and cultural norms from a distance," David says. Now the founder of ExecuVision International, David serves clients as a "Professional Outsider," using the insights of a broad and reflective external vantage point to help people step outside of their organizations and see them with new eyes.

ExecuVision is a facilitation and coaching business that has served over two hundred companies since its inception in 1998. Depending on the unique needs of the client, David will handle the case solo, or call upon partners with other areas of expertise. Many of his clients have been family-owned businesses, which he says brings an extra layer of complexity, often prioritizing loyalty over success.

His certification in Imago Relationship Therapy comes particularly in handy in these instances. "The Imago approach is about getting people into a conversation where they talk directly with each other about what they're really seeing, feeling, and experiencing," he explains. "Each party works through how much of the conflict is them, and how much of it is the other person. The role of the facilitator is simply to guide the conversation. The focus is on how things land, rather than who's at fault. Whether I'm working with family business partners, or executives who don't trust each other, I see tremendous success borne from getting things out in the open and investigating their origin."

David's approach usually begins with an analysis of who's in the room, including their motivations and strengths. ExecuVision uses the Core Values Index assessment to reveal a person's innate preference for a certain type of work. This leads to a better understanding of how each person can be engaged to contribute at his or her highest level of ability. Then, he examines the communication patterns within an organization, implementing systems to provide a feedback loop. Once an organization has a common vocabulary for the challenging conversations they need to have, actually having the conversation becomes much easier.

These considerations pave the way for replacing a "culture by default" with a "culture by design." "The culture of an organization isn't about a plaque on the wall with the company's mission statement," he says. "It's about how people treat each other, day in and day out. The key to an intentional culture is the daily behaviors of the people involved. Those behaviors must confirm the values the organization claims to have."

At its heart, his approach is exploratory, more interested in uncovering the root causes of malfunctions than finding solutions to superficial symptoms of discord. It takes an openness and acceptance of the shadows of life that isn't come by painlessly. He can still remember the day when, at 42, he experienced first-hand the Imposter Syndrome.

After working in several other countries, David had been asked by his French employer to take a position at the company's head office. When he walked into his new corner office in their grand tower in Paris, he suddenly had the distinct feeling that the next person who walked through the door would know he didn't have a clue what he was doing. "I felt paralyzed by fear that someone was going to figure out I was just pretending to be ready," he remembers. "I felt that I hadn't done anything to deserve this. I was sweating and racked with heart palpitations—classic signs of a panic attack. But then it struck me that nobody has all the answers, and that none of us really know what we're doing—if we did, life would be totally predictable, and it's far from that. The reality is that none of us know for sure what really needs to be done. We're figuring it out along the way, and that's what makes life exciting."

David inherited this critical, self-aware, restless

pursuit of understanding from his parents, who were incredibly hardworking. His father was one of twelve children growing up in a tenant farming family. He spent a year in prison for refusing to go to war and then became an impassioned civil liberties attorney, fighting for social justice for the impoverished. His mother, a dedicated educator, invested her whole heart and energy into her work as well. As far back as the 1950s, she was teaching high school students about contraception and encouraging them to get educated before starting a family. She later co-founded a community college and worked to change child protection legislation. Both his parents loved their work, and expected the same of their children. "Their only expectation of my four sisters and I was that we save the world," David laughs.

David was raised in a small town in Oregon, where few things were valued more than work and study. "We had a large family, and both my parents worked, so the children were responsible for cleaning the house, cooking dinner, washing clothes, and doing chores," he says. "The summer I was five, we lived in a migrant labor camp, where my father was working as a supervisor. I remember picking berries, beans, and crops in the fields alongside the migrants. That was where my family was, and it was expected that I would contribute. Work was an integral part of what we did—there was no separation between work life and family life. That has extended to my professional life today, and the way it's an integral fabric to who am I as a person."

Another early experience that would profoundly affect the gait of his professional step came when he was eight years old. David woke up to an empty house. The large, old dwelling had two pantries, and on that morning, he decided to take it upon himself to clean one of them. "I took everything out, wiped it all down, and washed the walls," he remembers. "My memory tells me I spent the entire day doing it, and when my parents came home, I couldn't wait to show them. My mother praised my initiative effusively, but, typical of my father, he said, 'If you had just cleaned the other one too, that *really would have been something*.' That became a defining moment for me. Most of my life, it has felt like, no matter how much I do, I need to do a little bit more. I've found that's a common trait among successful people—the feeling that you can always do more."

David's parents had always told him that he just needed to get through the monotony of high school, and he'd love the academic life of college. But when he graduated at age 17 and began classes at the University of Oregon Honors College, he was sorely disappointed. "I was expecting deep intellectual discussions, philosophical questions, and time to ponder," he says. "It wasn't like that at all. I lasted two terms and then heard Timothy Leary speak, whose tagline was, 'Tune in, turn on, drop out.' To an eighteen-year-old, that sounded like good advice, so I dropped out of college and leapt into the turbulent social and political currents of the day."

David engaged with the 1960s in all their glory—joining the Civil Rights movement, engaging the Vietnam War controversy, and working with a migrant labor group his eighteenth summer to help establish schools and education programs for the children. Later that year, he decided he would become a citizen of the world, traveling to Europe to write the next great American novel in the spirit of Hemingway and Steinbeck. He celebrated his nineteenth birthday in Canada on his way to Copenhagen, Denmark, where he would live for the next 24 years.

Embracing the life of an immigrant, David began washing dishes in the kitchen of a hotel for 85 cents an hour as he set about learning the Danish language and culture. Showing a penchant for organization and leadership, he was soon put in charge of coordinating the kitchen schedules, and then promoted to manager. "I never intended to be a businessman," David remarks. "I had always thought my career lay in academia. So when I naturally gravitated toward this career path and found myself starting to ascend in the business world, I spent a lot of time philosophizing on why it was interesting to me, why it works, and why I'm good at it."

After working in the hotel for three years, he was offered a job as a stock clerk at a small import-export company. He learned on the job by day and attended business school classes at night. He studied language and business, soon earning a promotion to Supplies Manager. Then, at age 25, he was hired as the Export Manager for a well-established Danish company, and was honored to be their first foreign employee. A year later, he was elected to the Board of Directors by his colleagues. "It was all a tremendous learning experience, as I didn't know anything about business," he says. "I read books and paid attention, and the lessons worked." He was then hired by a large family-owned engineering company that exported propane gas and supplies to 108 countries, each with its own trade regulations, consular invoices, and letters of credit. David had a mind for international trade, quickly learning to manage successful exchanges even with unstable countries like Nigeria, Pakistan, and Colombia.

His extensive work experience with international businesses drew the attention of a French company specializing in international trade facilitation—the inspection of goods exported to the developing world, ensuring that the right goods were shipped for a fair market value. They asked David to set up operations for them in Scandinavia to service their 38 clients, named by the World Bank as the most corrupt countries in the world. After that operation was successfully up and running, he was sent to establish new locations or assist floundering operations all over the world, leading to a host of adventures not for the faint of heart. "I was kidnapped in Nigeria and caught in crossfire in Pakistan," he recounts. "But overall, I loved getting to explore the world and learn so many different languages and cultures. Living in Taiwan was definitely a highlight—a country with only 20 million people, and yet the twelfth largest trading nation in the world. It was amazing to see how they do things firsthand."

By the time David moved back to the U.S. in 1996, he was thirty years wiser, and had the life experience to show for it. He had lived the life of a Dane—earning dual citizenship, assimilating that culture's proclivity for logical thinking and long-term sustainability, starting a family, and even winning election to the school board in his son's district.

What's more, David had studied philosophy and psychology at the University of Copenhagen. He wrote and defended a thesis in Danish of the existentialist philosopher Soren Kierkegaard. He studied Mandarin in Taiwan, German in Hamburg, and French in Paris. He lived in six different countries and worked in another twenty, using his status as an outsider to study business in a variety of contexts. "What I found was that there's a commonality in motivation for people," he explains. "The world is full of different cultures and different ways of approaching business, but there's a common denominator of motivation for all people that I've found in every society I've worked in, and it's this: *everyone wants to make a contribution at their highest level of ability.* Once I realized this, it became my mission, vision, and purpose in life to help people create organizations where every single employee is contributing at his or her highest level of ability."

David was recruited by a Swiss competitor of the French company he had started with. He was charged with turning around the worst performing unit of the enterprise's sixty operations. Within two years, he had transformed worst into best. "I had done five startups and three large-scale turnarounds by that point," he says. "The secret to any turnaround is simply identifying with the people involved what's going wrong. Ask people, what kind of an organization do you want? Then you decide together how to accomplish it, set everyone's sights on the future, and stay out of the way as they march forward."

David led the employees in achieving the team-based work environment they envisioned for themselves, establishing eight task forces to address specific areas of concern. The leader of each task force was chosen by a vote, and David modeled the approach after lessons imparted by his son—an elite Green Beret Operative in the U.S. Army and a member of the Commander's In-Extremis Force. "I've learned from him and my own experience to create Green Beret teams in companies to handle the chaotic situations in a targeted fashion, separate from the standard operating procedure of the regular Army forces," he says. "My son's team of only thirty people, for instance, succeeded in capturing and killing the top 200 Al Qaeda leaders, changing the entire course of the Iraq War. On a much less dramatic scale, I train teams to enact operations in an organization that change the entire course of a business."

Vistage International is a CEO peer group and leadership organization providing a supportive and constructive environment for CEOs to explore challenges and pursue personal growth. David became a member of a local group while struggling with a turnaround. "In the turnaround situation, I couldn't talk openly with anyone involved," David explains. "Vistage provided a forum to explore ideas with people who had no vested interest in the outcome. It was an amazing experience. When I completed the turnaround, Vistage asked if I would be interested in becoming a Chair—a facilitator of my own group of CEOs. I've been doing that now for 16 years, and still find it both stimulating and rewarding."

Around the same time, he was asked by another company to help develop their executive team on a long-term basis, leading David to launch ExecuVision International as a platform to realize his calling to design innovative, forward-thinking businesses that allow each employee to achieve their full potential.

Amidst these ventures, David spends time with the younger generation joining the workforce and sees that same eagerness to contribute at their highest ability. "It seems to me that young people today are seeking adult supervision—not parental supervision, but guidance from other adults," he observes. "I mentor several younger people, and many of my Vistage members mentor each other's children. We all find it very satisfying." He is also a certified Imago Relationship Therapist, basing his practice on the work of Harville Hendricks. "I frequently mediate disputes between executives, which are very similar to the issues couples have," David says. "The training in couple's therapy has been a great asset."

Much like Jean-Paul Sartre, who rejected the Nobel Peace Prize because he didn't value official honors and declared, "A writer should not allow himself to be turned into an institution," the honors and awards David's received don't hold much interest for him. "What means something to me is people benefitting from a conversation," he remarks. "When one of my Vistage members is having a hard time with something, and I know they feel better by the end of a conversation, those are the victories." Those victories extend far beyond the immediate experience of that person to transform family dynamics and community engagement.

And, David would argue, they reach even further. "It occurred to me at some point in my career that if we are to solve the multitude of problems facing the world, it will be through increasing exchange amongst all peoples," he says. "The path to international peace is through commerce. Savvy business people seldom see an advantage in killing their best customers. The internet has given us incredible access to people and the world. If we can move past issues of petty greed and short-sightedness, promote crowdfunding, and embrace the Conscious Capitalist movement, we can benefit everyone while remaining profitable and promoting the common good."

In many ways, David's story demonstrates how externally leading an organization begins with an internal focus of one's immediate mindset to examine the approach and perception from new vantage points. It begins with creating a good process, and then communicating with people to inspire, motivate, and help them achieve what they want to achieve—which, in many cases, isn't readily apparent. "Amazingly, very few people know what they want to do in life," he points out. "Many don't know why they're doing what they're doing or where they want to go. To me, leadership is helping people identify that. I think everyone is looking for a way to tell their truth. That's what I'm listening for. That's what I step outside to see."

Kathleen Benson

The Gifts That Aren't Givens

Growing up in the blue-collar town of Altoona in central Pennsylvania, Kathy Benson's family didn't have a lot of money, so she learned early on how to make a little go a long way. But it was only in retrospect, after working hard for what she achieved in life and reflecting back on the subtle sacrifices her parents made, that she came to understand things as gifts instead of givens.

One hundred fifty dollars was the cost of renting a small apartment five blocks from the beach in Wildwood for a week in the summer. For her father, who worked in a plant, and her mother, who worked in the Sears credit office at night so she could be home with Kathy and her two brothers during the day, the sum wasn't cheap. But they made other sacrifices in life so that the family could spend that time together each summer. And today, remembering her mother preparing sandwiches for a day at the beach and her father carrying the heavy cooler on his shoulder as the sand burned their feet, Kathy knows those memories are some of the most precious gifts they could have given her. "They were very positive, always choosing to look at the glass as half-full," she remembers. "At the time, I didn't realize how hard they worked to give us all they could."

Now the cofounder, President, and CEO of ORI, a market research firm that excels in providing innovative insights to drive results, Kathy's life's work is about giving people the opportunity to turn hard work into good lives for themselves and their families. "One of the things that motivates me most is the fact that we're able to offer a great working environment to so many people," she remarks. "It gives me a lot of satisfaction to know that I'm keeping people gainfully employed and offering them opportunities that other companies wouldn't, like the ability to have a good work/life balance."

The pursuit of that balance was exactly what compelled Kathy to pursue her entrepreneurial dreams in the first place, though she hardly could have imagined it would lead her to launch her own company. When she had her first child, Travis, at age 26, she took time off from her job working as the executive assistant to a business owner. It quickly became apparent that the office couldn't function without her, so at the urging of her boss, she packed up her baby and brought him in to work with her so she could keep the company running. "I loved my work, but after a month, I knew there had to be a better way," she remembers. "I needed a profession that gave me personal satisfaction while still allowing for the work/life balance I needed as a new mom, so I decided to start a word processing company."

Those were the days before the internet, so Kathy hit the library to do her research and contacted the newspapers to run her advertisements. When she spoke with her employer about her plans, however, he begged her to stay. She agreed to continue working for him, but under new conditions. She would work four days per week for her same salary, have the leeway to leave the office for other meetings as needed, and have her own phone line in her office, which she could answer with her own company name.

With these new arrangements established, Kathy decided that word processing might not be the best direction to take her fledgling business, so she phoned a friend, Susan Lynd. The two had worked together at an engineering consulting firm, and their aligned ethics and moral values made for an exceptionally compatible working relationship. They met at a McDonalds in Bethesda in January of 1988 to discuss a possible path forward, conceptualizing a data entry business on the back of a napkin. After more research and brainstorming, they decided to launch Office Remedies together, and their own mothers landed them their first two projects.

Several months later, the work began to trickle in. The Bensons had just bought their first home, and as a new mother who had to figure out how to balance the competing interests of family and finances, Kathy imagined there had to be other women in the community who felt just like she did. Carla, her sister-in-law, had just had a baby as well, so Kathy invited her to join the team. As more people sought the services of Office Remedies, she brought on neighbors and friends from church. "Suddenly we had a cottage industry of stay-at-home moms willing to work from home, which was an extremely novel concept back then," she explains. "I continued to cold-call, conduct meetings, and sell our data entry capabilities. Then, when I knew we had enough business that I could pay myself an adequate salary, I left my office job fully and worked from home for eight years, until we moved into our Herndon offices."

Kathy has always been driven by the thrill of strategy and the challenge of getting from point A to point B, and her team began bringing this insight to their work by pointing out questions in their clients' surveys that were generating mixed and ineffective data. The clients would ask for recommendations to improve the questions, and Office Remedies was happy to help. After about eight years, a light bulb went off for Kathy, and she realized the business was already so much more than a data entry company. With that, they brought on someone with survey expertise to help formalize the service, marking their transition into a research firm.

Before long, Kathy noticed that clients were asking for help with making sense of the data that Office Remedies was processing. She saw that companies were collecting massive amounts of data over time, but they didn't know what to do with it. Highlighting her needs-oriented approach to growth, she hired someone who could run the analysis and tabulations and teach the team how to really drill down to extract valuable information about customers, members, and the organization itself. In this fashion, the company continued to augment its services over the years, steadily evolving into the full-service research firm it is today.

Now known as ORI to reflect the firm's reinvented identity, the company has over 320 employees, with offices in Herndon, Atlanta, Dallas, Kansas City, Chicago, and Florida. With a team of seasoned statisticians and researchers, it utilizes traditional market research augmented with social media tools and technologies to help organizations make better business decisions based on qualitative and quantitative analyses of market penetration. "If a client wants to expand to new geographies, we show them how they would be perceived in those areas and advise on the best ways to communicate with those potential customers," Kathy explains. "We also do satisfaction studies to see how a company's customers or members perceive them. When it comes to data, we do deep dives to provide our clients everything they need to make good decisions."

ORI takes its work a step further by giving specific recommendations for implementing solutions, and then ties everything back to the reason the customer wanted to conduct the research in the first place, ensuring that their process is entirely outcomes-based. What's more, the company serves associations, commercial firms, and the federal government, drawing on the best practices from each segment to maximize its research principles and offer innovative solutions across spheres. "One reason Sue and I started this company was because we wanted to create a culture of responsiveness and empowerment," Kathy affirms. "If an employee comes to us with a great idea, we want to be able to act quickly and bring those benefits to our clients quickly. It's that flexibility and urgency that have kept us evolving to meet the needs of the entities we serve."

Though she never envisioned running a business like ORI, Kathy's entrepreneurial spirit was evident even in her childhood pastimes. She loved to sew and would sell the things she made. Then, in high school, she was charged with raising money for charity and decided to negotiate a deal with an office supplies distributer to purchase packs of pens for 30 cents. She then sold them for $1, and when her grandmother took her to bingo night at church, the packs went like hot cakes. In the end, she raised more money than any other classmate.

As the oldest sibling and only daughter, Kathy loved to boss her brothers around, cook for her family, and tend the garden with her uncle after school and on the weekends. Her parents prioritized family dinners together each night, and she remembers fondly the big Italian dinners the family had each Sunday at her grandparents' house. When she was 14, they started an annual reunion in the mountains of Pennsylvania, and they haven't missed a year in the decades since. "We have a series of pictures from each year, and it's great to see how the family has grown and changed over the generations," she remarks. "When we were younger, we'd sit and listen to the stories. Now I'm where my mom was when we first started going. Today, it's as important to my kids and nieces and nephews as it was to my grandmother 40 years ago. It's a platform for passing values down from one generation to the next through storytelling, and it's extremely important to all of us."

Fourteen was a transformative age for Kathy in other ways, as well. It was the year she began dating Shawn, the man who would become her husband, and the year her parents divorced. Watching them, she learned how important it is to pick up the pieces and do what you need to do to make it through hard situations. "Shawn helped me get through that difficult time," she reflects. "He was a football player, and I was a cheerleader, so we'd go to sporting events together. My family embraced him, and his embraced me. It was a very different way of growing up, with expectations that we'd stay in Altoona and settle down."

Having babysat for a number of business owners in the town, and having watched some of her own aunts and uncles move away and achieve different levels of success, Kathy knew there was more than one way to go through life. First, however, she wanted to master the art of hard work. When she turned 16, she was offered a job at the local drug store, where she was promoted to work in the pharmacy. Then, during her senior year, she participated in a co-op program, attending school in the mornings until eleven and then working in the data processing department of a manufacturing plant until 7 o'clock at night. "I worked for a really great family who would let me leave early sometimes for my cheerleading commitments," she remembers. "It was a good experience at balancing various priorities."

Neither of Kathy's parents had gone to college, and although she loved academics, it was assumed that she wouldn't pursue higher education. None of the college counselors approached her to open the conversation, and though she considered it, she was offered a full-time job with the manufacturing company upon graduation. She worked there for a year and then moved down to the D.C. area with her best friend to be closer to Shawn, who was enrolled at the University of Maryland on a full-ride football scholarship. The couple got engaged at age nineteen and married at twenty.

Kathy got a job with the government as a GS-2 in the secretarial pool making $8,000 a year, and Shawn's monthly stipend of $585 for room and board helped to make ends meet. "We thought we had so much money!" she laughs. "Nobody ever asked us if we understood what we were doing, or if we had enough to move to the D.C. area. We just made it work."

Kathy knew education was important, and because she hadn't had the opportunity to be a traditional student, she decided to take business classes at the University of Maryland in the evenings. She started doing sewing work for people in her spare time, and with football games on the weekend and family visiting from Pennsylvania all the time, the young couple was happy as could be.

The Bensons moved to Virginia when Shawn signed with the Redskins as a free agent in 1984, but when he suffered an injury shortly after camp started, he decided to resign. Drawing on the help of several great mentors, he was accepted into the sales program at Xerox and has been in high tech software sales ever since. Kathy spent three years working as an executive assistant for the engineering consulting firm where she met Sue. She then spent four years working in the finance industry before committing herself to ORI full-time.

In the intervening years of transformation, Shawn has become ORI's biggest fan. "He's always encouraged me to branch out and do what I want to do," Kathy affirms.

"He knows I get bored if I'm not challenged, so he always supports me in stretching my limits and doing what I need to do to get to the next level, personally and professionally. Our 33 years of marriage have been wonderful, and I couldn't imagine a better partner."

Together, Kathy and Shawn were active in the community through their children's school and sports. Now that Travis and their daughter, McCaul, are older, they focus on giving back in other ways. Shawn works with special needs young adults through a weekly weightlifting program focusing on health and fitness, while Kathy mentors women who own their own business or are looking to take the next step in their professional lives. As a board member of the D.C. Chapter of the National Association of Women-Owned Businesses, she's an important voice in the conversation of balancing work and family life, and as a leader, she aims to give alongside her employees as they participate in charity events like Relay for Life.

In advising young people entering the working world today, Kathy highlights the important role that failure plays in the road toward success. "A lot of our employees are afraid to fail, but mistakes are fixable," she explains. "They're important learning experiences for the whole team." She also embraces entrepreneurship as a force not only to start new companies, but to improve existing companies from within. "Some of our staff are very entrepreneurially-minded, and I encourage them to think of new products, services, and ways of doing things," she says. "Our employees come up with great ideas that have led ORI to conduct original research and pursue thought leadership that has been valuable for our clients."

This inclusive, proactive, forward-thinking approach and wonderful employees landed ORI a spot on the *Inc.* 5000 List of America's Fastest Growing Companies for five consecutive years—a badge of honor for a company that has seen many ups and downs in its 26 years of operation. And Kathy's and Sue's creativity and resilience have garnered spots on WPO and American Express OPEN's List of 50 Fastest-Growing Women-Owned/Led Companies, and on *Working Mother* Magazine's list of 25 Best Woman-Owned Businesses.

"It has been a real honor to be part of this," Kathy says. "I love what we're able to do for our clients and employees. And most of all, I love that I've been able to show my children what it means to be a mom working outside the home, running a company and leading a team. I've encouraged them to chase their dreams and try everything they want to try, because you have to experience lots of different things to really become who you are. That liberty is never a given in life, but it's the best gift one can give or receive."

BERNHARDT
WEALTH MANAGEMENT

Paul Boudrye

Asking the Right Questions

"Somewhere between your mind and your heart lies who you are, and that's what I want to know about," Paul Boudrye says boldly.

In a culture that often settles for the ease of surface-level exchanges and shamelessly self-interested networking, his words have a weight to them—the kind of weight that causes a conversation to sink deeper, past the formalities and how's-the-weather discourse so many of us have come to expect, to a place that is real.

"From as far back as I can remember, I've wanted to help people," he says. "If someone has a problem, a dream, or a goal, getting to the right place is about asking the right questions, but so often, people are taught to ask the wrong ones. That's why, when I meet people, I focus on getting to know the real them. I ask questions and listen to understand what their dream is and why, and then I think about people and opportunities I can connect them with to help achieve that dream. The question I enjoy asking the most is the *Wizard of Oz* question—if I was the Wizard of Oz and I could grant you one wish to solve a social problem that's important to you, what would it be and why? The responses to these questions are amazing."

As founder of HowToBe.Me™ and owner of ConnectorHub, a business development consulting firm serving the Washington, D.C. metropolitan area, Paul's success stems from the fact that he won't settle for the traditional networking styles pursued by so many of his peers. His approach is about getting to the soul of the matter—helping people improve their lives, further their businesses, and see in themselves the potential they couldn't see before. "People need to be asking themselves questions like, how can I change and do something better?" he says. "Or, how can I connect two things that have nothing to do with each other and create something new to solve a problem? I'm there to connect people—to the right questions, the right answers, the right people, and the right situations. Making these connections and watching people reach their potential is the *why* behind everything I do, and it's extremely gratifying."

Paul is passionate about seeing people take control of their destinies and success because he knows firsthand how difficult it can be when situations are at the whim of forces beyond one's control. When he was in sixth grade, the company his father worked for went under because the owner's father had been embezzling money. Paul's father, a chemical engineer and linear programmer by trade, was left struggling to find a new job, forced to uproot his family from Rockville, Maryland, to move to Blacksburg, Virginia. Paul had to leave the friends he had known since preschool, and it was a defining moment for him. "I saw my dad struggling due to something outside of his control," he remembers. "It led me to realize that you have to be in charge of your own destiny, and a great way to do that is to be your own boss. If you're not relying on someone else for a paycheck, no one can surprise you. In that sense, being an entrepreneur is one of the most secure jobs you can have. In my young mind, a seed was planted."

That seed would first sprout when he was in eighth grade. The family had moved back to Maryland, and Paul saw an opportunity to market candy in his mid-afternoon shop class. His mother would drive him to the store to buy bulk candy, and he would then sell it at retail, until the Vice Principle decided his venture was diverting too much business from the school store. "The Man came in and shut me down," he laughs. "But from that moment on, I was hooked on connecting a person with a need with a person with a solution, regardless of the product or service."

Beyond his entrepreneurial drive, Paul connected with the community around him through his humor. "The feeling I get when I make someone laugh is unlike anything else, and I really appreciate that as a way to get to know people and establish trust. The shortest distance between two people is through humor."

With diverse interests as a child that included piano, saxophone, psychology, baseball, football, soccer, and karate, Paul's focus settled into tennis in ninth grade and rooted itself as a lifelong passion. He played varsity tennis all four years of high school, and today, his game lends new meaning to the mantra, *Be the ball.* "When I play now, I'm in a state of Zen," he affirms. "There's a kinesthetic connection between the ball and me, and nothing else exists. I have no expectations, and I don't think, or my mind interferes with the natural flow of things. I just relax and let my mind and body work—I'm just along for the ride."

Aside from sports and his equally strong performance in academics, Paul launched a lawn and landscaping business in ninth grade after the sting of his thwarted candy operation had subsided. From the time he was 13, each summer found Paul hard at work. "I saw my father struggling to get his feet back on the ground, and I felt that if I didn't have to ask for money, that was my way of helping," he recalls. "The business grew to 20 lawns, and I'd employ my friends, paying them more than what they could earn in a store."

It was the early 1980s, and the computer was just becoming a household item. As Paul looked to expand, his father helped him use an electronic spreadsheet to build an optimization model that would show the right amount and type of equipment to invest in. His father financed him, and he bought the additional equipment that allowed him to expand from 20 to 40 lawns. "When he lost his job and went into consulting, my father became a reluctant entrepreneur," Paul remembers. "He was very smart to marry technology with entrepreneurship, and that rubbed off on me in some ways."

Paul continued running his lawn business on the side when he enrolled at the University of Maryland at College Park. But after four years of taking a full load of classes, managing his business, and commuting to school since he couldn't afford to live on campus, things began to take their toll.

Disillusionment was overwhelming. The lawn business was backbreaking work, and when Paul decided he instead wanted to make a living with his mind, he dismantled the company and took a year off to explore other opportunities. He also produced an entrepreneurship training video based on a class taught at the old Learning Annex by a local entrepreneur. He teamed up with graduate students from Maryland and interviewed entrepreneurs on camera to tell their story.

Inspired by this work, Paul decided to launch a traveling car detailing business to serve people who didn't want to spend time waiting in line at car washes. It wasn't long before he partnered with another local entrepreneur who did detail on cars in dealerships, and while doing that, the general manager of a Manhattan Subaru noticed his work ethic and offered him a position.

Paul had never sold cars before, but in his first month on the job, he sold 21 vehicles and made $10,000.

"I didn't know what the hell I was doing," he laughs. "But I had the same success again the next month, so by the third month, I thought I was a star. That's when I began overthinking things, and I tanked. I learned I didn't want to do that for the rest of my life, and when I married, bought a home, and decided to have children, I realized I needed to build something stable and long-term."

At the advice of one of his clients, Paul left the car business and was recruited into the life insurance industry. It was hard to make ends meet, and the pressures of fatherhood revolutionized his sense of responsibility, but he was a leader amongst his peers in number of policies sold and in the creative caliber of his ideas. He even came up with the concept of helping his clients leverage the cash value of their life insurance policies to help offset bankruptcy issues, and was commended by New England Mutual Life for his creative sales strategies. "People always say you should think outside the box, but for me, there is no box," he says. "When someone lays rules out for me and tries to put me in a box by saying I can't do something, I'm compelled to say, why not? You always have to turn things inside out and look at them differently."

It was this kind of thinking that compelled him to resign his position and launch an internet company just before his thirty-first birthday. His vision was a simple directory system that would serve as a virtual Yellow Pages for Delaware businesses. Companies would pay to have their websites posted in the directory, and Paul would cross-promote each company on radio, in print, and on billboards as well. His father loaned him $5,000 to get him rolling, and he then bartered over $200,000 in advertising with his vendors to make his vision a reality, promising to refer all companies that entered into the directory to the companies that helped him out free of charge.

Paul was then recruited by an accounting firm in D.C. to build an internet consulting practice, and it was here he taught himself web design and development. Three months later, however, the company decided to cancel the project, which led Paul to launch his own web site design and management business called ClikIt Web Solutions.

He grew ClikIt Web Solutions to 30 clients. When 2000 came and went, however, Paul saw the writing on the wall and knew web businesses were starting to become commodities. With that, he sold his business to an IT staffing company that wanted to develop its own web content management business, staying on to build that up until the dotcom bust of 2001 cut his salary in half and led him to walk away.

In 2009, he decided to explore and create another internet business, called BizConnect. "It was kind of like

LinkedIn meets EHarmony," he says. "I wrote a business plan, got funded for $50,000, and worked on that for several months before turning it over to my partner." Then Bond Beebe CPA and Advisors reached out to him over LinkedIn, ultimately offering him a position as Director of Business Development.

After a professional career of sampling different opportunities and work environments and getting to know his own strengths better in the process, Paul has an acute sense of what those strengths are, and he focuses every day on using them to further the success of his clients. With this in mind, he would advise young people entering the working world today to take the time to identify their own strengths early on. "Take the Predictive Index or StrengthsFinder tests," he encourages. "So much emphasis is placed on transcripts, test scores, and resumes, but we should be focusing on a child's strengths, motivations, talents, personality, interests, vocations, and passions. We should look at their natural strengths and then support those with all we've got. That's how we help young people reach their potential and live happy, purpose-driven lives."

Key in this equation of finding one's true strengths is the role of a mentor—something Paul never really had in his own life. Instead, he read the books of Ted Leonsis, Daniel Pink, Jim Collins, Mario Morino, Gerald Chertavian, Tom Rath, Jim Clifton, Richard Branson, Donald Trump, and Ross Perot, lining his bookshelves twice over with the thoughts of brilliant minds put to paper. "Soaking in these ideas through reading is important, but having a mentor is unparalleled," he remarks. "If you can reach out to people you trust and like, they can be invaluable in helping you mitigate errors you might make down the road."

Paul isn't just interested in studies and theories about youth, entrepreneurship, and education—they're his ways of paying forward his own success. He also works with the Network for Teaching Entrepreneurship, Build DC, and with Year Up, a program that helps at-risk youth transition into the business community. He supports Cornerstone Montgomery as a business mentor and the National Center for Children and Families in their mission to help foster kids, homeless families, battered women, and single mothers, as well as the Duke Ellington School of the Arts and various other organizations committed to helping children—whether through equipping them with marketable skills or simply making sure they have food to eat.

Paul's professional and personal journey is the aggregate of diverse steps that may seem, at first glance, to lead in a number of different directions. Yet every single step, and each choice that guided it, was streamlined by the understated style of leadership that focuses on raising people up with new solutions and new success. "Faith is the ability to believe in yourself and the choices you make, however hard they may be," he affirms. Learning to ask the right questions of life, and of yourself, is a way to take control of that story and guide it the way you want, and that's the kind of change I'm committed to bringing people. It's about writing the story you want with each word, each step, and each decision you make. It's like traveling down the yellow brick road of life—equipped with your brain, your heart and your courage—and ultimately reaching your personal Oz."

BERNHARDT
WEALTH MANAGEMENT

Khari M. Brown

Leveling the Learning Field

Growing up, Khari Brown's goal was to play professional basketball, so when he was cut from the high school team as a freshman, he was devastated. But the importance of the moment wasn't lost on him. "It fueled a fire in me," he remembers. "I decided I wasn't going to quit, and I kept practicing on my own. Luckily, someone left the team several weeks into the season, and the coach asked everyone who the jersey should go to. They asked me to join the team, and I was ready."

Though Khari rode the bench for much of the next three years, he worked hard and waited patiently until his big chance came his senior year. He had grown a few inches, and a teammate's injury gave him the opportunity to showcase the fruits of countless hours of practice. He suddenly became the star—not only of the team, but of the league. After playing all through college, he finally accomplished his goal of playing professionally by joining a team in Helsinki, Finland. "The whole experience taught me the importance of staying determined and using negative experiences as motivation toward positive outcomes," he says today. "It's a mindset I've used throughout my life, and one I've taught to young people along the way. The people who are most successful in life are the ones who don't give up under any circumstances, but instead look for alternate routes when they face setbacks."

Today, Khari's work is all about helping young people facing tremendous odds navigate alternate routes forward. As the Executive Director of Capital Partners for Education (CPE), a nonprofit organization dedicated to helping motivated, low-income students realize their potential and fulfill the dream of a college education, he is leading the effort in D.C. to level the playing field by leveling the learning field. "I firmly believe that, to whom much is given, much is expected," he affirms. "I came from a great family who nurtured and supported me, always pressing the importance of education. I've achieved some success, but if I had been born into different circumstances, I may not have achieved anything at all. That's why I'm committed to changing the odds for people who lack the advantages I had."

CPE was founded in 1993 by Ambassador Henry Owen and Ted Schwab with the mission of helping motivated low-income high school students get into college. In more recent years, it has added the goal of seeing those students through to graduating from college as well. "Despite the immense wealth in our city, and despite the fact that we're the most educated region in the U.S., we also have some of the greatest poverty in the nation," Khari points out. "D.C. has one of the greatest wealth disparities and income gaps, and because income translates to education and success in life, we find this unacceptable."

With this mission in mind, CPE works with poor children living in under-resourced neighborhoods where few kids go to college and begins by sending them to high-quality high schools. "If you want to go to college, you need to attend an academically rigorous school that has high expectations of you and will teach you the foundation to do college-level work," he explains. "The only options for those kids were magnet schools or private schools, so CPE began providing private high school scholarships and partnering with schools to cover tuition."

The organization recognized early on, however, that just going to a good high school wasn't enough. Many of these children were the first in their families or communities to set their sights on higher education, so the adults in their lives didn't have the background or knowledge to provide sufficient support through the college application process. Thus, CPE set up a volunteer mentoring program to match students with people who could guide them through the process one-on-one, filling in the gaps created by poverty. "Many kids don't have a network to draw on for career ideas, or someone to help them with their homework, or even a computer at home," Khari points out. "Many of our kids' families don't have bank accounts and don't know how to apply for financial aid, which means kids later find themselves having to drop out or transfer for financial reasons."

Indeed, while 82 percent of upper income college

students graduate from college once they've started, only eight percent of low-income youth see that success. While education philanthropy used to measure success by the number of kids an organization got in to college, it has since shifted its sights to measure success by how many are finishing, how much debt they accrue, and the kinds of jobs they're able to get once finished. Aiming to level the learning field, CPE's board and 11 professional staff members provide individualized support to its team of 180 mentors and also work directly with schools and families, hosting weekend workshops to promote college readiness, career readiness, and financial literacy. Thanks to these remarkable efforts, 99 percent of CPE's graduates enroll in college, and 72 percent graduate within six years.

"We're very proud of that success and are actively trying to expand our footprint," Khari affirms. "For years, we've been a highly successful yet niche program working primarily with kids in private school. But a few years ago, we took a step back and realized that a program as successful as ours has a responsibility to have a greater impact. Helping a few hundred kids isn't enough when there are thousands who aren't getting the help they need." With this broadened vision, Khari and his team adjusted their program model and became the only organization in the Washington area to adopt an e-mentoring platform, which allows its mentors and mentees to email each other on a weekly basis between monthly meetings. The tool has been transformative in establishing greater efficiency, standardization, and effectiveness, allowing CPE to serve more students at a lower cost.

To achieve a more expansive impact, the program also added a new point of entry. Whereas it used to work only with students who enrolled in CPE during their ninth grade year, it began accepting eleventh-graders as they entered their second semester, focusing on providing guidance through the last three semesters of high school. "These kids are on the college track, but they need help navigating the process," Khari says. "They don't have the social capital, the agency, or the social skills to succeed in college once they get there, and they don't know how to ask for help or handle the financial components of the equation."

As Khari rolled out these two advancements in 2012, he set his sights on raising seed money and doubling the program in two years. In 2013, CPE's student body grew by 40 percent, and the program raised the funds to grow a projected 40 percent through 2014. The growth is aggressive, but strategic, well-planned, and justifiably urgent. "Unless you're preparing for a technical degree, you'll be left out of this economy if you don't get a college degree," he affirms. "You won't make enough to support your family, thus perpetuating the cycle of poverty and setting your own children up for failure. The current generation is depending on CPE just as much as the next generation is, so it's imperative that we succeed."

This hard-driving, unrelenting, mission-oriented approach to life, legacy, and work was first modeled for Khari by his parents when he was a young child. Born and raised in the Boston area, his mother was a speech and language development specialist for young children, and his father was a photographer and professor. They instilled in him the value of hard work, honesty, empathy, reliability, and high expectations for all he did. "Every day, they got up and went to work, and I rarely missed a day of school," he remembers. "They taught me that, even on your bad days, you show up and make the best of it, because people are counting on you."

Khari's mother was a music major in college, and his father had a master's from the Rhode Island School of Design. Their passion for art rubbed off on their son to a degree, but he was drawn to athletics in a way they didn't understand. When he started playing organized basketball at age eight, he fell in love with it immediately. Through team sports, he learned the thrill of competing with others and the art of dealing with different personalities. From observing his coaches, becoming a captain, and later becoming a coach himself, he learned how to use different leadership philosophies with different people to help them achieve success individually, garnering success for the team as a whole.

For the active young boy, academics was far less exciting than athletics, but thankfully, Khari had a mother who sat patiently by his side in the evenings, teaching him how to write and reviewing his applications when college drew near. He was recruited by Division III schools and was accepted at Tufts University, where his father had been the first in his family to earn a degree after attending the institution as a night student.

At Tufts, Khari's interest in academics awakened. Gerald Gill, a professor of history and Khari's advisor, was a particularly important driving force in that awakening. After Khari turned in his first paper to the professor, Dr. Gill called him into his office and told him he wouldn't accept the work because he knew Khari could do better. Khari rewrote the paper, only to be told again that it was subpar. "I ended up getting a C- on that assignment," he laughs now. "But he saw something in me that I didn't quite see in myself. Now that I run a mentoring organization, I know that's one of the most important jobs of a mentor—to identify things in your mentee and push them toward those things. He believed in me in a way I didn't believe in myself at the time, and that was hugely powerful."

When Khari graduated and crossed the Atlantic Ocean to realize his lifelong dream of playing professional basketball, he felt he was on top of the world. But as he found himself struggling with both language and cultural barriers in his new home, he found that things weren't as easy as he imagined they'd be. The lack of sunlight in the winter left him depressed, and he was injured several times in games.

Still, he didn't quit. When he came home to the states for Christmas, he spent time reflecting and then returned to Finland with a new perspective and fresh approach. "I ended up having a terrific experience," he recalls. "In that case, perseverance and resilience were about stepping back and removing some of the emotion from the situation to take a more tactical approach to the problem. That process became another important tool in my business toolbox later in life, offering an objective and productive way of looking at problems."

When Khari finished up his year-long contract in Finland and returned to the U.S., he wasn't sure what he wanted to do. After identifying as a basketball star and investing his energy in that dream for so long, he suddenly felt like a nobody without any direction. "Growing up comfortably in the middle class, I didn't have the drive to make money," he remarks. "I had no clear aspirations, and it took me a while to figure it out, but I ended up getting into coaching because I thought I might want to go back overseas."

Khari began earning a good living as a personal trainer, but the idea of pursuing his entrepreneurial drive in the weight room, either as a trainer or a small business owner, wasn't intellectually fulfilling to him. What really drove him were the underprivileged high school kids he was coaching on the side. Over the three years he worked in that capacity, his kids won over 90 percent of their games, making it to state finals one year. They exhibited tremendous talent and motivation, and many went on to play college basketball.

One of the kids, David, was having a hard time breaking 700 on his SATs, so Khari began working with him after practice to figure out the problem. "I couldn't believe it," he recounts. "Though he was a B student, he was an eleventh grader operating at a fifth grade reading level. Because he was polite, handsome, charming, and a good athlete, his teachers had just passed him without giving him the help he needed. Nobody had expected him to do well in school and succeed academically, so he hadn't. There was no challenge to rise to because nobody was challenging him. I decided then and there that that was unacceptable. I would let kids like David know I had high expectations for them, and I would work with them to reach those expectations." Just like Professor Gill challenged him to do better, Khari vowed to see the potential in these kids that they couldn't see in themselves.

When Khari woke up the next morning, he knew he wanted to become a teacher. With that, he returned to Tufts to earn his Master of Education while working as a graduate assistant, coach, and residential life assistant. When he finished his degree at age 28, he decided he was ready to move outside the seven-mile radius where he had spent the majority of his life, relocating to Washington, D.C. When he was introduced to Ted Schwab, he set up an informational interview to learn more about CPE and his overall interest in education.

With that, Khari bought a suit, went in to meet with CPE's executive director to learn more about the organization, and found himself in the right place at the right time. It was the man's last day on the job, and the organization was looking for someone to replace him. As he reviewed Khari's short resume, he said, "You'd be great, but you've never really had a job before."

It was true that Khari had never interviewed for a job before, let alone accrued nonprofit management experience. Still, the fact that he was an ideal fit for the position couldn't be denied. "My athletic background speaks to my drive, discipline, and determination and I tend to view everything through the lens of being a coach," he explains. "To me, it's all about motivating people, management, and leadership. We discussed this informally, and I had no intention of selling myself to get a job, but something just clicked."

Doubting his own capacity to succeed in the position, Khari considered turning it down, but a close friend was adamant that it was one of those things in life he had to step up and say yes to. When he accepted the position in 2001, he hit the ground running, determined to rise to the challenge against all odds. It took a full five years to get the mentoring program running like a well-oiled machine, but it has since developed into one of the best in Washington, and Khari's own evolution as a leader parallels that journey. "Part of my leadership style is trusting people," he says. "I make sure to get the right people in the right seats on the bus, and then I give them a lot of room to operate. This gives them the freedom to be more creative, innovative, and effective in their work. I'm all about the power of "we," making sure each board member, donor, employee, and volunteer mentor understands the crucial role they play in our mission."

Indeed, CPE is all about the mission. Its Board of Directors are high-powered executives who choose to invest their time and money in the program because they understand that the difference that investment makes. Its mentors commit six hours a month for two years to a student for no pay because they understand the pivotal impact that a reliable, present role model has for these kids. They expect as much as they give because they understand how powerful expectations can be. "The entire CPE team is driving this program forward and transforming the future of D.C.'s low-income youth, one child at a time," Khari affirms. "They're the reason we were named one of the top local charities by *Washingtonian Magazine* and the *Catalogue for Philanthropy*. They're the reason we won the Neighborhood Builders Award from Bank of America, a grant that will help us reach our potential as we help these kids reach theirs."

Today, Khari and his wife, Yasemin, balance their lives as executives with the responsibilities of giving their own children the best possible chances in life. "We support each other in our careers and in parenting," he says. "She's loving and encouraging of all I do, and we've really made it a priority to be there to raise our kids together." They both support the Rosemont Center, an early childhood education program serving needy families in D.C. and aims to head off the cycle of poverty at its source at the very beginning of life. Their professional, personal, and philanthropic efforts dovetail in a mission that expects as much of society as they do of themselves, daring it to rise to the challenge and level the learning field.

Paula Calimafde

The Heart of Law

Almost every evening at dinner, Paula Calimafde's father would turn their dining room into a courtroom. A renowned litigator, he would "present" the case he was working on to his two daughters, and then ask them specific questions as if they were the judge or jury. "I recall he was working on a mine explosion case, where the mining company had wanted to increase its productivity, causing the machines to overheat. The workers had been told to override the safety feature," she remembers today. "He would ask us if we thought it was reasonable for a worker to turn off the safety switch even though there was a red sign over it that warned the user not to switch it off unless the entire machine was off. Dad figured if he could explain a complex case to us, or see how we reacted to a set of facts, he would probably do okay with a jury."

A decade later, Paula began law school at Catholic University in Washington, D.C., and realized she had already been taught most of the material. "I found myself thinking, 'I know all of this already because my father spent fifteen years teaching it to me, and I didn't even realize it at the time,'" she recalls. "It gave me such an advantage. I understood so much and was able to enjoy law school rather than struggle through it. It really made me grateful to have grown up that way."

Paula has since become a tax attorney and is now a Principal at Paley Rothman, the largest firm of estate planning attorneys in Montgomery County. Paley Rothman is a full service, primarily business-oriented law firm with tremendous capacity in commercial litigation, employment law, employee benefits, project development, real estate and tax. She currently chairs the firm's Retirement Plans, Employee Benefits, and Government Relations practice groups, and is a senior member of the Estate Planning, Tax, and Nonprofit groups. She has been nationally recognized on the "Best Lawyers of America" list, "SuperLawyers," is a charter member of the American College of Employee Benefits Counsel, and is a member of the American College of Tax Counsel and the American College of Trust and Estate Counsel. Being a member of all three Colleges places her in a very select group of attorneys in the country. She also serves as the Chair of the Small Business Council of America and is the President and General Counsel of the Small Business Legislative Council. She spends a portion of her time lobbying, but focuses more on education through position papers and testifying before the Ways and Means, Finance and Small Business Committees on Capitol Hill.

Paula began working at Paley Rothman almost immediately after graduating from law school when it was still a small firm of only five people. It was founded about forty years ago by Steve Paley and Mark Rothman, who met at the Justice Department. They decided to start their own firm together, and since Montgomery County did not yet have any tax lawyers, they selected a location in Chevy Chase to open shop.

Today, the firm has 37 attorneys, all of whom work collaboratively in a collegial company culture. "I feel extremely proud to be a part of the Paley Rothman team, where I have been able to play an instrumental role in helping our clients accumulate wealth and keep that wealth in a tax-advantageous way," she explains. "We help our clients maintain their wealth as much as possible during their lifetime, and at the time of their death, we preserve as much of that wealth as possible for their family or for other beneficiaries or charities they so desire."

In many ways, Paula seems to have been born for her career, as her parents immersed her in law and politics from an early age. She grew up in Old Greenwich, Connecticut, where she and her younger sister experienced a happy, carefree childhood. Her father was an intellectual property litigation attorney who instilled in his daughters an understanding that there was nothing they couldn't accomplish. "He always encouraged me to take risks," she recalls. "He would constantly urge me to go as far as I could and never to let fear stop me. I think he recognized my ambition early on and wanted to nurture it as much as possible."

Fortunately, Paula did not need much encouragement when it came to academics. As a child, she loved going to school and made excellent grades. Her mother, who stayed at home, was fiercely political, serving as town representative and being active in the League of Women Voters. Her parents' influence inspired Paula to dream big—at age three, she would often tell adults that she wanted to be the President of the United States one day. "My mother was a very strict, strong woman, and she taught me that no one can intimidate me," she recalls.

The encouragement she received from her parents was reinforced by the people she met growing up. Her father represented a major Japanese electric company, so the family traveled to Japan and met the heads of the corporation when Paula was a teenager. "We were exposed to many people who were highly successful at an earlier age than most," she says. "Being in that environment with those kinds of people to look up to was very defining."

Paula attended Swarthmore College for her undergraduate education, where she majored in political science. She decided to enroll at Catholic University for law school. "I've always loved D.C.," she recalls. "I thought it offered everything. Of course, politics was in the back of my mind, as I wanted to play within that arena as well."

During high school, Paula spent a summer in New York City working at her father's law firm. She enjoyed the experience, but decided early on that neither New York City nor intellectual property law was for her. This led her to Washington, D.C., where, at Catholic University, she had a professor who had just come out of working for the IRS with an impressive background in tax and corporate reorganizations. However, he had little experience teaching law students, so he approached the class at a much higher level than he probably should have. "A lot of people in class had no idea what he was talking about, but I really enjoyed it," she recalls. "I realized this was the area of law for me. I really like the intellectual kind of competition, but in a clean way where no one is getting hurt."

When she graduated in 1976, Paula began working with Steve Paley at Paley Rothman. She remembers her first assignment was a reorganization of a privately owned business. "I had friends working on Wall Street who were doing corporate minutes for several years, whereas we had paralegals to do that for us," she recalls. "The fact that I chose to work at a small firm allowed me to jumpstart my career and do complex and interesting work early on."

In 1986, Paula was selected as one of twelve commissioners for the White House Conference on Small Business, where she chaired the section dealing with social security, retirement plans, and health care. It was her first opportunity to work with the Small Business Administration, and in particular, the Chief Counsel at the Office of Advocacy, which assists small businesses on the Hill and with regulatory matters. She found she had a natural ease for talking with people and understanding the politics around the issues. "I had never given a speech in front of two thousand people before," she says. "The first time I did that, I felt like I had cotton in my mouth, but eventually I grew very comfortable giving speeches. I'm fortunate to have the skills necessary to work with disparate groups of people and find viable compromises."

Most recently, Paula has accepted the position of President and General Counsel of the Small Business Legislative Council, a large non-profit trade association that represents a variety of small business trade associations on Capitol Hill. "They represent an extremely diverse population, including associations representing those in construction, florists, petroleum distributors, electrical contractors, transportation infrastructure, printing, and so on," she says. "You have all these CEOs sitting around the table, discussing their issues and trying to agree upon an agenda that everyone feels comfortable with. It's a very powerful, permanent coalition of trade associations." She also serves as the Chair of the Small Business Council of America, which gives a voice to successful and stable small businesses throughout the country. The SBCA focuses exclusively on complex tax, employee benefits and health care issues that impact its members.

The Small Business Council of America has a business and legal advisory board comprised of professionals from around the country who specialize in and work with privately owned businesses, which can consist of small businesses or large family-owned companies. When an agenda is agreed upon, it meets with members of Congress and their staff to discuss its proposals. "If we are successful, we're able to turn an idea into a law to make life easier for small business. Often, we work to simplify the law and reduce administrative or unnecessary burdens," Paula explains. When the Small Business Council of America is not proposing new laws, it defends existing ones on the Hill that assist privately owned businesses, like those pertaining to retirement plans. "It's very easy to explain why I chose to join and represent the SBCA. I am able to work to make the law better for small or privately-owned businesses, and we see results," she explains. "It's very rewarding to look at a tax code section and realize that you helped bring it into being. It's a positive experience."

Paula's new position with the Small Business Legislative Council seems to be a perfect fit, considering her technical expertise in small and privately owned business taxation as well as corporate structure, qualified retirement plans, estate planning, and executive compensation. "I actually work in these fields, so when I go to Capitol Hill to speak to members or to testify, I'm not relying on a script that someone else has written," she explains. "When you actually do what you are talking about on the Hill, people sort of wake up and pay attention a bit more because they know they're talking to someone who's in the trenches. They know that what I'm telling them is from my experience, so it's going to be relevant."

Since taking on her new role as President of the Small Business Legislative Council, Paula has had the opportunity to refine her leadership style towards a more collaborative effort. "My alma mater, Swarthmore College, is a Quaker school, and it taught me to work on an issue until a consensus has been reached by everyone involved," she explains. "That's the style of leadership I prefer. In the lobbying world, I've learned that today's friends will be tomorrow's enemies and then, at some point, friends again. Whatever you say will eventually get around to that person, so I try to sit down with people when a problem arises and deal with the issues right away. It's so much more appropriate to deal with issues head on and up front."

Paula's husband, Alan Mark, is also a Principal at Paley Rothman, focusing on finance, project development, and biotech. They met when a fellow Paley Rothman partner set them up on a blind date years before Alan joined the firm, and the two immediately hit it off. "He's only a few years older than me, but he's been a great mentor for me," she says. "He is a phenomenal lawyer and has been known to close deals that seem to present insurmountable issues. We decided early on that we would only talk about law at home if something in our legal life was really important. We knew if we didn't do that we would end up only talking about the law and our jobs. We didn't want a relationship entirely dominated by the law. We enjoy each other's success, but our practices seldom overlap, even though we work in the same firm." When she and Alan are not in the office, they put family first, often traveling with their children and doting on their grandchildren.

As she shifts her gaze forward, the future looks bright, having spent a lifetime working toward her passions and building upon the foundation her parents instilled in her. "I can imagine most people would think sitting around all day doing taxes would be boring, but I don't see it that way," she says. "I've been fortunate to have very interesting clients. They are intellectually exciting and passionate, writing books and discovering new cures, so it's a really exciting way to practice law. You begin to care for your clients as friends or family, so caring about their best interest occurs naturally because for me, family has always come first." Indeed, having enjoyed a life where family, law, and lawmaking are sown together seamlessly, Paula's success comes from the heart as much as it comes from intellect and experience, lending it a rare and genuine nuance that is not soon forgotten.

BERNHARDT
WEALTH MANAGEMENT

Matt Curry

A Better Way

One Sunday after church, nine-year-old Matt Curry looked up at his mother and told her he was going to be fine. An active, interested boy with a strong inner compass, he was never one to sit still, and like many Sundays before, his fidgeting had led to his dismissal from the morning's service.

In his room later, his mother said she was worried about his future, but Matt never doubted himself for a minute. "I can't explain it, but I've always had this strong sense that I'd do big things in my life," he remembers. "I told her not to worry, because I was always going to be okay." Now the founder, President, and CEO of The Hybrid Shop, this inner fortitude and unwavering confidence have kept him steady through hard times and good, leading him to incredible success and into the uncharted territory of a brand new industry. "I like to create my own path," he says. "When faced with limits, I like to go beyond them. That's what entrepreneurship is all about—finding a better way."

Matt got his start in automotive work at his brother's urging when he was 15. Cleaning bathrooms and changing tires in the beginning, he worked his way up to apprentice technician and then transitioned over to management and sales, where he excelled. Over his career, he ran seven different stores with three different companies, tripling and quadrupling sales at each location. "I ultimately realized that, if I could garner that kind of success for others, I could do it for myself," Matt remembers. "I noticed that D.C. has a lot of high-end vehicles, but the quality of the parts and technicians you find at big box stores left much to be desired. D.C. needed a go-to operation for high-end, quality auto repair, so I decided to fill that niche."

The product of that effort, Curry's Auto Service, became expert at servicing all makes and models, including high-end European and import vehicles. Yet hybrid vehicles remained somewhat of a mystery. Such vehicles entailed a completely different set of operations—a craft that was not being taught in the auto repair world yet. "Hybrid owners wanted to take their vehicles to experts, but such proficiency was hard to find," Matt explains.

That's when he crossed paths with Dr. Mark Quarto, a PhD engineer, at a convention in October of 2012. Mark had been with GM for 28 years as one of the lead technologists in its hybrid and alternative fuel division. A scientist, inventor, software developer, coder, and programmer, he had established himself as one of the world's foremost hybrid experts and even created one of the first electric vehicles as a side project in 1987. As another side project, he created a battery discharge unit that conditions hybrid batteries to return to 95 percent of their original power.

"A nickel metal hydride battery can be reconditioned many, many times, but only according to a specific scientific process," Matt explains. "Mark put the hardware together, wrote the software programming, did the coding, and put together the training modules that could accomplish this, and he could prove it through before-and-after power and energy tests."

Mark had explained this achievement to Matt over dinner. At the time, Matt had ten auto repair shops, some of the best technicians in the country, and eight hybrid vehicles of his own. Mark offered to give Matt two days of free training on his machine and then let him test it on those vehicles to make sure it really worked. Matt accepted, and by the end of the training, his five top technicians were conditioning and rebuilding hybrid batteries on their own. "Mark is a world-class instructor, and he just blew us away," Matt recalls.

That was December of 2012. In January, Matt and his team brought Mark back in for an intensive four-day course. They put the machine to work for family and friends through February to test the technology further, seeing real improvement in their cars. "On day one, your hybrid vehicle might get 50 miles per gallon, but at year two, you might be down to 46," Matt explains. "At year four, you might be down to 40, because as the battery goes out of condition, the vehicle has to rely more on the gas motor, sacrificing efficiency and performance. Historically, the only solution has been to change the battery, which can cost many thousands of dollars, depending on the make. But our eight Priuses, which had been averaging between

37 and 44 miles per gallon, increased to between 49 and 52 miles per gallon after being serviced—even better than they were when we first got them."

After the results stayed strong through March, Matt and his wife, Judy, advertised a small notice for the machine in their electronic newsletter, which has over 28,000 subscribers. The customer response was one of excitement and enthusiasm, so Matt went to Mark, and his wife, Chris. "I asked for exclusive rights to the machine in North America, and I offered to sell it for them," he says. "Mark and Chris are incredibly smart, but I could bring to the table the business and entrepreneurial skills needed for success. They agreed, and we signed a contract."

With that, The Hybrid Shop was launched with the goal of creating an international network of high-end auto repair dealers to service, diagnose, repair, and maintain hybrid vehicles. Matt envisioned a company that didn't just condition batteries, but provided comprehensive hybrid care that spanned the gamut of services. They decided on a fractional franchise business model, or a business within a business. Companies like Curry's Auto Service are given the opportunity open a complementary business for a fee that covers the equipment and training, as well as operational, technical, marketing, and sales support. The machine and service can be up and running in four days, and The Hybrid Shop then earns recurring revenue each time it's used. Franchisees also get a five-day course with the Society of Automotive Engineers, a prestigious association that issues certificates of competencies that in turn strengthen the brands of the franchisees.

Now, when a consumer pays $1,299 to condition a hybrid battery instead of $4,000 to replace it, everyone wins. It's better for the environment because no new materials are used and nothing enters the waste stream. Manufacturers like Toyota, which spend $90 million a year to recycle their hybrid batteries and still have to worry about the resale values of their vehicles, have much to gain. Families are saving money, and green jobs are being created to help stimulate the economy—all because people like Matt and Mark believed there was a better way.

Even as a headstrong child, Matt was blazing his own trail and was the kind of kid other children looked up to. Born in D.C. as the youngest of seven children, his family moved to Vienna in 1972, into the house his parents still live in today. He was in second grade at the time and still vividly remembers the wonderful family dinners and holidays spent in that house, which will always feel like home.

"My parents are the best people I know, and my whole family has been a huge influence on me," Matt says. His father, an electrical engineer, was a civil servant who attained the rank of GS-15, Step 10 in the Department of Defense. He worked three jobs through the 1960s and 70s to support the family, while his mother took care of the children full time and then later cared for other kids to earn extra money. "We always had a house full of kids, and to this day, everyone in the neighborhood still refers to my parents as Mommy and Daddy Curry," Matt laughs. "People were always coming and going. That environment brought out my social side, which figures prominently in my affinity for sales today." As a very traditional Irish Catholic family, his parents taught him the importance of God, country, and family, with a focus on hard work and honesty.

In school, Matt preferred to be out in the world, actively engaging with his interests instead of sitting in a classroom. An avid athlete, he always wanted to win at sports, and often did. An early believer in focusing on one's strengths, he excelled at academic projects and challenges that aligned with his interests and was dismissive of those that didn't. "That philosophy wasn't celebrated when I was a kid, but it's very logical in a business setting," he remarks. "I focus on my strengths and hire exceptional people to do the things I'm not good at." Even back then, he was attracted to business aspired to one day be President of a company, dreaming of entrepreneurship rather than going the corporate route. "I couldn't see myself just sitting in an office," he remembers. "I'm a doer. I like to get things done, make things happen, and shake things up."

As a kid, Matt knew he would have to earn his own spending money, so he sold donuts, newspapers, and magazine subscriptions door-to-door. He cut grass, shoveled driveways, and later worked in a parts store. In high school, he was the first freshman in his school to make the varsity wrestling team in forty years, but a dislocated sternum clavicle landed him on the bench for the rest of the season. Then he played football, his true passion, until he tore all the ligaments in his ankle.

When he wasn't playing sports, Matt worked weekends at the tire shop his brother managed. "I learned how to be a general service technician, changing tires and oil," he remembers. "I learned I was not very good with my hands and didn't want to be a technician, so I got into sales when I was 17."

Upon graduating high school in 1985, he spent a year in college at George Mason University while working part-time at Goodyear, where he learned to be a go-getter and to pursue systems-oriented efficiency in his work. "We'd have to get through 50 or 60 cars in a day," he remembers. "If something unexpected happened—if a stud broke or the wrong part came in—I'd have to figure out creative solutions. To this day, I tell employees that when they run into a roadblock, they should be figuring out what's best for the customer, the company, and them. There's a solution to every problem, even if it means giving a customer a ride to pick up their kids from school while we finish up their car."

Matt then transitioned over to Craven Tire and worked in their wholesale division until, at the age of 18, he was offered a management position at their least productive location. Within twelve months, he brought the store's monthly revenue from $30,000 to $100,000, prompting Craven to promote him to their largest store, where he worked his magic again and raised monthly revenues from $160,000 to $250,000. "My strategy focused on all the things your mom teaches you to do," he remarks. "Be honest, be nice to people, and do good work. As a leader, you have to work hard and motivate people, remembering that they will only work as hard as you do. It takes process, procedure, follow-up, and making sure things get done right."

At Craven, it was normal to open the store at 7:00 AM to a line of 15 people waiting for service. Matt would work long hours and then go to school at night until he finally decided to stop taking classes and invest his full focus on his burgeoning career. He went all-in, and can still remember the day an employee picked up lunch for him. He didn't have time to eat it for several hours, and when he finally did, he bit into a french fry and realized that the oil had congealed in a revolting way. "I realized I couldn't live my life like that, so I put in my two weeks' notice," he recalls.

After brief stints selling insurance and used cars, distinguishing himself as the top used car salesman for several months in a row, he decided to return to the industry he had originally been drawn to. He took a position with Merchant's Tire and was promoted to Store Manager within thirty days. Of just over 120 stores, that location was ranked 69th in sales and 80th in profits. Per his specialty, he turned around the struggling store, bringing it to first in sales and second in profits within twelve months.

Three years later, Matt accepted an offer to run Craven's Tysons Corner location, which he did for about a year and a half. He then opened a door-to-door VIP promotion company for automotive repair shops in New Jersey. "That was one of my first businesses," he says. "It was fun for about a year and a half, but I was doing a lot of traveling, and I had a young family, so I sold it for $25,000 and went in fifty-fifty with a friend to buy a repair shop in Chantilly."

With that, Matt and his partner launched Curry's Tire and Auto, and over a nine month period, Matt worked 80 hours a week to bring the shop's sales from $30,000 a month to $100,000 a month. Unfortunately, however, the partnership didn't work out. "It's hard to put your blood, sweat, and tears into something, and to then have the rug pulled out from under you," he remembers. "Judy had just had our first son, and losing the business—and a friend—was one of the hardest times in my life."

Always one to make success out of a failing situation, however, Matt got back on his feet and took a job with Merchants Tire, bringing its Tysons store back from the brink until it became the company's best performing store. Then, over beers with a friend one evening, Matt was reading the Business Opportunities section of the *Washington Post* and noticed an advertisement for a Mercedes repair shop for sale. Behind an industrial park and with only four parking spots, it was in a terrible location, but Matt saw potential. "I knew I wanted to open another repair shop, so I figured now was the time," he says.

Matt spoke to the building's owners, who wanted to get rid of it and offered to finance him. With 13 credit cards, a $35,000 loan from his father-in-law, and a $200,000 equipment lease, Curry's Auto Service was incorporated in December of 1997. Through January and February, he would work from 6:30 AM to 5:00 PM at Merchants and would then work on cleaning, painting, and building a small showroom for the new business. Judy had just had their second child, Jenna, and she'd bring the baby in and help. When they couldn't afford to hire an accountant, she taught herself QuickBooks and took on the accounting and marketing responsibilities herself. "We were almost out of business before we were in business," Matt shares. "But with the help of friends and family, we worked our way through it and opened on March 16th of 1998."

In its first year, the shop did $1.6 million in sales, and Matt was able to hire additional help. He then opened his second location next to the AOL campus, where many of his customers worked, and a third store in Falls Church. They moved their original store to a better location with additional parking spots, and they opened a Reston shop. "One of the best things I ever did was buying the best equipment I could afford," he says. "Once, the President of the BMW Club needed to mount and balance the tires of his car, and we were the only ones in town with the equipment that could do it. He then wrote a full-page article about us for the local club magazine. I had also been racing cars since the 1980s and knew a lot of people from the racetrack, so from the beginning, our niche was European cars. Beyond normal service work, we were known for high-performance work, avoiding being pigeonholed into just one kind of service."

In 2005, with the four stores largely run by his partner, Matt noticed that the kids in his community had no sports league options. If they wanted to participate, parents would have to make long evening commutes to get them to games in neighboring towns. He knew there was a better way, so he co-founded Dulles South Youth Sports, raising $219,000 for a youth sports league and starting with his first love, football. They then added cheerleading, wrestling, volleyball, track and field, lacrosse, and soccer, drawing the participation of about two thousand kids. "It was great to run that program for several years and meet that need for the community," Matt remembers.

He then shifted his focus back to Curry's Auto Service, ultimately buying out his partner and opening a fifth location. "My leadership style is kind of like a bull in a china shop," he laughs. "I'm very direct. I know what I want, and I know that I'll achieve it. Honesty, integrity, and straight talk have been the cornerstones of my approach. I expect my employees to do a great job and maintain the integrity of our work." His philosophy has done more than garnered the respect of employees and the appreciation of customers. In 2009, Curry's Auto Service was named one of the top three independent tire shops in North America by *Tire Review Magazine*, and in 2010, it was voted Top Shop in North America by *Motor Age Magazine*, as well as Best Auto Repair Shop by *Northern Virginia Magazine*. They made the Inc. 5000 list of fastest growing business for three years in a row, were named one of the 50 fastest growing companies by the *Washington Business Journal* several times, and were recognized on the front page of the business section of the *Washington Post* in 2010.

All this attention caught the eye of Monro Tire, who made an offer that inspired Matt to enter a wave of enthusiastic growth before deciding to sell. He opened five stores in four years, and when he sold the business in August of 2013, the enterprise had over 150 employees and was on track to garner over $19 million in revenue.

Now, his focus is on The Hybrid Shop. As he works to pioneer a new industry, leveraging marketing opportunities and perfecting their robust internet presence, Matt and his team have become thought leaders in all things hybrid. With 22 franchisees up and running by July 2014, and another ten signed contracts in the works, they are poised for rapid growth as the hybrid market doubles and triples in the coming years. They've also received calls from all over the world, including Japan, Pakistan, Jordan, the Netherlands, and Australia, foreshadowing the global presence to come.

He's committed to moving and shaking in more ways than one, however. Matt also has a computer software development company that has built a tablet app, which allows auto repair shops to hold virtual meetings and webinars with customers. "The industry uses hundred-year-old equipment, and we're trying to promote technology and modernization," he explains.

Dulles South Youth Sports also continues to flourish, with ambitions to start a scholarship program to help bring sports into the lives of underprivileged children. "I hope all kids have the opportunity to grow up and have the lives I wish for my own kids—to become healthy, honest, good citizens who can really find true happiness in life." Named one of the top fifty philanthropists in D.C. by the *Washington Business Journal*, he's on the board of Final Salute, supporting homeless female veterans with housing and medical services. The Curry family has done tremendous work with a number of charities and has also traveled the world, finding ways to give back and transform communities in need while expanding their horizons and transforming their own world views in the process.

In advising young people entering the working world today, Matt underscores the importance of finding something you're passionate about and good at, starting at the beginning to learn it from the ground up, and then finding a better way to do it. "They say that, if you love what you do, you'll never work a day in your life," he says. "That may be true, but more importantly, you'll create passion, energy, and profits. The world will always need people who are passionate about finding better ways to do things, so as you walk your path in life, dare to look for possibilities past the traditionally paved routes, and dare to pursue them."

Robert Dickman

From Basketball to Business

Like most young boys, Robert Dickman grew up with the dream of becoming a professional athlete. Going to baseball games at the old Forbes Field with his dad, it was a Pittsburgh Pirate uniform he wanted to don. It wasn't until his freshman year of high school that he found his true athletic calling: basketball. Bob spent every day working on his game. He wanted to make varsity. He wanted to be good, and he saw himself getting better. With the opportunity to work hard at something he loved, he hoped his skills might open doors for him.

"There were no barriers for entry," he explains. "All you needed was a pair of tennis shoes and a basketball. The playground was always open." Coming from humble beginnings in Wheeling, West Virginia, this was important for Bob. Without the distractions of a TV or a car, he could really focus on his passion for the sport. Basketball was his ticket out, and he was going to make it count. He knew there were others better than him, but while Bob may not have been the best, he was always the hardest working. Going from a team hopeful, to a benchwarmer, to a starting player, he developed a strong sense of persistence, and this made him a leader on the court.

His dream of professional athletics paralleled the aspirations of many of his peers, and like the vast majority of them, Bob did not grow up to become a professional athlete. As a Principal at Avison Young, however, he uses what he learned on the court, as a team member and a captain, every day in his work.

A leading real estate services business, Avison Young promotes partner involvement with every client, and therein lays their competitive edge. Headquartered in Toronto, Canada Avison Young is a collaborative, global firm owned and operated by its principals. The company was founded in 1978 and comprises over 1,500 real estate professionals in 54 offices. They provide value-added, client-centric investment, sales, leasing, advisory, management, financing and mortgage placement services to owners and occupiers of office, retail, industrial and multi-family properties.

As a principal of Avison Young, Bob draws on his leadership skills in virtually every aspect of his work. He remembers a high school basketball game where he played point guard and was the leading scorer at the same time. Though his team lost, he couldn't help but reflect on what a great game he had played. His coach reminded him, "But we lost." In that moment, Bob realized how important teamwork is. "The job of the point guard is to get everyone involved," he says. "If this meant sacrificing scoring and not having my name frequenting the sports section of the local newspaper, then so be it." He learned that working together yields a greater outcome, and Bob sees this manifest in business all the time today. "Brokerage can be a very self-centered business," he explains. "You're paid by the transaction. You're paid above the company. Any chance to grow as a company depends on the ability to retain customers, and therefore it is critical to develop each member of your team. Some years you have to sacrifice income to keep that momentum growing."

Before he was a leader in business, and before he was a leader on the basketball court, Bob's first role as a leader was at home. When he was eight years old, his father passed unexpectedly, and Bob became the man of the house. With two older sisters and two younger brothers, he came to understand what that kind of responsibility really meant and sensed the fear in his mother. How was she going to make this work? How was she going to keep everything together? Bob had to be the point guard.

Wheeling was a steel town. Only 38 miles south of Pittsburgh on the Ohio River, blue-collar workers made up the brunt of the population of 85,000, and the Dickmans were no exception. Bob's grandfather ran an Atlas Van Line franchise, and after his father was the first to graduate college by earning a degree from the University of Pittsburgh, he returned to Wheeling to help run the family business. With the steel industry already in decline, the Dickmans' business was also struggling. When Bob's father passed, the family had a lot to overcome. His mother, Katherine, who until then had only known the work of a housewife, had a business to wind down, assets to sell, and a family of six to support on her own. Bravely, she got right to work as a bookkeeper for a senior home in North Wheeling. The books had never been balanced, and auditors were knocking on their door, but she was able to get everything under control within only two months. "She could stretch a dollar further than anyone," Bob describes, and for a family under such circumstances, this was crucial. With his mother's inspiration and his newfound responsibilities, he developed a strong work ethic.

If Bob wanted anything as a kid, he had to buy it for himself. He cut grass, delivered newspapers, did the yard work of all his neighbors, and between duties, he kept playing basketball. He won accolades for his talent on the town, county, and state level, and was ultimately recruited to Shepherd College in Virginia. Basketball proved to be the ticket out of Wheeling he was hoping for, but he was not granted the scholarship he needed. Fortunately for him, the college coach told him that if he made the varsity team, they would help him with financial aid. Bob made sure he did so, and played in that capacity all four years of college. By his senior year, he was varsity captain.

Bob's college life revolved around basketball, and he even chose his academic path based on which subject would allow him to make practice each afternoon. This meant majoring in business, which entailed classes in the morning, and in which Bob had never held a particular interest. After one Intro to Business class, however, he was sold. A former military colonel turned Wall Street guru, his first professor's unique perspective was captivating and sparked a real interest in Bob. Instructed to read the *Wall Street Journal* every day, he became fascinated, and soon his business major took on a concentration in accounting.

It was another professor, however, that further broadened Bob's perspective. "You're captain of the basketball team," the man told him. "That's great. But that's all going to end in two years. Then what are you going to do?" Approaching graduation, Bob realized he needed a job, but that he could use basketball as a tool to advance him. His coach took a look at his resume and suggested he put at the top that he was captain of the basketball team to highlight his leadership experience, and the advice proved solid. A job fair in Crystal City, Virginia landed him an interview at a company called the National Cash Register (NCR) in Rockville, and as fate would have it, behind the interviewer's desk was a basketball. The two talked about the sport for several hours, and by the end of the interview, Bob was hired. Within 48 hours of graduating college, he found himself employed and moving to Washington, D.C.

As an accountant, Bob helped the company collect money from the federal government, but he wasn't entirely enamored with the work. Doing the commission statements, he realized what kind of money the sales team was making—nearly the same in one month that Bob made all year. His hard work and persistence assured him he was capable of more, and he asked if he could get into the sales program. With no experience or computer engineering degree, however, he was not given the chance. As a result, Bob stayed only a year at NCR and went on to pursue his sales goals in telecommunications, where he truly excelled. It was in this capacity that he met his future wife, Ann, who began as a coworker, turned into a friend, and then turned into more. Life was taking off for Bob, and when NCR asked for him back two years later, he declined the offer.

While working in telecommunications, Bob had a coworker with an inspiring side hobby: he bought and flipped houses. At only 27 years old, this man had already acquired nine or ten properties and was renting them out. He had a game plan, and Bob was beyond impressed—he was fascinated. He had already developed a curiosity in real estate growing up in West Virginia, with all the talk of land and homes. Electing to take a real estate course in college had reminded him of that curiosity, but the work his colleague was doing in his free time piqued Bob's interest in a new way.

Given a promotion and the choice to move to either Cleveland or Buffalo to advance his telecommunications career, Bob chose neither. Instead, he decided to bite the bullet and give commercial real estate a try. With a friend working at a real estate firm called Danac in Bethesda, Maryland, Bob had an in. Though he didn't have any direct real estate experience, he had sales proficiency, a strong track record, and the unwavering confidence that his skills would translate. Lucky for him, they were looking for someone young to train who would accept a minimal salary. They took a chance on Bob, and unsurprisingly, he exceled.

In the first year Bob worked for Danac, the company was bought and sold four times. Once the dust settled after the final sale, it was in question whether or not they were going to maintain the brokerage aspect. With a new house, a pregnant wife, and an inherent drive for success, Bob demanded a commitment or threatened to look for work elsewhere. He was soon approached by Jack McShea Sr. to join the small real estate firm he was launching with big plans for the future, and it was just the kind of opportunity he was hoping for.

McShea & Company started as a typical father-and-son business. After a successful career in Real Estate Investment Trusts (REITs) and telecommunications, Jack McShea Sr. returned to real estate in 1983. With the help of his sons, Jack Jr. and Tim McShea, he began syndicating properties, but his visions for the company were bigger.

Jack wanted to expand and diversify. He sought to add brokerage, property management, and acquisitions to the list of services McShea & Company could provide. When Bob Dickman joined the company in 1986 as a broker, they were a staff of seven and had acquired only two properties. They grew to a team of 132 and managed over seven million square feet of office, retail, industrial, and residential space before Avison Young acquired them.

"I learned early in my career that the only constant is change, and that you always have to prove yourself and reinvent yourself," he affirms. Eager to stay at the forefront of the competitive real estate world, Bob is always trying to do things a little better, and he recalls from his days playing basketball that hard work does pay off. "Technological advancements help, but focus is more important," he explains. "Because people make their investments based on sound market data like vacancy rates, I'm cognizant of the fact that I'm very much in the information business, and I'm intent on gathering the best data possible for my clients." Salesmen solve problems, and with the investment he makes in his clients, Bob has set himself apart as one of the greats.

Bob also works hard to make sure each client feels taken care of because he knows what it feels like to have someone looking out for you. Growing up in the Catholic Church, attending Catholic school was all but expected. Even at $6 per week, however, his mother could not afford to keep her five children in the Catholic school system. The parish priest, Father Lee, did not accept this and told Katherine the kids would stay in his school. He told her not to worry about the money and that she would pay it back later in life, somehow. "I can vividly remember listening to that whole conversation and feeling the real effect of compassion," he says. "Knowing someone out there does care about you is a feeling I want my clients to understand at McShea & Company."

Bob and his wife Ann have found a way to pay back Father Lee for letting him and his siblings attend Catholic school, and today, Bob serves on the Board of Directors at the Catholic high school Our Lady of Good Counsel. The school requires students to involve themselves in community service, and when his own children were attending, they volunteered at SOME, So Others May Eat. In the last couple years, the Dickman family has gotten involved with the organization again and enjoys giving back in this way.

Today, Bob continues to live by a popular piece of advice his college coach gave him and his team. "To be early is to be on time," he recounts. "To be on time is to be late. And to be late is to be forgotten." In holding time as an asset, he also passes along his own bit of advice to young people entering the working world today. "Work hard and smart," he encourages. "Make yourself valuable by helping others. Be curious. These may be tough times, but if you do these things, they'll distinguish you in the long run." Bob and Ann's two children, Lauren, now 28, and Kevin, now 24, have found success heeding their father's advice—Lauren as a government consultant, and Kevin as a financial analyst.

From a young age, Bob learned how to take what you have and make it something bigger and better. Whether it was a penny, a chance to play basketball, or an opportunity to pursue business, this always meant hard work. "I don't think I'm a natural salesman, but I think I'm a great listener, and I think that definitely feeds into my success," he says. "To me, sales is more of a craft."

Honing a craft, as Bob has done, takes hard work and persistence. It also takes a great leader. First it was his mother, then it was his coach, then it was Jack McShea Sr. And then Bob Dickman became a leader himself. "I've always been inspired by Duke University's basketball coach, Mike Krzyzewski, who gave credit to the team for every win, but took full responsibility for every loss," Bob reflects. "He'd cite those losses as his own failure to prepare them correctly. That is the sign of a great leader, and I aim to take that kind of responsibility in my work at McShea & Company." From basketball to business, Bob has treated his life and his work the way his mother treated every dollar—stretching it far, making it count, and overcoming impossible odds through responsibility, enthusiasm, and the kind of commitment that comes from the heart.

BERNHARDT
WEALTH MANAGEMENT

Cameron Doolittle

THE PATH TO JOY

Cameron Doolittle can still remember being in first grade, when his father lost his job in construction. He was too young to understand how money worked, but he was old enough to know that "divorce"—a new phenomenon he had heard his friends talk about at school—was possible. As he noted the stress in his parents' voices and wondered if "divorce" was next, he made the decision that he would do whatever he could to be successful later in life. "I decided that wanting for money would not be my story," he remembers. "Financial security seemed like the path to joy—the best way to ensure that I wouldn't feel that way again."

As his family's situation stabilized and his father became a successful systems analyst, Cameron excelled in school and work, and sure enough, he was the Legislative Director to a powerful Member of Congress by the age of 24. When he realized that political power didn't hold much meaning to him, he switched to business, earning professional degrees from top universities and attaining remarkable success by the age of 33. But the business world didn't hold much meaning to him, either. A devout Christian from an early age, Cameron found himself understanding the Word of God with ever-increasing clarity. "Each of those experiences was a reaffirmation that the faith my parents taught me was, true and that the power and degrees and business success were meaningless without Jesus," he says.

It was these reaffirmations that led Cameron and his wife, Carolyn, to decide to put their trust in God and not money. "The freedom that came with that decision was incredible," Cameron notes. "I didn't feel like I had to chase that next promotion or big bonus. It was just this realization that enough is enough. Objectively, there's a level of money you need to be happy, and beyond that, diminishing returns kick in quickly. With that in mind, we've made a really intentional effort to live our lives for others."

Cameron is now the President and CEO of Jill's House, a nonprofit organization committed to bringing much-needed respite to the families of children with intellectual disabilities and weaving the story of Jesus into its mission and message. He has learned a lot about true security since his days as a first-grader. He's found that the path to joy isn't achieved through making money; it's achieved through bringing joy to others. "My joy comes from sharing the amazing news about God with people, developing great leaders, and building great organizations," he affirms. "At Jill's House, I get to do all of that, and more."

Jill's House was formally launched in 2010, but fundraising efforts for the organization began in 2003, when a young family in McLean, Virginia, received some news that would change its future forever. Lon Solomon was the senior pastor at McLean Bible Church, and he and his wife, Brenda, were the proud parents of three sons and a new daughter. Baby Jill seemed happy and healthy, until she started experiencing small seizures in her hand. They grew more violent and frequent, and life for the Solomons became an endless stream of doctors' visits, trips to the ER, and sleepless nights.

The stress was evident in their marriage, their parenting, and their work. One day, after Jill had suffered a particularly difficult seizure that left Brenda in tears, the phone rang. It was a woman named Mary. "I don't know you," came the unfamiliar voice, "but God told me to call you." Brenda's story came pouring out, and Mary immediately identified the missing piece. "What you need is respite," she said. "I know some people who can care for Jill to give you and Lon a little time to recharge."

With Mary's insight and assistance, life began to stabilize for the Solomons, and as they saw the tremendous benefit wrought by the simple gift of a few hours of peace, they knew there had to be thousands of other families out there who needed the same kind of help. Indeed, they were not alone. Families of children with intellectual disabilities suffer extremely elevated amounts of stress, which manifest in divorce rates 80 percent higher than normal. They experience higher rates of suicide, and siblings don't get the attention they need. "Our solution was simple and elegant," Cameron says. "We wanted to take care of children with intellectual disabilities overnight, giving parents a night or two each month to themselves. Even with that small break, stress levels plummet. We can't cure autism or cerebral palsy, but with God's grace, we can cure the stress gap that separates these families from every other family in the country."

Over the next seven years, the Solomons raised funds and built a center that would serve as a safe, fun place for children with special needs to stay, providing parents and caregivers with precious time to rest and recharge. With Cameron's help, the center opened its doors in 2010, and families began coming in droves. The 45-bed center began filling completely each weekend, so they rented extra space at a camp nearby. The organization then extended to Colorado Springs, Los Angeles, Austin, and Seattle, growing into a team of over a hundred employees with an annual budget of $5 million. Last year, they served 500 families, with a thousand additional families registered to receive assistance. "By God's grace, this idea of a rhythm of overnight respite is starting to change the face of disability ministry in America," Cameron affirms.

In the years since Jill's House first opened its doors, families have used their respite opportunities for things the team couldn't have imagined. A single mother brought her child to the center while she was recovering from chemotherapy. Some families used the extra time granted to them through respite to get their degrees, trying to build a better life for their family. Other families have used the time to attend the out-of-town graduations of their other children, since many children with intellectual disabilities have a hard time traveling.

Jill's House offers more than the gift of time—it offers the gift of God's grace to families who want to receive it. Ninety percent of the families who sign up with the organization have no connection to a church, and while some of them are not interested in engaging on matters of faith, others are. "Jill's House is certainly about providing resources to any family, regardless of religion," Cameron affirms. "But it's also about building relationships with those families, and through those relationships, we talk about the redemption and renewal that comes from living a life in Jesus. Giving the gift of physical rest gives us the chance to talk about that true spiritual rest and peace that comes from Jesus."

Indeed, while many people go through life pretending the world isn't fraught with pain and suffering, Jill's House is about confronting reality head-on, rather than denying it. "A lot of the families we serve are face-to-face with the brokenness of life every day," Cameron points out. "They recognize that the world isn't what it ought to be, and we have an answer for why that is. As Christians, our hope for a better future motivates us to love and support these families. We're not just talking the talk; we're walking the walk, and I think that leads to changed lives. It's not what I expected to be doing at 37, but it's absolutely incredible work, and I love it."

Though Jill's House wasn't exactly in Cameron's plans, it allows for a wholly faith-based lifestyle consistent with the very earliest days of his childhood growing up in Gresham, Oregon. His father was a pastor at the time of his birth, though he transitioned several years later to the construction industry. Even after the career change, his parents remained heavily involved with the church, routinely leading worship with his father on the guitar and his mother on the piano. "At first, my dad thought that, if you loved Jesus, you spent your life in vocational ministry," Cameron remembers. "But he came to understand that you can love and serve God in all different ways. When the recession hit in the 1980s, he went back to school for IT and found his calling, later becoming a systems analyst."

As his father went through those years of transition, young Cameron was being formed and shaped, observing the tremendous work ethic, industriousness, and integrity that were hallmarks of his father's spirit. "I remember him building our house with his own hands," Cameron recalls. "He'd go to work early in the morning so he could make it home in time to be there for my younger brother and me." Cameron's mother, a voracious reader, found ways to make sure her sons benefitted from cultural experiences, though the family was always strapped for cash. "I remember our church delivering a turkey to our home one Thanksgiving," Cameron says. "That was when I realized we were poor. Still, my parents always found time to support others who were going through hardship."

An avid football card, baseball card, and Legos collector, Cameron went on to earn his first dollar working a paper route. As soon as he was old enough to get his work permit, he got a job washing dishes at a pizza place. And as he matured, so did his faith. "In high school, I realized your faith can be more than something you just accept from your parents," he says. "I was reading the Bible myself, developing my own relationship with God."

Cameron's graduating class began with around 400 students, but had dwindled to 300 by the end of the year as students dropped out. "When you're not as affluent, you often know a limited number of stories about how life can go," he points out. "I didn't know what all was out there. I had heard people at church talk about the importance of having godly people in politics making good decisions, so I decided to study political science."

With that, Cameron enrolled at Wheaton College, a Christian school in Illinois. He enjoyed the experience but missed being with nonbelievers, whose eternity might actually be changed by what he said or did. With that in mind, he transferred to Stanford University. The summer between his sophomore and junior year, he landed an internship in Washington, D.C. with Senator Mark Hatfield, a man of great integrity and faith, and one of Cameron's heroes. "I was a kid from nowhere, but somehow, he and I connected," Cameron recalls. "I understood his philosophy in a unique way because we came from the same faith background. We were perfectly aligned on the concept that it's not the government who should be the agent of justice and mercy in society; it's the church. We agreed that the purpose of a charity isn't just to stabilize the needs of people; it's to be a vehicle for the spread of God's love."

When Cameron returned to Stanford that fall, he got a call from Mr. Hatfield's office asking him to write speeches for the Senator as he entered into retirement—a perfect way to help pay for his education. Upon graduating, he returned to Capitol Hill to serve as a Legislative Correspondent for Representative Joe Pitts from Pennsylvania. He moved on to serve as a Legislative Assistant for Representative Steve Largent, a former Seattle Seahawks player who had been another great hero through childhood. He then became the Legislative Director for Representative Lamar Smith. "It was fun, but in terms of actual meaning and impact, it felt lacking to me," he says.

During that time, Cameron met Carolyn, a Stanford student four years his junior who grew up in McLean. "A mutual friend told me about her, so we met for coffee one day while she was home for the summer," Cameron remembers. "By the end of the conversation, we both just had a really clear sense that God had made us for each other. I didn't know much at 23, but I knew how to pick an amazing woman." That spring, they got engaged, and Cameron pursued his graduate degrees in law and business at Berkeley so he could be near her.

The MBA program had been tacked on to his life plans almost as an afterthought. Cameron envisioned himself becoming a corporate attorney with a nuanced understanding of the business world. When he walked into his first MBA class, however, he fell in love. "I knew that this was what my mind was made to do," he recalls. "I loved everything about business—the problem solving, the data analysis, the pragmatism, the art of designing great customer experiences."

A couple weeks after Carolyn graduated from Stanford, they married and began to focus on Cameron's post-MBA plans. He was in the final rounds of interviews at McKinsey & Company when they discovered their first daughter was on the way. "The McKinsey job would have had me traveling all the time, and I wouldn't have been able to be the father I wanted to be," Cameron says. "We prayed a lot and then turned the McKinsey job down."

Instead, he took a position at a consulting firm called Corporate Executive Board, where he helped to launch new businesses for five fast-paced years. In 2006, he launched a group for Chief Financial Officers of mid-sized companies, which he grew to a $12 million business of 700 members. In 2007, he launched a General Counsel group that grew to 400. "I loved being that 'business launch' guy and was doing quite well, but I wondered if God had some other purpose for me," he says. "I expected I'd spend my life working there, trying to be generous to causes we care about and a truly loving manager to my team, but then a friend of mine who was on the board of Jill's House approached me. He explained that they needed someone to launch the center. They wanted to run it with a focus on Jesus's love, but with the excellence of a business. I decided to give it six months before returning to my real life."

Six months became a year. One year became two. And now, Cameron feels that Jill's House may be his life's work. "One thing I love about the organization is that it's fueled by people with a lot of philanthropic passion," he remarks. "It's a beautiful thing that, through the generosity of our donors, we can take the work of IT consulting or defense contracting and turn it into the work of mercy. There are many people who wonder what the meaning of their work is, and while there's certainly inherent value in doing well and being excellent at what you do, I think there's also a layer of joy that can be added to the tougher moments of the day-to-day work of our donors when they stop to realize, this work is also becoming the work of mercy. Lives are being changed and futures are being altered because of the emails they write and the meetings they have."

Now, as a leader, Cameron works to build a great spiritual environment for his staff that encourages people to surprise themselves. He assesses what people are capable of and then asks them to deliver on those abilities, giving them chances to accomplish things they don't think they can do. Many of his protégés have gone on to assume leadership roles at Amazon and Google; others have gone on to launch their own companies. "I like to give people big jobs with big responsibilities, and I expect big results," he affirms. "It's about loving people enough to know them, push them, and support them."

In advising young people entering the working world today, Cameron highlights the lessons taught by athletics—discipline, hard work, and an awareness of the power of delayed gratification. "Get a real job, and find ways to contribute without getting glory," he suggests. "Go in with the attitude that you have a lot to learn." Even as a leader today, Cameron remains deeply engaged in the learning process, having recently been selected as a Praxis Fellow for his excellence as a social entrepreneur.

His greatest honor, however, remains the accolades of the people Jill's House touches each year. On a scale of one to 10, the organization is consistently rated a 9.9 in its efforts to transform the lives of families all over the country. Yet local lives are never forsaken for national impact. Cameron and Carolyn are leaders in their small Arlington church, frequently hosting parenting seminars and mentoring young couples in marriage, even as the couple raises their own four children. "Carolyn is an incredibly wise, faithful, and giving partner," Cameron says. "I don't know why she chose me, but I'm so thankful she did. I make life efficient and well-planned, and she makes life beautiful and fun. It's awesome to have found the path to joy, and to walk together. It's not the life I expected, but it's a life lived for others and for Jesus. I wouldn't trade it."

Herbert S. Ezrin

Where There's a Will

By the time Herbert Ezrin started his eighth grade year at Jefferson Junior High School in Southwest Washington, D.C., his will to succeed in school had been deprived of oxygen for so long that it was all but gone. Growing up in the impressive shadows of three older siblings, and with his parents tending to his baby brother when they weren't hard at work at their convenience store, Herb struggled with his role as a student. He had attended one school until age seven, and then another when his family moved to Northwest Washington. When the family moved again, he relocated to another building and a new group of kids for junior high. He had friends and liked his teachers, but in some ways he felt lost, and it reflected in his poor academic performance.

Jefferson, a school in a lower middle-class neighborhood, was run by Hugh Smith, one of the top ten public school principals in the country at the time. He had gathered an exceptional team of teachers and among them was Robert Boucher. As Mr. Boucher got to know the shy boy in his algebra class, he saw something subtle hidden beneath Herb's self-doubt. It was will and potential he was seeing, so Mr. Boucher committed himself to helping Herb find his way.

Herb began to notice and appreciate the extra personal attention Mr. Boucher made a point to show him, and the lessons taught in his classroom that far surpassed book learning. He'll never forget the day Mr. Boucher wrote a long algebra question on the board, turning to the class of several dozen students for an answer. Herb raised his hand and gave his answer, only to be told by the teacher that it was wrong. Other students offered their solutions, but he rejected all of them. Finally, Mr. Boucher put the correct answer on the board—the same answer Herb had first given. "When I told him it was the answer I gave, he looked at me and then playfully tossed the eraser at me," Herb recalls today. "He said, 'Of course that was your answer. Remember that.' He was telling me that I had the ability; I just didn't know it. I just needed to have faith in myself."

The entirely singular education Mr. Boucher gave him lent Herb the confidence he needed to uncover the power of his own will. From his eighth grade year until he graduated from high school, he never missed the honor roll. "He was my all-time number one mentor," Herb affirms. "He drew out my capabilities in the best way possible. He meant so much to me, and we stayed in touch until the day he died."

By then, Herb was practicing law and living in Potomac, Maryland. Many years later, in the local Safeway one evening, he happened to notice that the nametag of the manager—a friendly young lady he spoke to from time to time—read Boucher. He asked her if she was related to his beloved teacher in any way, only to discover that she was his daughter. "All the gratitude I felt for the way he changed my life ran through me," he says. "She took the time that day to talk to me, and the next time I saw her, she came running up to me. She had told her mother about our conversation, and her mother knew all about me. That school and that particular teacher changed my whole life." Now the founder, President, and CEO of Potomac Business Group, Herb has dedicated his life to using his will to find a way, helping others navigate the roads they find themselves on and helping them build new ones when a fresh path forward is needed.

Herb launched Potomac Business Group in 1994 as an investment banking firm in Potomac, Maryland. With a team of eight business associates, the company specializes in M&A, capital raises, financing, loans, turnaround work, and the real estate transactions that accompany the sale of businesses that owns property. His daughter, a talented graphic designer, created his logo, and he set to work on branding—not only of his business, but also of himself. "I understand that, when I'm branding Potomac Business Group, I'm also branding Herb Ezrin," he says. "So much of my success is built on the reputation I've developed in the greater business community, and throughout the country." Herb also launched Tidewater Biodiesel, LLC, through which he's working to start a biodiesel business in Chesapeake, Virginia. "The will is there," he remarks. "Now we're working out the way."

Pushing through adversity toward achievement has been a hallmark of the Ezrin family ever since his great grandfather emigrated from Russia to Washington in the wake of the Civil War. Growing up in the D.C. area, Herb's grandfather set his sights on studying classical music, but as a Jew, he was barred from studying at a conservatory in Washington. Determined, he went back to Russia to study at the University of Moscow. There, he married and fathered 13 children, the youngest being Herb's father. In 1907, when his father was only five years old, a cohort of the family moved back to D.C., and while the Ezrin name still exists in Russia today, Herb was born a fourth-generation Washingtonian.

His mother, of Lithuanian descent, worked long hours alongside his father, modeling a strong work ethic that Herb readily absorbed and would pass on to his own children. Their store was located next door to a movie theater in Southwest Washington, and the Greek gentleman who owned the building had agreed to let the Ezrins' store sell all concessions to his moviegoers. Herb began working at the store at ten years of age to earn his allowance, where he met Sidney Kline, a gentleman who sold products to the store. The two took a liking to one another, and for $5 a day, a nice lunch, and an ice slush, Sidney hired Herb to ride around with him on his delivery truck, running parcels into customers as he idled in the street.

These experiences as a boy working for his parents primed Herb with highly marketable skills for summer jobs in later years. When he was sixteen, he was hired as the cashier at a busy store in Dupont Circle. "It was always jammed with customers throwing money at you, particularly at lunchtime," he remembers. "Everyone else who worked the cash register would crack under the pressure and come up short at the end of the night, but not me. I was used to the crowds that came into and out of the movie theater, so I was prepared for those later work experiences."

What Herb wasn't prepared for was the news he received in early 1961, when his local draft board let him know that his name was on the list and he'd be drafted that year. He was taking part-time accounting classes at American University (AU), and the Vietnam War was just gearing up. If he didn't enlist or join a reserve or guard unit, he'd be placed in the Army, the Navy, the Air Force, or the Marines, his fate lifted entirely from his own hands. With that, he began searching and finally found an opportunity in the Air National Guard at Andrews Air Force Base—the last opening they'd have that year.

Eight weeks of basic training in the dead of summer commenced. The Berlin Wall was erected, and a week after Herb was discharged back to the Guard Unit, he received a certified letter in the mail letting him know that his guard unit had been activated. He reported to full-time active duty at Andrews Air Force Base on October 1st, where he would spend the next year guarding the East Coast. "There were a lot of drills and exercises and things that needed to be done, but once we realized we weren't being deployed overseas, I got permission to continue with my courses at AU," he explains. "I had worked with an accountant previously, and I called him up to offer my help during tax season to make some extra money."

Herb finished up his accounting credits and made the Dean's List in 1962. Then, in June of 1963, he married Sandra, who he had been introduced to five years earlier by her cousin, the wife of Sidney Kline. When the two met on a blind date, it was love at first sight, and they never dated anyone else. They had promised their parents they'd wait to marry after Sandra finished her undergraduate studies, so the date was set for a week after her graduation. "She has incredible intuition and has been my rock through all the ups and downs of life," he affirms today. "She's incredibly supportive but will tell me when she thinks I'm wrong, which is important. She's incredibly strong and loyal, and operates with the highest degree of ethics."

Several months after the wedding, Herb started law school and kept working part-time in accounting. He became an editor for the Law Review. The month he graduated and earned his JD, President Lyndon Johnson signed a bill granting full VA benefits to all who served through the Berlin Crisis, so he went on to earn his LLM in Taxation at the Georgetown University Law Center. Between his time in the guard, the Air Force, and a reserve unit, he spent almost six years in service before being honorably discharged, and today, he keeps a piece of the Berlin Wall—a gift from his niece—as a token of the impact it had on the course of his life.

Herb began as an accountant and became a CPA, and then entered the legal profession, landing a job with a tax attorney in a small office. To start, he was given a tax court case, a district court tax case, and a Supreme Court case, which kept him challenged and engaged. He left the firm in April of 1967 with a job at an esteemed law firm, where he worked for three years before striking out on his own, renting office space from an accounting firm, and forming a partnership with a colleague.

The two worked together for several years before merging with another small firm and moving the practice to Chevy Chase, Maryland, where it remained for ten years. Three weeks before they were set to move out of their office space, however, their suite burned down, launching the firm into a mini crisis that ultimately led to its demise. "We had ten partners, plus associates, but the team wasn't pulling together the way I had hoped it would," Herb remembers. "It was 1984, and we weren't making our budgets. As the Administrative Partner, I laid out a plan that afforded a pathway forward, which involved cutting some overhead and developing a new culture of teamwork. I asked for a show of support, and not one hand went up. That's when I knew that it wasn't the place for me anymore."

With that, Herb called his original partner and proposed they start their own small firm again, taking one associate with them. He practiced for several more years and then got involved in some major business deals in the food industry. He was challenged more in that capacity than he was practicing law, and was met with great success from 1987 through 1990. All that changed, however, when the Federal Reserve changed its regulation of interest rates. "Ours went from eight to 18 percent," he says. "It killed our cash flow, and business deals dried up. We ended up liquidating everything and selling it off."

Now, Herb is free to focus his time and energy on Potomac Business Group, where each deal and each client challenges his mind in its own way. "I consider myself a problem solver," he says. "I go out of the box to solve a problem, whether it's getting a deal done or protecting a client in a litigation proceeding." Herb has also been a Board Member, Treasurer, and Committee Chair at the Association for Corporate Growth, and a Board Member of Exit Planning Exchange and of several charitable organizations. He finds himself always drifting naturally into leadership roles, as he has done his whole life.

In advising young people entering the working world today, Herb emphasizes the importance of honesty and openness. "Try not to be shy," he says, reminiscent of the lessons Mr. Boucher taught him. "Speak up for yourself, and remember that everything's always changing, so it's important to always keep learning. And when you decide what you want to do, be the best you can be at whatever it is. That's what people really want."

In striving to do his best through his long and varied career, Herb has found his greatest accomplishments and accolades not in awards or salaries, but in his family and friends. To him, success is when Sandra is out with friends, and one of them mentions to her that people stop and listen when Herb speaks. It's in the promise and potential of their three children and four grandchildren. It's in an article published in the local newspaper about his oldest son's avid involvement in the community. In the piece, the interviewer asked the source of his son's drive to work hard and stay dedicated to charitable and community affairs. "He said he got that from watching Sandra and me," Herb says. "That's one of the greatest accomplishments I could ever hope for." It's in the drive his second son has as an entrepreneur, and in the passion his daughter has for her charitable and community work. It's the Ezrin spirit, passed down from one generation to the next—the will that always finds a way.

BERNHARDT
WEALTH MANAGEMENT

Jon Frederickson

The Science of Art

Growing up in Clear Lake, a small town in Iowa, Jon Frederickson spent most free afternoons and weekends working in his father's blacksmith shop. Effectively an apprenticeship, his training focused on the technical precision and skill required for impeccable work in sawing, drilling, welding, braising, and forging. "In this sense, my father was my first teacher," he recalls now. "Every Saturday through the school year, and every summer vacation, I was watching him demonstrate excellence so I could learn the technique myself."

Jon recognized the same cycle of demonstration and repetition in high school, when he became an accomplished French horn player. His remarkable music career spanned college and extended into adulthood, when he became a professional musician, and though he had come a long way from the blacksmith shop, the recipe for success had remained the same. "When playing an instrument, you can have a lot of great ideas, but your work is nothing without technical mastery," he points out. "It's exceptionally technique-oriented. If I had trouble playing a phrase, the teacher would demonstrate it, and I'd repeat it back. There was constant attention to the tiny details that lead to true mastery."

When he decided to pursue his lifelong interest in therapy, however, things were different. His specific questions were met with vague answers, and his technical lines of inquiry were all met with brick walls. Finally, his professor lent voice to the issue. "He told me I was too focused on technique, when psychotherapy is more of an art," Jon recounts. "I was playing as an extra in the National Symphony Orchestra at the time, and I knew a little about art. I knew it wasn't vague and wholly intuitive, as many in the therapy field would have you believe. There is a tremendous amount of technical mastery that's needed, and a number of critical decision points along the way. It was like a light bulb going off in my head. I knew that true excellence in art and craft has a science to it. I wanted to learn and teach psychotherapy like my father taught blacksmithing, and like my teachers taught music—through repetition, diligence, and metrics for success."

The data spoke to Jon's observation, with success rates in psychotherapy outcome research remaining relatively stagnant through the last fifty years. While other experts—chess masters, baseball pitchers, and world class surgeons—have grown more effective in recent decades thanks to advancements in technology, analytics, and training, psychotherapy has been held back by privacy and protectiveness—not by concerns around the confidential information of patients, but more by an innate aversion in therapists to videotaping and sharing their work. "Psychoanalysis, which I'm trained in, is a fairly conservative group within psychotherapy, and when I first considered videotaping sessions, I was nervous for the confidentiality of the patient," Jon says. "But then I realized I was more nervous about violating my own confidentiality, making my work a hundred percent vulnerable to viewers. When people see your technique like that, their criticisms are systematic, detailed, and incontrovertible. There's no way to hide—you are held completely accountable for your work."

Yet in that vulnerability and scrutiny lies the power of Jon's approach. Intensive short-term dynamic psychotherapy, or ISTDP, is a form of therapy that utilizes video-recorded research to develop and highlight empirical techniques, and its success is a testament to the idea that there is science in the art of the work. "In reviewing the tape from a session, I can see exactly where a patient and I get stuck, and I can assess how to move forward," Jon says. "It's a form of quality control. Top performers are always getting feedback, and these videotapes are a crucial tool for teaching students to recognize their blind spots in assessing the physiological signs of anxiety."

Now the founder of ISTDP Institute, an organization focused on alleviating human suffering through psychotherapy, psychotherapy training, and supervision, Jon continues to invest his life's work in elevating the standards of his field, dedicated to transforming a profession that can transform the lived experience for people around the globe. Recognizing that pain from illness, loss, and death is a natural part of life, ISTDP focuses on the alleviation of suffering. Jon himself became acutely aware of the difference between the two at age five, when he was in his bedroom taking a nap with his younger brother and sister. When he heard a strangled choking noise coming from across the room, he looked to see his brother tangled in the cords of the curtains. He jumped out of bed and rushed over to help, but he wasn't able to save him—his brother died in his arms.

The next 24 hours were a blur, with the arrival of the emergency crew and the somber faces of the neighbors who cared for Jon and his sister through the night. Through the funeral the next day, his worldview took on the endlessness that comes from realizing that some questions in life have no answers. "At five years old, I found myself confronted with death in that profound way, and began wondering where people go when they die," he remembers. "What does it mean that some people disappear and we don't see them again? What is the meaning of life and death? What are the connections? I saw my parents go through this devastating loss, and through these many questions I was exploring, I wanted to help those who were suffering."

Growing up in a town of only 6,000 residents, where everyone knew everyone and lighthearted jokes were traded with each handshake, Jon had an intimate window into the tragedies that befell members of his community. Yet paradoxically, there was no outlet to talk about the events and the feelings they induced. When a neighbor committed suicide, or when a friend's son died in a tragic tractor accident, the town maintained a stiff upper lip and put one foot in front of the other. "I remember one visit to my uncle's house when I was twelve, and I overheard my father say that he had almost killed himself many times, but suicide was a coward's way out," Jon recalls. "It really affected me, realizing people just had to gut it out because there was no help to be had. When I came to D.C. many years later, it felt like I was arriving from a different planet, there were so many services available. I've remained very mindful that, in this country and around the world, therapy isn't as available as it is in urban areas."

Jon's grandfather had been a blacksmith from Denmark who immigrated to Iowa and set up a shop there. He died in 1943, but Jon's father returned home from the World War II and reopened the shop. As a small boy, Jon would sweep up, take measurements, set up the jigs, and slice iron. By first grade, he could sharpen the sickles of hay mowers used by farmers. When he was in sixth grade, his father suffered an injury in the shop that meant he couldn't work for two weeks, so Jon ran things on his own. By high school, it was clear that he was being primed to run the shop one day—perhaps after several years of community college.

Though he saw no problem with this future, Jon had always had a remarkable studiousness about him. Neither of his parents had gone to college, yet he was a voracious reader, spending all of his earnings from the shop on books. He had a particularly compelling English teacher at his Catholic high school who posed an extensive reading list to the class, requiring that every student pick twenty books to read each semester. Amongst the Shakespeare plays and existential pieces, Jon happened to come across the works of Erich Fromm. "In reading *Escape from Freedom* and *The Sane Society*, I was struck by the brilliance of economics and philosophy woven into psychoanalysis," Jon recounts. "I thought it might be cool to become a psychoanalyst someday."

At the time, however, Jon's talent lay in music. Amidst blacksmithing and a stellar academic performance, he had been inspired to practice his horn relentlessly by the remarkable kindness of his high school band director. As luck would have it, he began to show real talent for the instrument, making all-state band during his sophomore year. When he was a junior, he became the first horn in the all-state band, and he began paying for his own classes with a talented teacher in Cedar Falls, Iowa—an eighty-mile drive from his home. The teacher convinced him to apply to the National Music Camp that summer, where he was awarded a scholarship. "It was the first summer I didn't have to work," he laughs. "For eight weeks, I was in this amazing place, surrounded by music and people from all over the world. It was a great experience, and I wanted to get out there in that world."

Fortunately, when Jon's horn teacher heard he wasn't planning to pursue music through college, he hopped in a car and paid a visit to Jon's parents, ultimately convincing them that Jon had real talent. "He really changed my life," Jon affirms. "He's living proof that you can make a difference, person by person. I don't know if he fully realized what he did for me, but he changed the course of a life." With that, Jon started studying at the University of Minnesota, continuing his classes at Indiana University and then finishing at the University of Washington. Upon completing his undergraduate degree, he became a freelance musician in Washington, D.C. When an extra horn player was needed in the Opera House Orchestra or the National Symphony, Jon was ready to take the stand. It was in this capacity, drifting from engagement to engagement, that Jon met Kathleen, the oboist who would become his wife. She was also a freelance musician, and they dreamed of getting into the same orchestra.

The National Symphony had five relevant openings over the next several years, and Jon and Kathleen made it to the finalist stage each time, but neither of them landed the job. Finally, as Jon decided he was tired of freelancing, a new thought dawned on him: what if Kathleen continued to try out for orchestras, while he went back to graduate school to become a therapist like he had wanted? With that, at age 28, he enrolled at Catholic University and played concerts every night to help cover the costs.

Jon graduated from the Washington School of Psychiatry in 1982 and worked for four years at the American University Counseling Center before going into private practice full-time. He developed some prominence throughout the D.C. area, teaching at the Washington School of Psychiatry and presenting frequently. By chance, he happened to attend a class in 2000, in which the speaker showed his work using ISTDP. "As soon as I saw his presentation, I was dying to know everything about it," Jon avows. "I had never traveled overseas for a conference before, but I promptly signed up for an ISTDP conference in Italy. I thought it was incredible; I couldn't believe patients were improving so quickly." Empowered by his belief in the philosophy, Jon approached one expert and asked to study with her. He then approached one of the leaders of the conference and asked to host the next one in D.C. "I was going to make this happen," he affirms.

With the supervision of leaders in the field, and with the guidance of ISTDP experts in Montreal, Jon found his own effectiveness improving dramatically. He had an opportunity to present his work at a 450-person conference in Denmark, with attendees from all over the world. "I was presenting the case of a dissociative patient—someone many people would have given up on as untreatable," he says. "But I showed my videotape, which demonstrated a pretty dramatic change in him." When the presentation ended and the crowd honored him with a standing ovation, Jon realized he had turned a corner. Having worked tirelessly in relative anonymity for 25 years, he was suddenly a superstar, receiving invitations to present all over Europe. "How does the son of a blacksmith end up presenting his research at Oxford University?" he says. "My life exploded with an entirely new career, and ever since, I've spent over two months each year training people abroad."

The training element of his work is crucial, magnifying the potential for positive impact exponentially. Indeed, research indicates that a significant percentage of therapists actually harm patients, so he sought prospects for raising the bar of proficiency by disseminating training materials to others around the world. With this vision, he launched the institute in 2009 as a way to train trainers, educate stakeholders, host webinars, sell books, and make information available. "I wanted to help as many people as possible by leveraging the internet and my time," he says. "Now, through the institute, I have a team of six people who help host webinars and conferences, and a core group of 12 people doing trainings all over Europe."

With a leadership reach that spans oceans and continents, Jon's influence is powered by inspiration. "In teaching others about my work, I show them what I believe in, what we do, and what we see," he says. "If people want to do the same thing, I invite them to join me and offer them a viable and verifiable path forward. I'm always struck by the fact that most people really long to do something meaningful. The only question we really care about answering is, can we actually help this person we're seeking to help?"

Though his wife, Kathleen, has continued to invest her passion in music, the inspiration that fuels her has the same power as the dedication that drives Jon, allowing them to understand each other on the most fundamental of levels. "I'm truly blessed by this woman," he says. "To be a professional musician in the Opera House Orchestra, she has to practice three hours a day, even on vacation, so she totally understands what psychotherapy means to me. She understands that I could never treat it as a job, or just a way to make money. Some of my colleagues think I'm crazy because I'm always working or reading about the field, but she knows. We're two people incredibly passionate about what we do, and incredibly excited for each other that we've been able to find so much success in our respective careers."

In advising young people entering the working world today, Jon emphasizes the importance of pursuing meaning in work. "It's kind of this idea of having a vocation," he explains. "Too few people think about what their vocation is, and too many people do work that's not really meaningful to them. It's a hollow point in their life. I would urge people to find something that's meaningful to them, because passion, more than money, will make you happy. Even if it takes a while to find what's meaningful to you, give your life the natural time it needs—it's worth the time and energy to find it."

Beyond this, Jon underscores emotional intelligence as the best predictor of success, focusing on persistence as a key element often overlooked. "As a youngster, I remember turning 25 and cursing the day because I hadn't achieved anything yet," he says. "I didn't realize that success would come with the next 25 years of persistence. I had gotten on my path—now it was time to work my tail off and remember that the race goes to the long-distance runner, the person who's willing to pursue passion and work hard every day. In many ways, success is about the discipline to follow through. It's about dreaming without limitations, but firmly grounding those visions in the empirical observation that creates real, lasting, life-changing results."

Steven Freidkin

Transformative Technologies

It all started when Steven Freidkin absentmindedly donned a red collared shirt one morning when he was 13 years old. He had always been drawn to technology, often stopping by CompUSA to check out the latest products and software on the market. On that particular day, he was traversing the aisles, when a customer mistook him for an employee and began asking for his advice on which computer to buy. "I don't work here, but tell me about your needs," he said, excited to be putting his knowledge to work for the first time. Steven helped the customer pick the right product and, upon request, helped set it up as well.

With that, a passion and pastime evolved into a job. Over the next several decades, that job flourished into a livelihood, and then into a company that now fuels the livelihoods of almost a hundred full-time employees—Ntiva, Inc. As its founder and President, Steven continues to combine his passion for entrepreneurship and business with his gift for using technology to solve problems, providing clients with tech support that reaches to the heart of each enterprise, the root of each problem, and the transformative power of each technological solution.

Steven's first customer, the man who mistook him for a 13-year-old CompUSA employee, was so impressed that he offered the whiz kid an internship in his large company's IT department that summer. In the fall, he retained Steven's services for personal IT matters and began referring him to other executives in McLean, Potomac, Rockville, and Bethesda. "I developed a pretty good business providing information on custom computers—what people should get, how to order the products, how to set them up, and how to solve whatever issues might arise," Steven recalls. "I did all of this through my sole proprietorship, Custom Computer Creators."

Eventually, a customer—someone Steven had been serving for four years—sold his company and decided to launch a mortgage business, asking Steven to handle the technological aspects. While Steven was not familiar with the business world yet, he was committed to working hard and providing value to the business. Through that commitment, he assisted in building the technology to allow the company to scale rapidly to meet its business volume. That mortgage company referred other companies to Steven, and before long, he found himself helping an organization scale from four to 400 employees. "It took me a long time to figure it all out because I didn't know what I was doing," he laughs. "But I kept trying till I got it right, and with the experience came proficiency. I developed a recurring revenue model, where I got paid a monthly retainer fee, and through word of mouth, lots of other mortgage companies contacted me to take over their IT support. By the time I was 19, I had 60 hours a week of recurring revenue."

As the work piled up, Steven began hiring contractors and took his clients' advice to charge more for his work. One of the contractors, 20 years his senior and boasting extensive experience in technology and large corporate networks, began moonlighting with Custom Computer Creators on evenings and weekends. When he realized he couldn't continue the contract work while keeping his full-time job and raising his family, he and Steven decided to launch a new company. With that, in December of 2004, Ntiva was born.

In formally launching a company at only twenty years of age, Steven was bound to make a mistake or two along the way. "In my infinite wisdom, despite advice to the contrary from every smart person I knew, I made him a 50/50 partner," Steven recounts. "I thought we would need his technical skills and age to really legitimize us in the eyes of businesses we hoped to serve. But as time went on and we hired more people, it became apparent that he didn't have the same work ethic, drive, and commitment to the company. He was a great technician, but he had a different approach to business. I was committed to growing Ntiva based on profitability, even if it meant I had to work 80 hours a week. My partner's philosophy was to borrow money to build up the infrastructure and services, and the business would follow. Maybe he was right, but I didn't want to owe anyone anything."

By July 2008, the partners decided to separate, again

running into disagreements over the company's worth. It was an ordeal that ultimately lingered for seven years, underscoring the dangers of a 50/50 partnership. "It was an extremely expensive life lesson," says Steven. "I'm happy to have been able to afford it, but I wouldn't wish it on anyone else."

Through this challenge, Ntiva was nurtured by Steven's intuitive foresight and indelible commitment to leading his company according to his own sense of reason and responsibility. Observing the rapid growth of many of his mortgage company clients, he noticed that the unbridled success seemed unnatural, and even illogical. By 2006, he noted that over half of his revenue came from the mortgage industry and made an immediate commitment to diversify. "Even though I respected the owners of those companies and continued to support them, we stopped taking on new mortgage company clients and focused on bringing in other types of businesses," he explains. "Something just didn't feel right. We grow exclusively by word-of-mouth and referral, so it was hard to change that cycle, but succeeded. It's a good thing we did, because only one or two of those companies still exists today."

Instead of facing certain desolation when the housing market collapsed in 2008, Ntiva was appropriately diversified and poised for success. As a result, the several years that followed were among its best yet as they delivered on their value proposition of a high touch, high response, high accuracy technical support services for companies looking to outsource their IT departments. The experience was a huge lesson—not only in trusting his intuition, but also in the importance of contributing real value through business. After watching mortgage company after mortgage company collapse because they ultimately weren't creating value through sales, Steven developed a keen eye for business value that allowed him greater discretion in choosing which clients to take on. "If a company doesn't add value in what they do, we're likely not going to succeed in adding value to them, so they won't be a long-term fit," says Steven.

In assessing good long-term fits, Steven and his team serve small to mid-sized businesses and nonprofit associations. "Our ideal customer is someone who recognizes that technology is strategic, and that it needs to be part of their company to grow and evolve," he explains. "It's a company that has a vision for their technological capacity but lacks the internal resources to carry it through themselves. That's where we come in." Ntiva's average customer size today is around 38 employees, but its clients range from as small as two employees and as large as 15,000. With 85 full-time employees, the company generates around $15 million a year in revenue, and is driven to maintain its commitment to excellence every day through the examples set by its own clients. One of them, Dennis Ratner, Founder of Hair Cuttery, has been a client since Steven was 14 years old. "At the core of his business, he has always wanted to wow each customer with every touch, and to make sure his internal team is equally wowed, because he knows they're the ones facilitating those interactions," Steven recalls. "As a trusted advisor, I've been so fortunate to have the opportunity to learn how all my exceptional clients run their own companies, and to bring those lessons back to my own business."

Steven's business acumen is also modeled by the example set by his parents. His father launched a CPA firm which he operated for forty years, while his mother ran a boutique eye care and optometric practice starting in 1976. His father had three children from a previous marriage, but all were considerably older than Steven. Growing up in Potomac, Maryland, in the middle of nowhere, his interest was cinched for life the day his older brother showed up at home with a computer when Steven was six years old. "I took every opportunity to play with it, learn about it, take it apart, and put it back together," he remembers. "I was completely fascinated by the technology that was transforming the world just as my mind was developing enough to figure it out."

Around that time, Steven's father took him to a large philanthropic event and promised he'd pay his son $1 for every person the boy walked up and introduced himself to. With that, young Steven went marching around to as many people as he could, gaining a new level of comfort with the act of extending his hand to a stranger. "I was disappointed I only made $220 at that 500-person party," he laughs today. "But it was extremely rewarding—not only for the dollar incentive, but more so because I got an idea of how important relationships are in business. Lots of people can provide similar products or services, but having a relationship allows you to truly understand a client."

Steven's other primary source of income through those early years was selling rocks—an endeavor he launched at the age of seven. He would collect rocks on the street and sell them at every opportunity, amassing $1,500 by the time he was 13. He used that money to invest in DJ equipment—a move that outraged his father, but eventually proved profitable as he became a hot commodity for Bar Mitzvahs, weddings, and other events. "I made a few hundred bucks per event, and for a geeky kid, it was great to have girls excited about what I was doing and wanting to be involved."

In his spare time, Steven worked as a busboy at Potomac Pizza, got a job scooping ice cream, and was no stranger to helping out at his mother's eyeglass shops, where he had stamped envelopes since he was four years old. He got a job at Woodside Deli in Rockville when he was fifteen, working Friday evenings and all day during the weekend. By the time he was sixteen, he was managing the business's catering, operations, and restaurant. He did that until the age of eighteen, when Custom Computer Creators began demanding all of his time. "Up to that point, I was making $500 or $600 a weekend, and then $1,000 or $1,500 a month on computer work," he recalls. "I had no social life, and the Dean's assistant let me leave school as needed to go to work. I didn't do it because I needed the money, but I knew that I needed to be financially independent in order to pursue my own path. Otherwise, I would have had to become an accountant and followed the goals of others."

As he neared the end of his high school career, Steven decided to apply only to the University of Maryland's Smith School of Business. The school had a one percent acceptance rate, and Steven mentally prepared himself for the high likelihood that he would not be accepted, yet his precautions were unneeded. He was admitted, and ultimately decided to live in Tysons Corner to be near his office and commuting to College Park for class. Adapting the pattern he had utilized in high school, he attended lectures as needed, studied prolifically, and got near perfect grades. "It was really rewarding because I could apply the information directly to technology and what I was doing at work," he remarks. "Technology is always changing, so I decided not to enroll in their computer sciences program. Instead, I majored in Accounting, a field of study that has remained virtually unchanged for hundreds of years. I decided that if I could get accounting as my core, I could apply it to the ever-changing field of technology as a great differentiator."

By 2005, Steven had only a couple classes left to finish his degree, but they were in subjects that had nothing to do with his major. Having studied opportunity cost in a number of economics classes, he decided the value added of finishing his last couple courses wasn't worth it, and opted to drop out before finishing his degree. He was eager to shift his complete focus back to his clients—an impulse he became particularly thankful for the night he got a call from Solarus Salon and Spa in Arlington, Virginia. The company had been experiencing network problems all day and needed to be operational again by the time they opened the next morning, so even though it was midnight, Steven headed over to the site with his new puppy, Radar.

Upon arriving, he met Heather, the daughter of the salon owner. As he worked, she played with the small silky terrier, and by the end of the late-night maintenance session, Heather and Radar had become fast friends. Steven had Heather watch the puppy over the next several months as he made frequent business trips to Los Angeles, and before they knew it, the two began dating. Four years later, they adopted another dog, Doppler. Heather took a job in Ntiva's accounts receivable department, and the couple married on May 26, 2013. "She's incredibly focused when it comes to getting things done," Steven says. "She's very free in sharing her thoughts and feelings, which allows me to be a better leader and a better person. She's great at picking through a situation and providing insight I wouldn't have thought of otherwise." The couple welcomed their son into the world on April 30, 2014.

In advising young people entering the working world today, Steven underscores the value of hard work and consistency. Having observed people who jump around from thing to thing, driven by instant gratification or the simple thrill of trying something that seems different and exciting, he believes much can be lost to those gaps. "If you're consistent in what you want to do and you dedicate yourself to it, you'll get better and better," he explains. "You'll never be the best, but you'll place yourself on that upward trajectory, making more money and achieving a level of mastery you can't get otherwise. Find what you're passionate about, and then don't worry about anything else. If you really love that thing, you'll push hard for it and have fun in the process."

Ntiva is the living proof of that philosophy's potential. And as Steven's approach as a leader has evolved over time, so has the company's prospects. Indeed, it grew through its early years thanks to his micromanaging tendencies. "Through sheer hard work, I was able to grow the company to $10 or $12 million a year by having my hand in every single pot," he affirms. "Everyone reported directly to me. But as time went on, I realized that our company doesn't have value if it's structured this way. I decided to create an entity that can stand on its own, with or without me. Now, I'm focused on getting the right management in place, defining expectations, holding people accountable, and giving them more running room."

Despite the changes wrought by this evolution, some things will always stay the same—things like it's commitment to maintaining a top work environment for its employees. Named by Washington Business Journal as one of the top medium-sized D.C.-area businesses for two years and one of the best places to work for seven years running, Ntiva's success has taken on a snowball effect. "We're creating an environment that attracts and grows rock star employees, who deliver amazing support to our customers," he explains. "As a result, our customers refer more people to us, and we all grow together. We feed that success back into training, or raises, or career advancement, and the cycle is perpetuated further."

Equally critical to Ntiva's core values—and in Steven's own priorities—is the importance of giving back to the community in both dollars and time. "My father taught me that it's the times when you feel you can give the least that you should actually give the most," he remembers. In this spirit, the Freidkins launched a foundation through which they donate to multiple charities. Likewise, Ntiva holds quarterly business innovation group meetings, where the agenda inevitably includes ideas for giving back to philanthropic organizations.

The results take Ntiva's mission of transformation through technology to another level. One year, the company provided a computer lab to a group home, and several technicians went on to provide classes to teach residents how to use the machines for employment searches and job skills. Another year, Ntiva partnered with a client to build the first computer lab in a hospital in Ethiopia. The client sent a doctor to teach in the hospital every two weeks, and Ntiva provided electronic test-taking and preparation materials to keep the students engaged and learning. On yet another occasion, Ntiva revamped the IT infrastructure of a suicide hotline, allowing the organization to field eight percent more calls.

"At the surface of our business, we're making sure networks are running and making sure people have the right operational tools," Steven says. "But at our core, that translates to tangible, meaningful results. It means a nonprofit can do more with the dollars it has. It means absorbing lessons and insight from one CEO and using it to improve the experience of another. And in the case of our philanthropic ventures, keeping IT services functioning and optimized means lives saved. With technology transforming itself at an increasingly rapid pace, we work to ensure that the world transforms right along with it, ready to turn today's challenges into tomorrow's success stories."

Wendy Gradison

IN THE NAME OF BELONGING

As a young girl growing up in Cincinnati, Ohio, Wendy Gradison came to realize at an early age that some of the hardest barriers to overcome are also the hardest to see. She first began to notice the invisible constraints that separated her from her peers when she entered a private elementary school, where she became the only Jewish child in her class. As well, her parents were barred from joining organizations in their community because of their religion. "Growing up in an environment that was very prejudiced and discriminatory, I didn't ever quite feel included," she recalls today. "It gave me firsthand experience of the invisible barriers and hidden discrimination that so many people in our society face, and I knew I wanted to pursue a career that helped people overcome those obstacles to achieve a sense of belonging."

Now the President and CEO of PRS, Inc., a psychiatric rehabilitative services organization that provides a path to wellness, recovery, and community integration to individuals living with mental illness, substance abuse disorders, and other hidden brain diseases, Wendy has dedicated her life to the deconstruction of these barriers. In the rubble of the aftermath, she designs pathways to success for her clients, helping them lay the pavement that allows for a smoother journey through life. "So many of our clients have suffered silently as they live with the stigma of mental illness," she remarks. "Even though it's a brain disorder, it's not treated like other medical conditions, which are talked about openly. Instead, it's often forced underground until a person's life is shattered and it's impossible to keep hidden any longer."

Clients thus present at PRS with the most damaging diagnosis of all: hopelessness. As mental illness often emerges for the first time between the ages of 18 and 25, many are only at the threshold of adulthood, yet feel that they will never realize their goals or dreams. The PRS platform, however, is all about realization—that recovery is possible, that success is within reach, and that hope is founded. "My staff and I are driven by the facilitation of transformation in peoples' lives," Wendy affirms. "Our success is tangible, and meaningful, and powerful, because it means people are moving forward with their lives."

PRS was first developed in 1963 in a church basement. The Community Mental Health Act had just been signed into law, releasing patients from the debilitating grip of psychiatric hospitals, institutions, and asylums, to be brought back to their communities in the hope of rejoining society. Yet there were no services set up in those communities to meet the needs of these individuals, prompting local mental health associations in Northern Virginia to ask a brilliant visionary, Vera Mellen, for help. Vera began holding meetings for former patients, where they would play cards, drink coffee, and socialize in an environment of skilled training and support. Thus marked the beginning of the field of psychiatric rehabilitation, and PRS.

Psychiatric rehabilitation has nothing to do with medication or 50-minute therapy sessions, instead focusing on building relationships between clients and staff through working side-by-side on a client's chosen goals. For this reason, a key pillar of Wendy's work is the growth and development of her employees. "I love that I get to be part of creating a culture of mentorship and coaching at PRS to help young people advance their careers and learn what it means to change our clients' lives," she says. "Our clients' success depends on the development of engaged and trusting relationships by our clinical staff, so it's critically important that I'm focused on our team's well-being and nurturing. We hire and train for emotional intelligence, placing a primacy on our staff's understanding of how they're experienced by other people and how to modulate that experience for the greater good. I also focus on maintaining a fun, dynamic, rewarding, and open culture, where staff can make mistakes and challenge the status quo without apprehension. They're the change agents, not me, so I'm working every day to make sure they have the tools and support they need to be exceptional."

PRS began as a small program in Fairfax County helping clients recover from serious mental illness, and has since evolved to serve clients with substance abuse disorders, autism spectrum disorders, mild intellectual disabilities, or a life crisis at hand. The organization provides Recovery Academy Day Program services, community support services, employment services, and community housing, serving clients throughout Northern Virginia and Washington, D.C.. PRS also recently merged with CrisisLink, a 45-year-old nonprofit that runs a 24/7/365 crisis hotline. The operation makes outbound calls to seniors and individuals living with mental illness, and has recently added an innovative texting platform to appeal to young people.

PRS is largely funded through government grants and contracts, supplemented by fundraising efforts that allow them to provide services they believe in but which fall outside the scope of government resources. The Virginia Department of Aging and Rehabilitative Services, for instance, can understandably only fund employment support services cases where individuals meet certain metrics that indicate high likelihood of a successful employment outcome. Some of Wendy's clients, in contrast, are very early in recovery but want to begin the process of getting a job immediately, so fundraising allows PRS to take those chances on those clients. It also allows them to provide services to clients who can't cover assistance costs themselves but aren't poor enough to meet Virginia's Medicaid eligibility requirements. Thanks to these efforts, PRS has grown to over 80 employees and utilizes its $6 million annual budget to serve over 1,000 clients.

While PRS helps its clients with a host of considerations that include medication, housing, nutrition, budgeting, and behavior management, its key focus is supporting people in choosing, getting, and keeping jobs. "Employment and vocation are some of the most powerful frames through which we view ourselves and our lives," Wendy points out. "Being employed allows someone to feel productive within a valued role, which does so much for self-esteem. A lot of the work we do is helping clients find that valued role of their choosing, whether it's in a job, or getting involved in their faith community, or as a family member, volunteer, or student. We empower people by helping them find that place where they feel energized, and where they feel like they belong."

For Wendy, this feeling of empowerment and belonging first came from her family. Born in Cambridge, Massachusetts, she spent the first several years of her life in Washington, D.C., and still vividly remembers her parents' decision to move to Cincinnati when she was four. As the second oldest, she was assigned the important role of copilot to her father, who was driving the family's station wagon. They stopped at a motel for the night, and the next morning, he broke from the family's staunch nutrition standards and let his young daughter add sugar to her Rice Krispies. "We were never allowed to have sweets—only a single bowl of ice cream on Sunday nights," Wendy remembers. "We weren't allowed to watch TV either. We were required to play a musical instrument, take ballet, and have an hour of alone time in our room each day to look inward. These traditions—and those memorable little moments when we were allowed to break from them—were hallmarks of our extremely close family, which provided comfort in Cincinnati as I confronted anti-Semitism and discrimination for the first time."

Wendy and her four sisters had the tremendous benefit of watching their parents pursue interesting and meaningful work. When Wendy was small, her father, a graduate of Yale University and Harvard's business school, was assistant to the Undersecretary of the Treasury, and then the assistant to the Secretary of Health, Education and Welfare (now known as HHS). He then served on the Cincinnati City Council while also working at the stock brokerage firm his father founded. Later, he was elected as mayor of Cincinnati, and then to the U.S. House of Representatives, where he served for eighteen years and focused on healthcare on the Ways and Means Committee. "He's a top expert when it comes to the complexity of our nation's healthcare system," Wendy avows. "One of the things I respect most about him is his ability to grasp the grays, the blacks, the whites, and the inconvenient truths about any issue. He was always open-minded, willing to listen to others' views even when they conflicted with his own. He taught me that things are never simple—that the more closely you're willing to look at an issue, the more complex it becomes. I really loved watching how he would synthesize all the facts, figures, opinions, politics, realities, and environments at play, in an effort to solve some of the toughest problems in our country."

Wendy's mother taught her the equally critical skill of marching to the beat of her own heart. A dancer and Tufts graduate, where she received her Bachelor of Science in Mathematics, she never lived by anyone else's rules and instead followed her own soul and voice, which led her to pursue law school when her daughters were still young. "She was one of only four women in her class," Wendy says. "She's always been a role model for me through her confidence to trust her own judgment and find her own way, even as society was telling her she should be a homemaker who wore makeup and used curlers."

Even immersed in the experience of growing up, Wendy sensed that her story was unique. She recalls the day the first President Bush came to speak on behalf of her father at one of his campaigns, and she was responsible for picking him up at the airport in the family station wagon. She would help out with the political campaigns that elevated her family's presence in the community, even as she noted the discrimination against Jews that left her feeling like an outsider. She grew up with a silver spoon and access to the best education, even as she remembers vividly the riots that shook Cincinnati after the assassination of Martin Luther King, Jr. "I remember looking out the back kitchen window and seeing a building burning just a couple blocks away," she says. "The city was on fire. It really impressed upon me the principle of equality—that people deserve an equal chance in life."

From nursery school until her senior year of high school, Wendy was taught in the same private school setting, where high school students were required to wear uniforms, but where a visionary Head of School for her elementary years preferred that girls wear pants and shorts just like the boys—a revolutionary move at the time. Wendy's parents expected their daughters to be top in their class, and the girls rose to the occasion. From seventh grade onward, she went to school with only girls, which proved a great environment for her science and math skills to flourish. She thought she might like to pursue a career in dance, but ultimately decided she didn't have the raw talent for it. She then thought she might pursue math, until she enrolled at Williams College and took her first advanced calculus class. "Unlike one of my sisters, who knew from the age of eight that she wanted to be a doctor and took a very straight path toward that goal, I wasn't sure what I wanted," Wendy recalls. "I felt lost, in a way, but I was very interested in human nature and in the ways people relate to one another."

Psychology, then, was a perfect major for Wendy, supplemented by courses in diverse subjects like music and math to reflect her wide-spanning interests. Williams had just gone co-ed, and Wendy's freshman class was the first to admit women. The hard lessons of youth and growing up were learned against the striking backdrop of the Berkshire Mountains, and Wendy emerged a seasoned young lady to land her first job as a counselor at the Family Planning Council of Western Massachusetts. "I had never worked before, and I really didn't understand what being an employee meant," she says. "My employers, as well, weren't in a position where they could realize the importance of teaching and mentoring me."

Wendy went on to accept a position with Carl Sagan at Cornell University, where she worked on the Voyager Interstellar Record Project. The two Voyager Spacecraft were being launched out into the universe, and the project entailed coding 120 photographs and an assortment of music and information onto a record in case the vessel was ever found by intelligent life. "He was such a great visionary, and it was so much fun to be in his orbit, so to speak," Wendy recounts. "Yet I was directly reporting to his office manager, whose leadership left much to be desired. I had not yet had that mentee experience with a superior who was invested in my personal and professional growth. I feel that these challenging early experiences in the workplace informed the kind of employer I wanted to become."

Then Wendy came to Washington to live with her father and work on Capitol Hill for Senator Bill Cohen of Maine, who went on to become the U.S. Secretary of Defense. "It was a great office environment to work in, and I had a wonderful boss there," Wendy says. "At that juncture, I realized that what I loved about the various jobs I had held was the interpersonal piece. The common thread between all of them that seemed to give me energy in any setting was the act of relating to people and helping them in any way I could." That's when a friend suggested she get her Master of Social Work—a degree Wendy had never heard of before.

Learning that it was a good degree for those interested in working with people and with an eye toward social justice and giving back, she enrolled in Catholic University's two-year program, where she interned at a mental health center called the Prince William County Community Services Board. Working with young people afflicted by serious mental illness, she began to see the marked impact of the programs and services she was helping to administer. Upon completing the program, she was hired by that agency, where she spent the next seventeen years of her career.

Wendy's boss during that time, Jan Holton, was an incredible influence on her professional path, teaching her invaluable lessons about management, leadership, and organizational culture. "She was a keen student of organizations and taught me how to think about staff, how to have difficult conversations, how to hold people accountable, and how to make an office environment a great place to be while maintaining very high standards," says Wendy. "When you spend so many years working for someone that exceptional who's always taking you to the next level, you internalize those qualities over time."

After fifteen smooth years there, the board brought on an executive director who didn't mesh with the culture of the organization. Wendy had to work with the new individual directly, and noted the negativity that emanated from the new style of management. "From that situation, I learned how important it is to be incredibly welcoming and have my door wide open for anyone to come talk with me about anything," she says. "I want each of my employees to feel that they're welcomed and appreciated."

Serendipitously, Wendy found herself unable to grow further in her current position just as Vera Mellen was looking for a new program director. The two hit it off, and in 1997, Wendy joined PRS as a member of its management team. Vera then announced her retirement later that year, and Wendy threw her hat in the ring for consideration. "After a year with PRS, I had been with the company long enough to form my own opinions about what we needed to do to move to the next level, and I had spent enough time in a different work environment that I offered a fresh mindset," she explains. "I also really believed in the work and understood psychiatric rehabilitation, given my extensive background in the field. Most importantly, in my interview, I was not someone who said we needed more money to accomplish our goals. Instead, I said we needed to make different choices with the resources we had."

After completing a national search, the board chose Wendy to fill the position of CEO, marking a new chapter in PRS's evolution. And since she took the helm, her signature initiatives have revolved around bringing business practices into an organization that's all about heart. She has focused on efficiency, workflow design, restructuring, accountability, and deliverables, taking the nonprofit to the next level by accentuating the business mindset that must underlie a mission focus in order to maximize effectiveness, sustainability and impact. "What Vera created and grew was her gift," Wendy affirms. "Now, this is mine. And whoever succeeds me will bring a different set of gifts. But for today, while I'm here, we're focused on the idea that our work is never done. We're always about, what's the next thing we can learn to do better? How can we improve that client outcome, improve the bottom line, and better meet the mission? How can we serve more people in need more effectively?"

This leadership was instrumental in landing Wendy the 2011 Excel Award for Nonprofit Leadership through the regional Center for Nonprofit Advancement. The organization was also a finalist for the *Washington Post* award for nonprofit excellence. But to Wendy, true success is measured in joy, abundant in her life not only thanks to her work at PRS, but also thanks to her family. Her husband of thirty years, Lee Goldman, is a clinical psychologist with a private practice in Mclean, Virginia. "I'm intense and focused and can be very anxious, whereas he's extremely laid back, relaxed, calm, and steady," she says. "My work gives me great joy and is very dynamic, but it's also hard and intense, so it's really good for me to be around him and his calming presence."

A renaissance man, Lee spends his weekend's woodcarving, fly fishing, or tinkering with technology. Both Lee and Wendy treasure their roles as parents to their children, now age 25 and 27. "I'm so proud of them and how we co-parented such joyful, competent, curious, funny, confident kids," Wendy says. "It's such a gift to watch them evolve and take their own journeys through life. My daughter is getting her Masters of School Counseling, while my son recently chose to leave the corporate world to explore working in a mission-driven organization. They make me prouder every day."

In advising young people entering the working world today, Wendy underscores the importance of following your heart. "Pay attention to fit instead of salary," she encourages. "Be respectfully assertive. Don't let the hard stuff go underground, but instead express it in a productive and encouraging way. Find mentors and pursue places and environments that give you energy, where you can have fun and be joyous. As your job responsibilities and stressors increase, preserve your commitment to finding those people who are centered and calming, and to paying attention to nutrition and exercise. Take time to find gratitude every day. Life is short, so pursue work and a life that makes you feel more alive—that gives you that true sense of belonging and making a difference, to which we all aspire."

Tom Guagliardi

The Fighter

Tom Guagliardi was one of six children growing up in his childhood home in Toronto. It was a tight fit sometimes, but that didn't stop him and his brothers from clearing all the furniture out of the living room on Saturday afternoons to make a homemade wrestling ring. Then, when the television lit up with the bright lights of the stadium and two men poised to fight for victory, the Guagliardi boys transformed into the greatest wrestler they knew—their own grandfather. "We would good-naturedly beat the crap out of each other, scaring our mother in the process," Tom laughs today. "Friends from the neighborhood would sometimes come over and get involved; it was like a ritual."

Tom's grandfather, a former drill sergeant, professional football player, and worldwide heavyweight wrestling champion, was a mountain of a man in every sense of the word, and Tom was determined from his earliest years to emulate him. When, at four years old, Tom came home and asked his parents to sign him up for soccer and hockey teams, it was his grandfather who paid his registration fees. His grandfather taught him how to fold his clothes every night, make his bed every morning, respect his mother, and stand up for his family. He taught him manners, discipline, humility, work ethic, and perseverance. "I learned all my life lessons from him, and to this day, he's my hero," Tom says. "Most important, he taught me to accept defeat externally, but not internally. With grace, you accept that you may have lost the round, but not the match. You analyze what went wrong, and you strive for perfection, always. That's what it means to be a fighter."

Through his extensive and varied career, Tom has worked to be for others what his grandfather was for him: a true catalyst, promoting the success and development of individuals and companies alike. "I can sit back and smile when a person I've mentored moves on to bigger and better things, or when a company I've supported goes through a successful transition," he explains. "Great mentors and coaches change lives, and that's what I've always aimed to do—protecting, leading, and bringing people with me into successful outcomes."

The fibers of his character, as competitive and relentless as they are nurturing and gentle, were forged in the shadow cast by the most life-changing event of his life—the sudden death of his father. His mother and two older siblings had gone out on errands, coming home to find his father deceased on the floor beside Tom, a sleeping baby. To those who knew his father, the event was a tragedy cast in a painful, negative light that would haunt them their whole lives. But Tom would come to think of the event differently—as a catalyst for future positivity and personal growth.

Tom's father had been a paratrooper in the US Army, but the family had since moved to Canada and fallen on hard times. As a very young boy, he was raised with the help of a foster mother until age four, when his mother remarried a friend of his father who had lost his own wife suddenly. The man had two daughters just a little younger than Tom, and given the impact of loss, blending the two families proved especially difficult.

As a result, Tom was a contradiction—a troublemaker who also sought to break up fights instead of start them. As well, the stern nature of his stepfather led him to the feeling that his efforts and accomplishments were never good enough. "In one of the first soccer game I played when I was four years old, I scored three goals and was smacked in the head for not scoring six," he remembers. "I think I was born with an innate aversion to anything other than first place, so my stepfather's demands didn't teach me excellence. Rather, they gave me a firm resolve down the road to never treat my own wife and children that way. But I also realized down the road that it wasn't a problem with me; it was just his personality."

Despite the challenging dynamic between the two, Tom deeply loves and appreciates his stepfather, recognizing that his childhood experiences shaped him in school, business, and sports. "It's like they say in the movies," he remarks. "Get busy living, or get busy dying. Always being in trouble like that was like a fire licking at my heels, and I remember one pivotal moment in my life where I flipped the coin of perception and began to see everything in a positive way, instead of a negative way. Instead of thinking I couldn't do anything right, I began seeing it as, I won't stop till I get it right. That shift was pivotal in defining my work ethic and my worldview."

Just as Tom's stepfather was demanding of Tom, he was also demanding of himself, working construction all day and then handling a side venture in the evenings doing carpentry, plumbing, and electrical work for a list of clients, all to provide for his family. As a boy, Tom often went along to help, serving as the cleaner when he was too young to assist with the actual labor. "The blue collar work ethic is strong in all my siblings, and even my own three daughters demonstrate it," he remarks. "They're all exceptional students and athletes. One of them was an excellent soccer player. Another was an excellent soccer player and competitive swimmer. The other was an Olympic-level gymnast, who had this incredible self-awareness, mental calm, and inner gauge of work and success. All three girls measured their progress not by the medals they won, but in quiet internal inventories of what they had done well, what they could improve on, and where they were in relation to their goals. I'd say that's very characteristic of our family and how we work toward success."

As a kid, Tom reserved most of his effort for sports and invested less than he should have in school. The soccer team he played on stuck together from the time they were only four, and the same group of kids would play on the same team through adolescence. When the kids weren't busy doing chores for their families, they were practicing in the park. They played before, during, and after school, until it was too dark to see. Tom's youth soccer team became one of the best in Canada and traveled all over the United States, playing in a worldwide tournament in Philadelphia and the Bicentennial Tournament in D.C.. To everyone's surprise, they beat most of the European teams as well, and Tom landed a spot on a semi-pro team when he was only 15.

That was the year he got his first job as well, working on the railroad for the summer. He gave his mother a portion of his earnings and then saved the rest, having learned strict austerity from his grandfather's example. By the time he started high school, he had nearly $6,000 in the bank, which allowed him to pay the $750-per-year tuition for the small and selective Catholic high school he had gained admittance to. "As well as demanding top-level academic performance, the school also supported its students in becoming top-level athletes," Tom says. "They groomed you to be a success in the world, either with your brain or your body."

Thanks to these standards, Tom received a number of scholarship offers to pursue higher education in other countries, but he decided to stay in Toronto to attend York University. He deferred his education to play soccer and met Barbara, the woman who would become his incredibly supportive and inspiring wife. Soon thereafter, he was injured and returned to school, where he at first studied to become a physical education teacher. But when he learned the bleak job prospects for the profession, he decided to switch and major in science instead, transferring to Ryerson University to earn a degree in public health. During that time, he interned at the regional health department for eight months to gain field experience, which prepared him to accept a job with the Health Department upon graduating.

For the next six years, Tom worked as a public health inspector specializing in STDs for six years, rapidly rising up the ranks until he hit a roadblock and would have to wait for others to retire before advancing further. "Through that time, everyone I worked with kept offering me sales jobs," he recalls. "I had never thought of myself as a salesman, but when I talked to Barbara about it, she pointed out that I can talk easily with anyone, and that I'd be a natural. With that, I decided to try switching careers in the hopes that I'd be able to provide more for my family."

Tom was offered a job at 3M, and his first foray into business turned into a 15-year stint accented with breakout moments of success. For each of the first several years he was there, he was given the company's Gold Disk Award for top salesperson. Then he won its Everest Award, given to the top salesperson globally. At 32, he became the youngest person in the company to take on a business portfolio when he was given the worst case in the whole corporation. If he didn't turn it around in six months, the business would be shut down, and Tom would be out of a job.

Tom was nervous at first, but he quickly learned that there's much more to learn from a bad business than from a good business. With the encouragement of his brother-in-law, a successful CEO, he let his instincts guide him, as well as several great mentors and teachers. At the end of the six-month period, the President of the company said he had done a great job and gave him another six months to continue his efforts, selling off land and unprofitable contracts and trimming up the business. After the first year, he had stopped the bleeding. After the second year, the business was profitable. After the third year, 3M was able to sell it, and by working his magic on the divestiture team, Tom was able to fetch a price 50 percent higher than the number his colleagues were willing to settle for.

From that moment forward, the firm gave him bigger and bigger businesses to run, culminating in a highly profitable pharmaceutical company. "People called me the Sunset Kid because they knew that, when I came in, I'd clean things up," he reports. "It meant some people would have to go, and things were going to be shaped differently. I was good at it, but there came a point where I needed a change. I was gone all the time, and even though I was doing good things for the corporation, I was tired of being the bearer of bad news for many people."

When Tom got a call from Cedara Software, one of the first developers of 3D software imaging for brain surgery, he decided to take the opportunity, which would allow him a global business experience. Tom, Barbara, and their daughters move from London to Toronto, where Tom was put in charge of a global portfolio that spanned the Middle East, Europe, and the United States. Within thirteen months, he helped grow the company from 80 to 440 employees, but he wasn't optimistic about the firm's ethics and prospects. When 3M asked him to come back and run several businesses, he saw it as a parachute and agreed. A year and a half later, after completing his tasks there, he dove into the distribution world by becoming VP of Sales for a company called Digital Storage, growing it to a nice size before selling it. He then became the VP of Sales for a manufacturing company before taking the helm of Digitek as President in 2008. He led the company as it grew from $90 million to $150 million in annual revenue, and as the team grew from 40 to 110 employees.

That growth revolved around the creation of core values and culture. "I want to go into a building and feel that the energy and culture is palpable," Tom says. "People undervalue culture because they think it's something you can just change with a nice company Christmas party. But it's so much deeper. It's everything—how you treat people each day, how honest and open you are about what's going on. It's no different from raising a child. What you want, you have to show. You have to live it and demonstrate it every single day, and show that you care about the things that matter to your employees. It's about details and knowing each person as a person."

In assembling Digitek's cultural identity, he put integrity at the very foundation, followed by respect and partnership. Innovation marks the last key principle, with a premium placed on execution of good ideas. "I live by the motto of excellence and execution," Tom says. "I lead as I coached soccer and hockey, with an emphasis on teaching and understanding that different people achieve on different levels. If we were short-staffed in the warehouse, I pack boxes so they could be shipped on time. You help each other out, just like you do in a family."

Outside of work, Tom and Barbara's life together over the years has been a mirror image of these values and worldviews. When their daughters were children, Barbara hung signs in their bedroom to remind them how to live good lives—phrases like *Attitude is everything* and *Because nice matters*. Every day, Tom stops and asks himself, "What have I done to enhance someone's life today?" Even if it's as small as holding the door open for someone at the mall, he understands the power of positivity in a world where so many people tend to focus on the opposite. He plays hockey on a traveling team and can still hold his own, even alongside players half his age. He's done charitable work for muscular dystrophy research, with paralyzed veterans, and through the Knights of Columbus. Barbara, on the other hand, decided to learn how to play the harp several years ago. "We've never said no to each other, so I encouraged her to do it," Tom recounts. "She took lessons from a world-renowned harpist, and now she plays in hospitals for cancer patients and their families. Hers is the music that flows out from behind a curtain or in the waiting room, bringing peace and humanity in the direst of circumstances. She's a real-life hero to me, and I would not be half the person I am today of not for her."

In advising young people entering the working world today, Tom ranks enjoying the journey as the most important thing, and notes the value of persistence. "Understand that where you start is not where you're going to end up," he says. "Do the best you can at the job you have, and be open to learning all you can. Kids now are under so much pressure these days to get into college, but entering the business world is different. You can take your time, listen, and learn. Don't invest so much of your life in your job that the rest of your life becomes secondary."

Beyond that, Tom's success springs from the source. As his grandfather taught him, character is built from the very first attempt, the very first stroke, and the very first breath. "The way you're shaped when you're young determines the way you develop, like the way you shape your business determines the way the business develops," he affirms. "The tiniest detail at the beginning changes everything if you're not paying attention. It's like building a house—if it's off a quarter-inch on one end, it'll be off three feet on the other. That's why we're fighters—for family, for success, for the positive."

BERNHARDT
WEALTH MANAGEMENT

Bill Jaffe

Each One: An Entrepreneur®

Bill Jaffe can still remember the sound of the tree branches rattling in the wind and rain outside his childhood home. It had been a dark and stormy night in South Florida, and the ten-year-old boy was home alone with his three younger siblings. His mother was ill at the time, requiring hospitalization at Johns Hopkins in Baltimore for several months, and his father, a pediatrician, had to make frequent house calls, often relying on the Jaffe children to take care of themselves. "The four of us were afraid, huddled in a big overstuffed chair, when suddenly, something in me changed," Bill remembers. "That was the moment I picked up responsibility and accepted it as part of who I am."

Now the Executive Vice President and General Manager of Technical and Project Engineering, LLC (TAPE), a systems engineering, modeling & simulation, training, cybersecurity, and program management government contracting firm, Bill has worked to model and instill a sense of personal responsibility throughout the company similar to what arose in him all those years ago. The company employs around 200 people, and each one is given the leeway and support to listen to each customer, determine what they really need, analyze the market space, and use that information to help the team overall. "Our mantra is, 'Each One: An Entrepreneur®,'" Bill says. "Everyone has the power to embrace the entrepreneurial spirit, and at TAPE, that spirit is part of the company culture."

TAPE was incorporated by Bill and his wife, Louisa, in 2003, building on Bill's successful consulting practice. It opened for business in 2004 and initially did proposal and capture work for other corporations. One of those early customers was converted into a long-running subcontract, still active to this day. During that time, TAPE planted the seeds that allowed it to become a prime contractor, acquiring multiple award schedules from GSA and laying the appropriate infrastructure. "Louisa and I discovered a genius and synergy in our partnership," Bill explains. "My ability to identify customers and figure out the next move pairs perfectly with her exceptional capacity to manage the company's overall strategic objectives, day-to-day operations, long-term decision-making, employee relations, and strategic marketing. She understands cost drivers and how to keep things moving forward. We're a perfect match."

TAPE won its first prime contract in 2005, and in 2006, they landed a blanket purchase agreement that allowed them to expand the business to the Department of Homeland Security. Serendipitously, the Army also put out for competition a contract for which Bill had written the software twenty years before. The project had marked his initial foray in the federal contracting industry, analyzing cost effectiveness in Army training spending. "The software developed a process for training exercise choice optimization, achieving maximum readiness for the least amount of money," Bill recounts. "It also supported the Army in its defense of spending choices to Congress."

Thanks to Bill's background in the subject matter, TAPE won the $15 million per year contract—at the time, the largest single award contract given by the Army to a Service Disabled Veteran-Owned Small Business. As the company had only been doing between $3 and $4 million a year in revenue, the win represented a quantum leap. "Whereas, before, we only had to manage ourselves, now, we also had to manage big companies like CACI and L3, who were subcontracting for us," Bill remembers. "As TAPE more than quadrupled in size overnight, we had a lot of learning experiences. I considered our management of rapid growth to be the testing ground to see if we could survive. In many ways, that change was the crucible in which TAPE was formed."

Indeed, it was during that time that Louisa and Bill established the company culture that sets TAPE apart today. The company had always been process oriented, but they put those processes in writing to ensure streamlined, cohesive operation. Working on a mission critical application that affects the way each soldier gets trained, TAPE was essentially touching the lives of every soldier in the Army. They spent the next several years absorbing that contract and honing their identity as a business.

Ironically, TAPE grew so much as a result of that one

contract that it surpassed the North American Industrial Classification System's definition for a small business in that category, launching them into an entirely new world of competition. "One day we were competing against companies our own size, and the next, we were up against companies like Lockheed Martin," Bill explains. "But the thing is, it's still all about relationships. Regardless of the size of your competition, success is still built on an interpersonal basis, face-to-face, so that's what we're concentrating on now."

TAPE focuses not only on growing its own business, but also on helping others grow theirs. A service-disabled veteran herself, Louisa is passionate about finding ways to support veteran entrepreneurs, helping them translate the leadership skills they learned while on active duty into project management skills in the civilian marketplace. Bill works as a small and mid-tier business advocate, managing an advice blog for that population called *The Fish Don't Jump in the Boat*. "We went to several conventions for service-disabled veteran entrepreneurs, and I was struck by how people were more focused on getting certifications than on putting in the work to get contracts," he remarks. "It's not enough to have a boat—you actually have to go out on the river with a hook and bait and be willing to put in the hard work to fish. Whatever it is you want, you have to go out and make it happen."

This enterprising spirit has been a hallmark of Bill's character since he was a boy growing up in a close-knit Jewish community in North Miami Beach. Shortly after he was born in Brooklyn, New York, his father was drafted for the Korean War. However, because he was a pediatrician, the Army decided to have him perform draft physicals instead of deploy overseas, and his tours were mostly Southern towns. Dr. Jaffe so much preferred the weather in the South to the chill of New York that he moved with his family to North Miami Beach, a community of New Yorkers who had taken up root in South Florida. At first, the town didn't even have phones. When people needed Bill's father's medical services, they would call the police, who would in turn let Dr. Jaffe know that a house call was required. This impressed upon young Bill a commitment to service that would last his whole life. "Why am I doing what I do with TAPE today?" he says. "It's in my blood. It's my way of giving back in service to the federal government and to my country."

Bill's mother went to college and got a degree in an era when such accomplishments were not the norm for women, and she went on to become a nurse. Also an avid painter, she was an early "women's libber," who embraced an ethic of equality between the sexes and was the logical and rational counterpart to Bill's more emotionally-driven father. She worked as an accountant at her husband's 20-employee pediatric practice, which he shared with two other doctors. "Both parents were very much about building things together," Bill says, echoing the highly effective partnership he shares with Louisa today. "My parents' work was a model for how to treat people, how wealth should be managed, and the importance of focusing on efficiency."

Even as a boy, Bill was an excellent salesman and could sell to anyone. He delivered newspapers and then graduated to selling Tupperware. "I was kind of an academic, nerdy guy in school," he says. "I was a little too smart for my own good, but I spent a lot of time outside and owned a small sailboat that I'd take out on the lake." The family also enjoyed piling into their van to go on road-trip vacations together.

Bill was 13 years old when Castro came to power, and the Cuban population began to immigrate to South Florida in earnest. There was such a large and growing Cuban community that Spanish language lessons were taught over the PA system while Bill was in elementary and middle school. The U.S. university system didn't recognize advanced degrees from Havana, so Bill and his high school classmates were taught by PhD professionals who did not qualify as college professors. The students became bilingual, and Bill set his heart on becoming an international businessman, aiming to learn all about Foreign Service and international law.

This dream led him to Georgetown University's School of Foreign Service. Fluent in Spanish, German, and French, he earned his Bachelor of Science in Foreign Service in three years and intended to go on to an international business master's program. At the suggestion of a friend, however, he shifted his sights to an MBA and enrolled in Dartmouth's Tuck Business School immediately upon graduating from Georgetown. He was eager to finish up his schooling and formally launch his professional career. Thanks to Dartmouth's intense focus on U.S. business issues like total quality management, organizational innovation, and industrial engineering, his dreams of international business transitioned into something else.

Upon graduating in 1972, Bill moved to Reston, Virginia, and started working for Amtrak just after it was first formed. Accepting a position in their payroll department, he was attracted to the company because it offered free travel, and he would rail up and down the Northeast Corridor frequently. "It was exciting to be part of the early infrastructure economics of the D.C. metropolitan area," he remarks. "I remember a time before the Dulles toll road had even been built."

After eight years working for Amtrak, Bill took a

position with Marriott Corporation and became their worldwide office automation manager. In that capacity, he managed the logistics, delivery, and installation of office automation equipment for Marriott Hotels across the world. He then accepted a position as a programmer with CACI, where he built the original Army Training Models that would become so pivotal to TAPE's success two decades down the road. Several years later, he went to work for the federal contracting arm of a small company called CompData. This was followed by a ten-year tenure at Sita Corporation, a new 8(a) business.

During those professional ventures, Bill appeased his entrepreneurial spirit on the side by launching several businesses that bought and sold board games and Pokémon cards. "I was a great salesman but a poor buyer," he laughs. "Those businesses never made a cent, but I really loved the experience of going to conventions and sitting behind a table, laying my wares in front of me and selling. In government contracting, we build our business around relationships, which is a different phenomenon from the usual dynamic of wholesale and retail sales. But as I've gotten older, I've begun to embrace the possibilities that come with relationship-building with customers and staff."

After helping Sita Corporation move to Number 3 on *Washington Technology's* Fast 50 list, Bill accepted a position in Columbia, Maryland, for a company that set up large accounting systems for airlines. Bill was tasked with helping them bring that expertise to the federal sector, but things changed dramatically for the business when planes hit the Twin Towers on 9/11 and the airline industry shut down. "When it reopened, it was a completely different environment," says Bill. "The company simply didn't have the money to continue, which prompted me to go into business myself."

In 2002, Bill launched a consulting practice, and it wasn't long before he met Louisa. She had come to Washington with the Army Reserves in the immediate aftermath of 9/11, just before the time of her retirement from active duty, and she then began working as a supervisor at a helpdesk. She didn't have a vision of a future there, so Bill suggested she get into contracting as well. "The next logical step was to go out to Vegas, get married with Elvis, and then come back and launches TAPE," Bill laughs. "That's exactly what we did. Now, as CEO and President, Louisa brings a strategic vision, sunlit spirit, easy rapport with customers, and an enormous sense of pride to the workplace—all of which have been instrumental to TAPE's success. We were Number 2 on *Washington Technology's* Fast 50 list, and I think this really speaks to Louisa's status as a rising star in the community, and to our success in conveying that all of our employees, subcontractors, and customers are an integral part of the TAPE family."

For Bill, TAPE is about the ability to affect management and make a difference in the direction of an organization. Indeed, he and Louisa model the kind of difference they hope to make for their clients in the way they run the organization. "We're not naïve in understanding that success in business is driven by profit, but we also aim to bring a lot more than that," he explains. "We want TAPE employees to want to come to work and feel like they're making a difference, and to understand that we're there to support them in doing that."

As the company continues to grow, it is now faced with the challenge of preserving the culture that makes it so unique and successful. "The more you harden the arteries of an organization with processes and procedures, the harder it is to preserve the agility and family focus that made it successful as a smaller enterprise," Bill says. "So we're very cognizant of that and are taking strides to make sure that TAPE employees still feel entrepreneurial and vital."

In advising young people entering the working world today, Bill emphasizes the importance of maximizing skill sets without focusing too much on a specific profession. "Whatever you think you want to do today is hardly likely to be the thing you will be doing five years from now," he points out. "Between technological advances and our own inherent capacities to grow and change, it's impossible to predict the future, so we focus on building the skills that will keep us versatile."

Beyond that, Bill points out that every success and failure has the seeds of things that work and things that don't, so from everything, we can learn. Having the courage and wisdom to look at our mistakes long enough to learn from them comes from the awareness that people are not their mistakes—a lesson Bill learned from a Special Forces Colonel. "There are always things we'd like others to do better, but people are distinct from their mistakes, and understanding the difference between the two is the key to successful management of a staff," Bill explains. "Just the simple act of saying hello to others and getting to know them as people is so important." Believing in the future of their employees and their customers alike, Louisa and Bill's company is showing the federal contracting space that each person can be an entrepreneur, and that each person matters.

BERNHARDT
WEALTH MANAGEMENT

Sid Jaffe

The Best Work of Life

Sid Jaffe was a highly successful 40-year-old national accounts manager at AT&T the evening his ten-year-old son, J.D., engaged him in a conversation about baseball and values. "Dad, you and I like baseball," the boy said. "Ernie Banks said, 'It's a great day for baseball—let's play two.' But we never even play one!"

It was true. Sid's 17-year career with AT&T had led from one thing to the next in rapid succession, to the point that he was traveling three weeks a month. Something in his son's voice struck a chord deep within him, and the very next day, he submitted his resignation. "There's a tremendous amount of personal freedom in being able to enact balance in your life," he says today. "That decision put me on the path to starting my own business, which meant I could invest the time I wanted into my family and community service. I live to work in the community. It's something deeply rooted in our family, strengthening our bonds with each other while we strengthen the families, organizations, and positive efforts around us. As I learned in the Jaycee Creed years earlier, it's the Best Work of Life."

Today, Sid is the founder and CEO of Sid Jaffe & Associates, LLC (SJ&A), a consulting firm that specializes in breakthrough solutions for government contractors to help a business grow its revenue, margin, and valuation. This is accomplished through educational efforts like training and support on matters like proposals, back office software, coaching, or clinics. "We work shoulder to shoulder with people, helping them through business problems and providing special expertise to younger companies that can benefit from the perspective of someone who's been through it all," Sid remarks. "Each of our consultants has thirty years of experience, at least."

Launched in 2011 as an outgrowth of Sid's previous company, Advantage Consulting, Inc. SJ&A works with a host of clients, ranging from embryonic startups up to a top multinational government contracting company that was starting a multibillion-dollar commercial practice. "We're great at turning a boulder on its axle very quickly," says Sid. "We've helped firms of one or two people grow to over 700 employees. We've helped large firms launch ventures that go from zero to millions of dollars in revenues within a couple years. Our sweet spot isn't the size of the company or the effort; it's the need to grow revenue, expand margin, increase valuation, or overcome obstacles."

With its core team of seven primary engagement associates, supplemented by the expertise of 120 available subject matter experts in proposal writing, consulting, pricing, and other areas of interest, SJ&A is about making sure its clients are ready for the future—a mission that was cemented in Sid's own life in the wake of the most traumatizing moment of his life. He can still remember with crystalline detail what it felt like to fall through a window he was working on at his parents' house when he was fifteen. The glass cut a large gash around his arm, and as he saw the amount of blood leaving his body and noted that he was the only one home, he thought, *I'm going to die.*

Somewhere in his subconscious, he remembered the question his father had asked when he was ten years old. "Sid, are you ready?" The boy had replied, "For what?" His father had answered, "In that case, you're not ready." Five years later, with life quickly leaving his body, he realized what his father had meant. "I finally understood that I had to start being ready," he recalls. "You're never really ready for everything, but you have to put yourself in a position to be ready."

Sid certainly wasn't ready to die, and that could only mean one thing: he was ready to live. With that, he tore off the sleeve of his shirt and made a tourniquet to stem the blood loss, and then called an ambulance. He lost consciousness on the way to the hospital, waking up behind the surgery curtain just long enough to hear the doctors tell his parents that he would survive, but they didn't know if his arm was salvageable, or if the blood loss would cause permanent brain damage.

When he finally woke up in a hospital room, he was acutely aware of the life in him, and of the life he had left. "By all rights, I probably should have died," he remembers. "I had a very clear sense that there had to be a reason God let me live, and it was not to be the person I had been to that moment. I had been coasting through life, drifting from one event to the next without any purpose or drive. I wasn't a kid who was going to be something."

Born in Washington, D.C., he and his two younger sisters were raised in a rough neighborhood, and Sid never had grand ideas for his future. His father had been in pharmacy school when World War II broke out, so he dropped out of school to enlist in the military at age 30, serving as a radio operator on a B-17 plane. After the war, he repaired radios until he had saved enough money to open a small delicatessen with his wife. There, the Jaffes modeled incredible work ethic, sense of humor, and the highest possible integrity for their children. Sid can still remember the book his father kept by the cash register, where they kept track of the names of customers who owed money and the corresponding amount. "People would come into the store that needed something to eat but didn't have any money," Sid explains. "Dad's policy was that nobody left his store hungry. Most of the people in the book were never able to pay back my father, and debts totaled thousands of dollars. But it was okay; that was his way of doing community service."

Sid worked at the small shop from the time he was tall enough to see over the counter. It was his way of helping out the family, and the notion of getting paid for the work was absurd. For many years, the Jaffes lived in an apartment above the store. "Our neighborhood wasn't exactly a bastion of security," Sid remembers. "A lot of my neighborhood friends didn't have a home that felt secure, like I was blessed to have. I got involved with Habitat for Humanity in my adult life because I came to recognize that my strong family and home let me become the person I am, instead of the person I could have become growing up in that environment."

As a student at Calvin Coolidge High School, Sid never thought of college as a given. But after the accident, he decided he was going to do something with his life, even though he didn't know what it would be yet. "I had nothing to work hard for—until then," he says. "I had come pretty close to not having any more moments, and each one has been a gift since then. I'm paying them back. There's a sportscaster, Tim Brandt, who said, 'I've lived life on a scholarship.' I feel the same way. I've had a few injuries along the way and I've taken some penalties, but I've been lucky, and sometimes it's better to be lucky than good."

When he came out of surgery, Sid's arm resembled a claw, with severe nerve damage and a grim prognosis. The family found a doctor in Texas, however, who worked with veterans and performed a surgery that returned some flexibility and motion to his arm, but none to his hand. The doctor said he wouldn't improve further, but Sid heard the words as a challenge rather than a sentence. Another doctor said shock therapy might restore some additional movement, but not to count on it. But with each doctor who told him things were as good as they were going to get, Sid got better. Drive had found its way into his life with a vengeance. As more and more movement restored, he found a way to carry his hand so people didn't stare. He couldn't play clarinet anymore as he had done in years past, so he picked up trumpet, and then had a custom clarinet built. "I knew there was a reason I was moving past all those obstacles," he remembers. "If you have any sense of spirit within you, you know it's not just you, because there are a lot of people who aren't given that chance. I was determined to find my reason—which I learned is the best work of life."

Amidst his long recovery, Sid attended American University, but his real education didn't commence until he landed his first truly professional job at AT&T. He had applied for a position as a central office employee, but a battery of tests landed him a position as a communications representative in the marketing department, where he ultimately met his wife. He was upset by the placement only until he realized that, as a top craft job with lofty prospects; it was a better position than he had originally hoped for.

Thus, a career in sales and marketing was launched that would hold incredible learning opportunities. "I worked in a company of a million people," he reflects. "A lot of senior managers just came in to sit around all day and then leave. They didn't want to take risks or be bothered. I learned quickly that it was far easier to apologize for a screw-up than ask for permission, so I became accustomed to doing what I believed was right."

At the time, telephone companies were controlled by the Public Service Commission, so the practice of actively pursuing new sales was virtually unheard of. That didn't stop Sid and several colleagues from launching a small operation in D.C. called Company Initiated Sales, through which they went out and talked to people about getting a new phone system. As his sales skills developed, he learned the then science of data sales, which was volume, usage, data, frequency, language, accuracy, and cost. As he mastered the sale of data, computerized phone systems came out. Once he mastered the sale of those, UNIX and computers hit the market. By the end of his tenure at AT&T, he was selling the most advanced communications computers in the world to firms in the U.S. "Through all of that, I kept pushing myself to keep taking the next step forward," he says. "It was about always being ready for the next thing. Thanks to that practice, I left with the confidence that would one day allow me to start my own firm."

Upon resigning, Sid agreed to stay on three more months, but he was offered his next job within hours. He had mentioned to a client, Computer Data Systems, that he was moving on and the company promptly extended an offer. Captivated by its culture and potential for growth, Sid accepted, spending the next several years experiencing the workings of a mid-sized commercial company and the dynamics of the government marketplace. Then, in 1992, he and a partner, Doug Allston, launched Advantage Consulting, Inc.

The company started as a consulting firm offering business development services to accountants, but quickly realized that their skills were better suited to the government contracting community, which was underserved at that time. The firm did quite well until Doug decided it was time to retire. Around that time, a top client sought to enlist Sid's services full-time to help them win a major contract, so they bought Advantage Consulting. Sid stayed on a couple years longer and then moved out with his team to launch SJ&A. "Starting SJ&A has truly allowed me to do the things I'm good at, and to do the best work of life," Sid affirms. "When I can help individuals and businesses succeed, which in turn helps families and communities succeed, I know I'm doing the best work of life."

Inextricably intertwined with this concept is the theme of community service that so deeply pervades his family, from generation to generation. In 1974 Sid was "learning and earning"—trying to establish a life for him and not giving much back to the community. When he and his wife, Missy, had their first child, they grew close with another family who had adopted a daughter around the same time. Together, the Jaffes and the Joneses got involved with their local Jaycee Chapter as they raised their daughters. "I remember our infant daughters wearing tiny Jaycee vests our wives had made," he recalls. "At that moment, family and community service fused for me, and I adopted the Jaycee motto, *Service to Humanity is the Best Work of Life.*"

Before long, Sid was encouraged to run for president of the Virginia Jaycees, which was comprised of 120 chapters. Women couldn't be a part of the Jaycees at that time, and his stance against this discrimination further solidified the connection between family and service for him. Throughout his active leadership in the Jaycees, their house was a haven to community members of all denominations, with Missy very active in the Catholic Church. She would always set an extra place or two at dinner for whoever they happened to invite over that night. Both Sid and Missy remained highly active in Scouts for their son and daughter, Jenn, who went on to launch one of the first special needs Girl Scout troops in Northern Virginia. "What's important is that this sense of commitment to community service transcends to the next generation," Sid says. "My daughter, son-in-law, son and grandchildren are all very involved in their communities and schools. We didn't have to ask them to do it; it's just innate for them. It's the number one thing our family does together. Some families go to the beach or to movies together; we like to do community service together."

Living this way, Sid and Missy have set a tradition for future generations of the Jaffe family—one in which children are raised with their eyes ready to see and their ears ready to hear. His own son, keenly attuned to hear the call of the best work of life, entered the priesthood, and when he was studying for ordination in Rome, he arranged for Saint Pope John Paul II to bless the chalice, which he would use for a lifetime, when he was given the pontiff's white zucchetto. After his ordination, J.D. gave the zucchetto to Sid, and gave Missy a stole blessed in holy oil—the traditional gift for mothers who give their sons to the church.

Tremendous meaning for the Jaffe family comes not only in symbols of service and spirituality, but also in humor. Sid can still remember teaching J.D. how to play baseball, when the five-year-old would pick up the ball and examine it instead of throw it. When Sid explained that the object of the game was to pick up the ball and throw it back right away, J.D. asked why. To help get his point across, Sid took the ball and wrote "bomb" on it. "Think of the characters in your cartoon shows, which have to get rid of the bomb immediately," he told his son. J.D. thought that was funny, and one morning, he put the ball in Sid's shoe. It became a running joke between the two, with the ball finding its way into briefcases and under pillows. When J.D. studied in Rome, somehow the ball magically appeared. In Nat's Stadium, Screech handed it to J.D... Later, when Sid received an Association of Corporate Growth (ACG) meritorious service lifetime award in California, he was handed the bomb ball in front of M&A leaders from around the world. "It's of no value to the outside world, but it's of infinite value to us," Sid avows.

In advising young people entering the working world today, Sid emphasizes the priceless nature of the balance he's achieved today. "For me, being involved with the community, and having my family involved with me, is a richness that can't be duplicated any other way," he says. "I'm not saying it's the only thing, or the best thing, but there's nothing else like it." Indeed, in Sid's eyes, the highest value of SJ&A has been its facilitation of his work in the community. When it comes to starting a business, he notes four key things that must be accomplished. "First, you have to bill something to somebody so you're making some money," he explains. "Next, you have to sell something to somebody so you're making money in the future. Beyond that, you have to network with people to secure customers and see what's out there. And finally, you have to do the administration. People often fall in the trap of focusing on one of these things at the expense of the others. But it's absolutely imperative that you find a way to make it work and keep all four plates spinning at once."

It may seem like a tall task, but Sid has managed to keep all four criteria met, while defining his legacy through a remarkable list of service commitments. He's been a member of the George Mason University Century Club, a board member of the Greater Reston Chamber of Commerce, a committee chair of the Northern Virginia Technology Council, and President of the National Capitol Chapter of ACG and on their International Board in Chicago. Within the nonprofit community, he's also been State Vice President of the Virginia Jaycees, a board member for Habitat for Humanity of Northern Virginia, and President of the Annandale Lions Club. Worldwide, he has been recognized as a Jaycee International Senator, a lifetime achievement award bestowed on only 60,000 people total across the globe since the organization's launch. He and his family also support numerous smaller projects in the community. "I'm willing to listen to almost any opportunity, and to help if I can," Sid says. "For all that I've done up to now, I'm still on the journey toward fulfilling my purpose in life. It's about family, service, and helping people do the best work of their lives by focusing on doing the best work I can in my life."

Dalena Kanouse

Staying the Course

As Dalena Kanouse's sneakers hit the pavement in syncopated rhythm, the chaos of downtown Houston bustled around her. She was grateful for a break from the synthetic smell of hospital corridors and the hum of medical equipment, even if it meant honking cars and rushing buses. And Dalena knew that, as long as she stayed the course, it would lead her to a small garden shielded from the din of the city by several large trees. There were benches for rest and reflection—a kind of oasis for people like her, who were more worn out from trials of the soul than from a daily run.

On that particular day, Dalena decided to stop in the garden. Her husband's leukemia had come back a second time, and after weeks of chemotherapy and a bone marrow transplant, they would find out later that afternoon if the treatments had worked. They would find out if there was still time left, or if it had run out for them. Sitting on one of those secluded benches, Dalena closed her eyes and prayed. She asked Heavenly Father for a sign, but then tears came to her eyes as she was flooded with guilt. She knew she should have enough faith not to need confirmation.

Then, suddenly, a vibrant red bird appeared out of nowhere and alighted on one of the branches above her. It seemed to be watching her, and as she got up to leave, it didn't fly off. "From then on, red birds, or cardinals, have been a symbol of hope, peace, and strength for me," Dalena says today. "They remind me that everything's going to be okay. We found out later that day that Sam's treatments had worked, and we had another six wonderful months together."

It was late September of 2009 when the Kanouses returned to the University of Texas M.D. Anderson Cancer Center and found out that Sam's leukemia had come back for the third and final time. Knowing it wouldn't be long, the hospital released him so he could live out his final days at home. "For the entire three-and-a-half-hour drive back to our house, we left the radio off and just talked," Dalena recalls. "We remembered the past and all the great times we'd had. It was as if time disappeared."

Just a few days later, Dalena awoke to find that Sam had already gotten up. As sick as he was, she could not imagine where he could be. She walked around the house and discovered him at his computer typing up a job description for her. In the sixteen months he had been sick, they had never discussed the idea that she would take over his government contracting firm, Management and Training Consultants, Inc. (MTCI). But that morning, he made his wishes clear, reviewing every responsibility with her to make sure she understood. He had her print off the job description and read it through with him, line by line. The next day, he passed away.

At the time, Dalena had a career of own, having worked for nearly two decades as a civilian employee at the Department of the Army. For the previous sixteen years, she had served in public affairs. In the ten years since Sam had started MTCI, he would come home after work and tell her about his struggles or victories for the day, and now that he was gone, she chastised herself for not paying closer attention or taking notes. "But hindsight is 20/20," she says. "I was determined to keep my promise to Sam—to continue his legacy and try to do the best I could at growing what he started. With that, I threw my whole self into staying the course and seeing this mission through."

Taking over as President and CEO of MTCI meant resigning her civilian work to eliminate any conflicts of interest, and to focus her time and energy on the 130+ MTCI associates who had just lost the company's founder, and a friend. They knew of her, but they didn't know her, and Dalena knew there would be hurdles to overcome with the transition of ownership. To complicate matters, her husband had served 25 years in the military and had launched MTCI as an 8(a) Service-Disabled Veteran-Owned Small Business. "When companies graduate from 8(a) status, many of them go out of business because they don't know how to operate outside of that space," Dalena explains. "We overcame that, and the transition from Service-Disabled Veteran-Owned to Women-Owned. It was a tough time."

Through the transition, one of the company's contracts went up for recompete, and MTCI lost it to a lower bid. Dalena and her leadership team also took a step back to refocus and streamline the firm's expertise. While Sam had cast a wide net resulting in forays into logistics and IT contracts, they decided to hone in on MTCI's three core competencies of training, human capital, and program management. With excellence in recruiting and retention, the company's mobile training teams have achieved outstanding results with the Army National Guard. They also work with the Department of Defense to assess colleges and universities who have MOUs to participate in the tuition assistance program. In this capacity, MTCI ensures that military personnel receive the same treatment as their civilian counterparts.

By strategically streamlining its focus, and by strengthening its commitment to its high-caliber associates by formalizing a competitive benefits package, establishing a bonus program, and adding Dalena's own personal touch through small thank-you notes and gift cards, MTCI was able to weather the transition without losing any additional contracts, and without any layoffs. "We're not casting a wide net anymore in the hopes that we'll catch something," Dalena affirms. "We've gone back to the basics, so to speak, and are really focused on doing what we do best. We've developed a pipeline we're very proud of, and it's sustainable." On an uptrend that has brought them just under $14 million in contracts for 2013, MTCI now has 110 associates, with locations in 27 states and Belgium. And it's those associates who have made all the difference, earning the trust of MTCI's clients and filling in Dalena's blind spots. "I really didn't know anything about running a company, much less a government contracting firm," she recounts. "I really had to dig deep into my soul to be able to do what Sam asked me to do, and I know I couldn't have done it without our outstanding staff. It took me a while to realize that I didn't have to know everything, but the truth is, we have outstanding people who do a phenomenal job. I'm so thankful for them."

MTCI remains a successful company today because Dalena refused to quit, and the decision to persevere has been a constant theme throughout her life from the time she was a child. Her parents—a strong and lighthearted mother and a beloved gentle giant of a father—divorced when she was three, and her mother remarried a man in the Air Force. They moved frequently, spending time in the Philippines, Florida, and Texas. As the youngest of seven children—her mother's three children, plus four stepsiblings—and an exceptionally quiet young girl, her parents didn't notice that she was struggling in school. Even today, she still remembers the quiet trauma of being held back in first grade, of her fourth grade teacher accusing her of not doing her homework in front of her entire class, and of being the last student to be picked for spelling bee teams. But in those hard moments, Dalena got to know her own capacity for resilience. She had to work harder than everyone else to get that A, but she learned how to do it, and in the process, she learned how to persevere.

"My parents concentrated on the problems my older siblings were having, so nobody really emphasized the importance of education for me," she remembers. "They didn't know I was having trouble, but I kept on trying. Now, education is an important part of my legacy. I was determined to give my children all the attention and education I possibly could so history didn't repeat itself, and I'm on the board of Smart Beginnings Greater Prince William to help kids get a great education before school even begins, during the most formative and critical years of life."

Dalena spent her junior high and high school years in Killeen, Texas. By that time, her mother had gotten divorced again, and her older siblings had moved away, she focused her time on playing basketball and working. She was 16 years old when she met Sam Kanouse, one of her coworkers at Kentucky Fried Chicken. The two fell in love and were married the following year, in 1976, when she was still in high school. Sam joined the military, and Dalena graduated early. Aside from brief stints in Germany and South Korea, he was stationed at Fort Hood, so Killeen remained home for them. They had their first daughter, Domonique, when Dalena was 19, followed by a second daughter and a son by the time she was 25. Sam joined the National Guard, and Dalena started taking courses toward her Bachelor of Business Administration.

The Kanouses moved to the Northern Virginia area in 1993, where they remained for 12 years. Thanks to the time and stability, Dalena was able to land a public affairs job at the National Guard Bureau, impressing her employers with her work ethic and determination. As she worked her way up the GS schedule to a GS13, she finished her bachelor's degree after 13 years and then immediately began working on her Masters of Public Administration. "I was one of the first in my family to get my bachelor's, and the only one who went for a master's," she remarks. "Aside from simply wanting to do the best job I could with my education, my children and my husband were my drive. I wanted them to be proud of me, and I wanted my kids to see that it's important, and that it's possible. Now, all three of them have gotten their bachelor's and gone on to get their master's. I couldn't be prouder."

Sam launched MTCI in 1999 in the unfinished basement of their home in Manassas, Virginia, with only a desk, a phone, a computer, and a very large whiteboard. He had just retired from his position as the Recruiting Retention Sergeant Major for the Army National Guard and wanted to give back to the organization that had given so much to him: the military.

Sam was born in South Korea. When he was twelve years old, his mother married a military service member and moved to the U.S. Even though he knew no English, he never let it stop him from succeeding. He dove into all the opportunity his new country had to offer. He became a member of the National Honor Society in high school and was admitted to West Point, though he turned it down to marry Dalena. He started MTCI with the goal of giving back to the military, and his first contract allowed him to hire four people. Today, the company still holds that flagship contract, which has now expanded to a 29-employee-project.

When Sam and Dalena returned to Texas for his thirtieth high school reunion, they remembered how much they loved it. They decided to move back, so Sam relocated the company's headquarters, and Dalena got a job at Fort Hood. It was there that Sam was diagnosed with leukemia, and there that Dalena saw the red bird in the garden.

After Sam's passing, Dalena moved back to Virginia, whose state bird is the cardinal. Tasked with finding a new local bank for MTCI, she set up a meeting with the bank that had believed in Sam from the very beginning, Cardinal Bank. "They wanted to meet me before we solidified the relationship," she recalls. "I had to pass that test, and I was nervous, but as I walked through the door for the meeting, I realized their mascot was a red bird, and it filled me with that same strength I felt in the garden. I knew everything would be okay."

Now, Dalena and the MTCI team are looking toward the future and embracing change. Domonique, who helped Sam through the company's early years and then sought to broaden her experience by working at other contracting firms, now serves as MTCI's Senior VP of Business Development, and is a true driving force behind the company. She recently revived a selling tool for recruiters that Sam created, called *Step by Step to Success* and refurbished it into a holistic recruiting and leadership training program called *Road Map For Success* that will be piloted in 2014. MTCI is also looking to expand its services to other arms of the federal government, like Health and Human Services, the Department of Homeland Security, and Office of Personnel Management.

MTCI also remains a leader in its community of Prince William County, partnering with the Prince William Chamber to sponsor events like the Salute to the Armed Forces, the Women's Leadership Conference, and Valor Awards, which recognize first responders. They support the Military Spouse Employment Partnership Program, the Military Child Education Coalition, and the Association of the United States Army. Dalena, herself, serves in the Business and Professional Women's Foundation – Joining Forces Mentoring Plus program, sharing her experiences to help women veterans and military spouses make their way into the world of business. "Resiliency has been a constant thread through my own life, and it's at the heart of MTCI's culture," Dalena avows. "Not only do we provide resiliency training through Central Texas College to our Soldiers at the Wounded Warrior Transition Brigade at Fort Hood, but we support organizations that encourage resilience. What's more, we're part of Virginia Values Veterans—73 percent of our associates are veterans, and 18 percent are family members of veterans. In 2013, we won the SmartCEO GovStar Award for supporting our military. It's an honor to be recognized for something that comes naturally. And as we continue Sam's legacy in this important way, we are reminded that MTCI's narrative is, itself, a story of perseverance. In 2010, the year after he passed away, the company was named to the Inc. 5000."

In advising young people entering the working world today, Dalena emphasizes the importance of self-improvement all through life, regardless of one's age. Her example shows that it's never too late to pursue a degree, because you never know what demands life might place before you in the future. Her story is also a testament to the power of her perseverance, which is rooted firmly in her faith. "It takes a lot of strength not to give up, but it also gives you a lot of strength," she affirms. "I truly have stepped outside of my comfort zone to carry this torch, and I'm better for it. Sam always believed in me and told me I could do anything, and in rising to meet the challenge of continuing his legacy, I've shown myself that he was right. Life is short, and by persevering and never giving up, we make it the best it can be—and we become the best we can be in the process."

BERNHARDT
WEALTH MANAGEMENT

Grace L. Keenan

The Dynamics of Success

There's something profoundly different about the manner and mission of Dr. Grace L. Keenan's approach to medicine. Raised on an Irish potato farm in Canada, she has the grounding of the good earth in her touch. Familiar with diving into backbreaking work even if she doesn't have all the answers, she has the confidence not to decline the toughest of challenges. Trained at a medical school in Newfoundland, she has a breadth and nuance of knowledge as vast as the windswept terrain she was taught to serve. She has a resoluteness of spirit that keeps her standards of care unyielding, and a common sense that most players in the health industry today are only beginning to wake up to.

Now the founder and CEO of Nova Medical & Urgent Care Center, Inc., a thriving, multi-facility, integrative medical provider in Northern Virginia, Grace grew her practice the way her parents accrued their own success—from nothing into something. Her father, the eldest of 15 children, grew up in a poor farming community and dropped out of school in third grade to help care for his younger brothers and sisters. Her mother, a teacher in a one-room schoolhouse, grew up the daughter of a butcher. When they married, they were gifted $100 in cash from friends and family. Her mother had her heart set on buying a bedroom set from the Sears catalogue, but her father insisted on using it to buy a flock of sheep. His new bride was in tears for weeks, though she would later come to realize that this was indeed a wise decision.

That winter, Grace's father cleared a hundred acres of land that had been given to him. In the spring, he removed the stumps and planted a hundred acres of potatoes, which grew into a bountiful harvest. Once they sold the crop and the flock of sheep that had since multiplied, they had enough money to build a potato house to shelter future harvests. As time passed and their farming business grew, they moved into a large Victorian farmhouse on 500 acres of land. Over their lifetime, they amassed 5,000 acres for farming, a family plane, packaging plants, and a trucking company, building an impressive farming operation.

Grace's father was the symbolic leader of the family venture, but her mother was the real mind and might behind the business. Deeply devout to her Roman Catholic faith, and known to speak with perfect diction, Grace remembers her mother as strong and unbreakable. She was also a quintessential lady of the era, keeping a copy of Emily Post on the kitchen counter for her daughters' frequent reference. She believed the best thing she could do was raise them to be good wives and mothers, teaching them all manner of domestic skills. Grace didn't mind cleaning or baking, but she hated sewing, and refused to learn how to darn socks. "I was filled with fury at the idea that any man would expect me to darn his socks!" she recalls. "My mother could never get over the fact that I didn't learn how to properly sew until medical school."

Grace grew up the youngest of eight siblings in a family that would meet at the table three times a day for meals, where the discussion revolved around productivity and the tasks each person hoped to accomplish. The nanny who cared for her through her girlhood was very gentle and taught her a great love for animals, lending a charmed air to her interactions with the world and a rich connection with nature. "She taught me that touch and humanity are integral to growth and healing," Grace affirms. "We would heal animals on the farm at times, which kindled my interest in veterinary medicine. I also had an uncle who was schizophrenic, which sparked my interest in mental illness. Everyone else considered him an embarrassment and didn't want to be around him, but I would sit with him through his psychotic episodes, asking him about his experiences and developing great compassion for him."

This compassion was part of a larger thread running through the family. Each morning, the children would traipse down to the community bunkhouse, where the homeless sought shelter. Grace and her siblings brought breakfast and an invitation to work on their father's farm to earn a day's wage. Her father also employed inmates from the local jail, who came to assist with the backbreaking work of farm labor. The women of the household, in turn, prepared elegant meals for the workers, and Grace had the opportunity to get to know people from all walks of life. "I took an interest in different types of people and how they got to where they were in life," she reflects. "I had this desire to help people improve the general caliber of their lives."

Grace was twelve years old when her father had the first in a series of heart attacks. Her mother sat her down to discuss what would happen when they passed away. The farm would be split between her five brothers, while the daughters were guaranteed that their tuition for school would be paid for. "At a very young age, I understood that I would need to be responsible for my financial wellbeing," she remembers. "I decided to rely upon myself to feed my children and put a roof over my head, committing myself to working hard."

With only a limited understanding of the world, Grace imagined she had two options: business, or health and science. Having watched her own parents run the farm business, she was disillusioned with the former, so she considered the latter. She got a job in a pharmacy but found it exceedingly boring, and she didn't want to follow in her sister's footsteps to become a nurse. Her mother suggested she become a school teacher or a secretary, but neither appealed to her. She met with the family doctor in her hometown and asked if he thought she was smart enough to become one herself. "He said he didn't know, but he explained to me what I'd have to do," she recounts. "So I applied to the most prestigious school in Eastern Canada, Dalhousie University."

After gaining admittance and earning her Bachelor of Science degree, she applied to medical school in Newfoundland, though she was fairly certain she had no chance of getting in. The program's ten seats for residents of New Brunswick garnered around 500 applications each year. "I did not ever dream that I'd get in, but I did," she says. "It was a true life highlight—an incredible moment that I've never forgotten. I imagined myself living a Norman Rockwell-type existence, romanticized and heroic."

Though her experience as a doctor would be a far cry from the idealized concept she emulated at her journey's start, it lends credence to the refrain that beauty is truth. In Newfoundland, she was trained to care for big city residents and rural Inuit people alike. The Inuit patients didn't speak English, and Grace wrestled with cultural differences that compelled mothers to cancel necessary treatment regimens when their children didn't like the taste of the medications. She was taught to think of medicine as caring for all parts of the patient, and with minimal equipment and support.

Grace completed medical school in 1985 and her residency in Ohio, where she was trained as an internal medicine specialist. In that capacity, she learned to care for complex patients in both hospital and outpatient settings. "I was essentially functioning as an intensive care doctor at the time," she remarks. When she came to Loudoun County, Virginia in 1988, she was a 28-year-old board certified internal medicine specialist credentialed to work in the ICU. "I was a foreigner with a British background who dressed like a French girl and seemed culturally out-of-place," she reflects. "No one wanted to hire me, so I decided to take out a $30,000 line of credit, lease a 1,200-square-foot space, and start my own practice."

Grace had no idea how long the money would last, and she hadn't done a market analysis, but she compared all challenges to a winter in Newfoundland, certain they would be less difficult. With no idea of what to expect, she put an ad in the local paper. She didn't have a graphic artist, so her contact at the local paper offered to design a rudimentary advertisement featuring Grace's graduation photograph, a brief biography, and a note that she was accepting new patients.

Much to her surprise, the phone began to ring off the hook. A sizable population of local residents had previously been stationed at a US Naval Base in Argentia, Newfoundland, and Grace's picture conveyed the familiarity of a long-past lifetime in its wholesome, unassuming invitation. "They're very loyal, and immediately became my patients," she remembers. "On the day I opened the doors of my practice, I had eight appointments. The patients had to walk over boxes to get in, and I couldn't believe all those people wanted to see me."

Though business continued to escalate, Grace found time to give birth to her first child, David, in 1990. She returned to work a month later, leaving David in the care of a nanny. Several months later, however, she walked in on the nanny shaking the baby, and vowed to never leave her child at home again. With that, she rented out the 1,500-square-foot commercial space next door to her practice and turned it into a nursery. Each day, her patients would come in for their appointments and then go see the baby.

Three years later, Grace's practice had outgrown its location, so they moved down the street to a 9,000-square-foot space spread between two floors. There was an urgent care center at a hospital a half-mile down the road. She asked them to refer those patients that didn't have a primary care physician, but they refused because she wasn't affiliated with their building. With that, she decided to open her own urgent care practice in 1991, which became Nova Urgent Care. "I modeled Nova Urgent Care after the cottage hospitals I had seen in Newfoundland, where the small rural towns didn't have ICUs," she says. "It wasn't realistic to transport people hundreds of miles away for care, so excellent and holistically-minded medicine was practiced in these little cottage hospitals. I didn't see the point of admitting someone to the ICU for an asthma attack. Rather, the patient could be put on the right medications and monitored in the urgent care to prevent unnecessary expense and hassle. Almost always, they didn't need further hospital care, and thousands of dollars were saved."

Patients were drawn to the one-stop-shop model that her practice endorsed, and they were drawn to the simple customer service skills she had learned as a waitress and bartender through medical school. "Customer service is often lost in medicine," she remarks. "It has always been important to me to do little things that respect the dignity of each person I serve, such as offering a patient a nice warm blanket, or learning some rudimentary Spanish and attempting to speak the language as needed, and enlisting the patient's opinion in their care."

As the Nova Medical and Urgent Care model expanded, its culture and brand were maintained by Grace's hiring standards. "I strive to hire people who feel the same way I do about medicine," she notes. "If a person does not share the same mission, vision and values, he or she is not a good cultural fit for us. We are dealing with patient lives, and I take great pride in that. I often tell prospective employees that I cannot pay them for what they're expected to do, so their drive has to be genuine and inherent. I expect people to care genuinely about our patients and protect their best interests. I ask our staff to serve our patients as their authentic selves. Our patients deserve it."

Amidst continued growth and expansion, Grace's personal and professional life came in ebbs and flows. Having learned what love was when David was born, she was committed to having more children, but faced complications that led her to consult a reproductive endocrinologist. She was put on an overzealous regimen of medications and treated like a number, giving her a vantage point of the patient experience that revolutionized her capacity for empathy. "I spent a year in bed, thinking I could just go to these specialists and they'd have the magic sauce," she remembers. "I learned a lot about medicine from the patient's eyes as I was being charged exorbitant amounts while being treated horribly. I almost died several times, and I ended up losing the twins at age 39."

While on bed rest, Grace ran her company from her home and coached her staff through a massive influx of patients when the competing urgent care center down the street went bankrupt. They outgrew their space yet again and moved into an old emergency room nearby. To pass the time, she decided to take a Harvard distance learning course on complementary medicine. The material covered alternative forms of medicine she had never considered, but which resonated deeply with her. Since the 1940s, homeopathic medicine had been systematically removed from the healthcare landscape. Yet alternative forms of medicine, including naturopathy, had been scientifically proven to be effective. "I was so impressed with the idea of working with teams of people with such different philosophical approaches to help patients," she says. "And mind-body care really emphasizes the power of belief in medicine. Patients and doctors need to trust and believe in each other if things are to go anywhere. I think that without believing in something, we don't get better. Medicine is a science, but there's also an art to it."

After five years of failure with reproductive endocrinology in Northern Virginia, Grace sought the care of Dr. Schoolcraft, a doctor in Denver who had grown up on a Kansas wheat farm. After the first treatment, she was pregnant with her daughter, Beatrice. One year later, at 42, she was pregnant with twins. "There's a 2 percent chance that a woman over 40 will give birth to twins, and it has a much smaller chance of happening for someone with the kinds of challenges I had," she explains. "It was a sad story turned into a happy one, and I feel that belief played a role. You can't just wish and make anything come true, but there's a lot of power in positive thinking."

A month before she gave birth to her twins, her company suddenly found itself in need of a new location in Leesburg, so they moved into an abandoned pet shop space in town. "It was a simple rectangular space with windows at one end, and I remember drawing up the plans for the architect while on bed rest," she laughs. "That was the new site in Leesburg for Nova Urgent Care, and we weren't sure if anybody would want to see us there, but pretty soon, we had so many patients that the hinges wore off the doors." The operation now includes four locations: Gainesville, Leesburg, Ashburn, and Sterling.

Through that time, Grace's company hadn't only grown vertically, but also laterally. After growing fed up with rent culture, she purchased a 60,000-square-foot building in Ashburn, Virginia, to house the medical group operation she relocated from Sterling to Ashburn. She turned the rest of the building into a condo regime, retaining 75 percent ownership. Around that time, she launched a third component to her company, The Medical Spa at Nova. "We needed a facility where people could heal, not through the sole help of prescription drugs, but instead with a focus on diet, lifestyle, exercise, and other key solutions to chronic disease eradication," she says. "The question was, were we going to keep treating reactively with drugs and surgeries, or were we going to treat proactively by focusing on prevention? The latter made sense to me."

Integrative care is commonly accepted today, but when the spa opened in the early 2000s, naturopathic and other alternative approaches to medicine were not as common. When the practice opened, patients who had exhausted all other options began to see results, giving them the power to reclaim their lives. "Many times, your health is directly connected to the whole story of your life," Grace points out. "You look at the age of the patient, the time symptoms occurred, and what else was happening in their life at that time. You begin to piece together the parts like a car mechanic, connecting the dots to reveal new discoveries about a patient's condition."

Now, Grace's four locations employ approximately 270 people, who serve between 500 and 600 patients each day. A 100 percent Employee Stock Option Plan company, Nova operates with an emphasis on ownership, accountability, and the company's core values: compassion, excellence, collaboration, and integrity. It has naturally attracted tremendous diversity, with 36 languages represented in its staff. Its success draws not from over-prescribing and over-charging, but rather from the good will and loyalty inspired by the team's commitment to cut costs and deliver practical, thoughtful, intentional care. "Not everyone needs to have an MRI scan or an expensive procedure," Grace says. "If you have good bedside diagnostic skills and you know how to use a stethoscope, you don't always need a lot of expensive technology."

Good business and management practices, compelled by good hearts and minds, lead them to provide $60,000 in free care to Loudoun County residents who can't afford treatment. "We don't turn away people who are suffering if they don't have money," she affirms. "We feel that it's important to give back to our community, and we support a number of local fundraising efforts and events.

We also host an annual breast cancer awareness event at our spa in October, and have worked with beneficiaries including the Tigerlily Foundation and Breast Cancer Network of Strength. This year, we've selected the Cherry Blossom Breast Cancer Foundation as our beneficiary."

Her sensitivity to the woman's experience is straightforward and comes without frills, informed by a lifetime of observing various gender norms. "I feel very strongly about gender equality, both for men and women," she says. "I've never felt that I was a woman in a man's world—all my mentors were men, and we got along great."

In advising young people entering the working world today, Grace encourages a harmony between passion and practicality. "It's important to pick a career that will put food on the table," she says. "I think it's wholly possible to love what you do and do what you love while also providing for yourself and your children. Always be true to your authentic self, even if that means making hard decisions and rerouting your life's course." Leading by example in this regard, she remains fiercely motivated by the opportunity to see each patient as an individual, with their own story, beliefs, afflictions, and solutions. Her work is not merely about prolonging life, but optimizing it. It's not only about making people well, but also about making them whole. "Recovering from afflictions in life, whether physical, emotional, or psychological, is a complex process," she remarks. "Maybe we don't ever fully recover to that naïve person we were before we experienced the affliction. But maybe true healing is recovering into something more wonderful when we weather difficulties. Maybe those hardships help us understand what's really important in life. At its root, that kind of wholeness is what I work to bring my patients every day."

Max Kryzhanovskiy

The True Journey

When Max Kryzhanovskiy moved to the U.S. from Ukraine at age eleven, he knew no English. Along with his parents, grandparents, great grandmother, and uncle, the small family of immigrants settled in Albany, New York, with no friends, family, or roots in the area. "My parents had always talked about how America is a land of opportunity where you can live your dream and achieve anything you set your mind to," he remembers. "It sounded so easy. I imagined I'd start a business and be a multimillionaire in the blink of an eye. Now, twenty years later, I'm living proof that, although it's not quite as simple as that, you can achieve anything you want here. Achieving success in America is a true journey, but it's one worth taking."

Now, Max is the cofounder, President, and CEO of MOS Creative, a full service creative and digital media agency that focuses on data analytics to build high quality user experience, mostly in the digital space. Since his first days in the country, learning the language from classmates at school and watching cartoons at home, his interpersonal skills have flourished into an understanding and mastery of expression so complete that, today, his success revolves around the power and nuance of communication.

In essence, MOS Creative is in the business of capturing and conveying emotion to help people understand and connect with the products and services of their clients. As much a science as an art, its work utilizes data and analytics of the various pieces of information that inform a consumer's buying decision. "Some people don't believe in the power of marketing, but we have so many channels for gathering information today and so many ways of reaching people, whether it's through smartphone devices, computers, TV, radio, or something else," Max points out. "Through the digital landscape, it's incredible how we can capture data and follow a sales process from A to Z to increase the bottom line. Every step of the way, through granular data, we can see where people are coming from, what they're reading or downloading, and what they like or dislike."

Max and his team use this knowledge to nurture the consumer experience and serve better content, which might mean writing specific copy or designing specialized video and animation. "We aim to create the highest quality experience for the customers of our clients, but also for our clients themselves," he says. "We work hard to understand their needs and design a perfect fit product for each client."

Underlying Max's devotion to his work is a lifelong passion for sales that runs in his family. Though his mother had a background in nursing and his father worked in the taxi business, both began traveling to Poland, Bulgaria, and Turkey, where they would purchase goods cheaply and then bring them home to Odessa, Ukraine, to sell. "They really connected with the hustling mentality of Jews living in the city at that time," he remembers. "They were about buying low and selling high."

From his parents, Max learned the value of strong interpersonal skills, loyalty, honesty, transparency, and deep relationships. Their pursuit of sales brought out his own innate ability for the craft, and as a young boy, he would organize his friends and set up car wash stations to earn money. When his parents brought him unusual trinkets from their trips to other countries, he would sell them instead of collect them. "I always knew I wanted to be in business for myself, and I always loved sales," he recalls. "I understood how to talk to people and bring out the value of a product for others."

When it came to pastimes, Max enjoyed a happy childhood, developing a wide network of friends and reveling in the competitive nature of European soccer, field hockey, and track and field. The world around him, however, was far from stable. As the Soviet war with Afghanistan came to a close in 1989, the government fell apart, giving way to mob violence and pervasive killing. "It was like the Wild West," Max says. "I remember in vivid detail the soldiers coming home in boxes and the funerals that were held in the entrances of buildings so people could come pay their respects. It was a crazy time."

Max's father had seen the success of Russians and Ukrainians who had immigrated to America in the early eighties and wanted that future for his family. As conditions in Ukraine worsened, Max's grandfather finally consented to leaving their homeland, and through a Jewish organization, some old friends from Odessa sponsored them to cross the Atlantic and settle in Albany.

In this new life, Max's mother worked in a restaurant and then as an office assistant. His father got a job at BJ's and then assembled furniture for Cheapo Depot. The language barrier was hard, and the once-talkative and social boy found himself cut off from his peers by the cultural and linguistic divide. He was ultimately expelled from school for defending himself from bullies through fighting, so the family decided to move south to Pikesville, Maryland.

Max's grandmother had always pushed him, reminding him that he was a smart boy and could ascend to that next level if he wanted to. Starting high school in a new town, and with the support of his close-knit family behind him, he began to make that ascent. His social nature was revived, and he immersed himself in sports and social life. "I made a really successful traveling team called the Thunder Football Club, which had state championships several years in a row," he recalls. "The dues weren't cheap, but my parents paid my way. In retrospect, I wish I had dedicated myself more to sports. I had the drive and athleticism, but my mind was on other things at the time."

One of those things was work. Max always had a job, whether it was selling reproductions of antiques, windows and siding, or knives. As members of a Jewish fraternity, he and his friends also got considerable experience throwing parties to raise money so they could travel to visit chapters in other cities like New York, Philadelphia, and Chicago. With the help of his parents, he began investing some of his savings in real estate. His entrepreneurial ideas centered around technology and forecasted the social media boom that would later change the fabric of society so drastically. Meanwhile, his mother became an aesthetician, and his father purchased his own truck to make deliveries. The Kryzhanovskiys were living the American Dream—a reality cemented when Max began his college studies at Towson University.

Max took courses toward a finance major that were supplemented by a job at Morgan Stanley. The experience, however, turned out to be everything he didn't want in a future career. "I was on the fixed income side, sitting in front of two computer screens all day comparing debits and credits," he remembers. "I wanted to be on the floor dealing with brokers and actual clients. I always knew I was a people person, but I didn't realize how important that was to me until they asked me to start training the temporary employees who were coming in. I realized that I get so much energy from working with other people that I don't even need coffee."

One of Max's college courses routinely invited business leaders from the community to come speak about their experiences. He'll never forget the day that Brian McCardy, the owner of a printing supply and document management company, came in and challenged the students to collect used laser toner cartridges from businesses and organizations around town. When the man said he'd pay between $5 and $85 per cartridge, a light bulb went off in Max's head. After class, Max went directly to the Towson Library to speak with the woman in charge of printing services. She had a room full of old toner cartridges she didn't know what to do with, so Max made arrangements to come pick them up and set up a recycling box there for incoming used cartridges. Max didn't have the contact information for Brian, but he quickly found other businesses willing to buy the used cartridges. With that, he began visiting businesses all around town, offering to pick up their used cartridges on a routine basis and pay them a cut of the money he made from their sale.

When he told his friends about his big idea, the only one who didn't write him off was Alex Kutsishin. The two decided to join forces and launch Maximum Refills, the earliest iteration of MOS Creative. After several successful months, they decided they wanted to start selling toner cartridges as well, generating profit on both ends of the operation. They flipped through the Yellow Pages, found a company that might be interested, and went in for a meeting. When Brian McCardy himself happened to walk by the meeting room, the whole effort seemed almost divinely inspired. "We recognized each other immediately," Max laughs. "He told me that running into me was one of the greatest things, because he saw that one of his presentations inspired someone to actually go out and build a business. It was unbelievable how it worked out."

As the modest company began providing more services and reaching for new opportunities, Max and Alex changed the name to Maximum Office Solutions, or MOS. As the cofounders grew more entrepreneurial, they were offered the chance to run a nightclub, having spent their days in college hosting glamorous nights out that attracted good crowds. "That actually became a great marketing strategy for MOS, because people want to do business with people they like," Max points out. "As people came to our nightclub and had a great time, they asked what we did during the day and wanted to support us that way as well."

MOS continued to grow, adding creative services like business card, promotional material, and website design. The business became less about selling commodities, and more about identity creation for other companies.

With that, two years after Maximum Refills was launched in 2007, the company came into itself as MOS Creative. "Our experiences in different industries really informed our awareness," Max points out. "Our night club business was about building an experience, while our MOS Creative work became about building an experience through serving specific content. In marketing and advertising, the pretty stuff you see and experience is just the tip of the iceberg. I was intrigued by the data and details that drive creative."

Always driven to press the entrepreneurial envelope, Alex suggested they begin pursuing the new and rapidly growing digital space. "We envisioned building a platform for easily designing mobile websites—kind of like the Godaddy model for creating mobile websites—and then scaling it," Max recounts. "We built a system that worked well, so we decided to take it to market by creating a new company. At that point, we didn't understand the difference between a service company and a product development company, which needs lots of capital for building, testing marketing, PR, sales, and support."

Eventually, the partners realized they were investing all their time and money into this new idea, diverting important resources away from MOS Creative. One of their clients became an investor, and then the CEO of the new company. Ultimately the CEO decided he wanted to keep the company's software components but not the services like custom design and development, so MOS Creative acquired those aspects of the business. Then, toward the end of 2013, all three decided to go their separate ways professionally, leaving Max to lead MOS Creative toward its goal of building high-quality experiences across platforms and delivering content to desired profiles.

Now, Max works each day in the exhilarating environment of an industry that is evolving at an unbelievable pace, breaking down the silos that exist between platforms to create unified, compelling company analytics and identities. Working to bring their clients into the creative process in avant-garde ways, MOS Creative has its own green screen studio which they plan to rent out so people can start creating videos of their own with the help of the firm's staff animator and videographer. "It's all part of working with clients to develop a full solution," he affirms. While companies between $5 million and $50 million are a perfect fit for MOS Creative, Max also loves working with startups. "It's such a joy to help them build into something," he says. "I love working with passionate people who love what they do."

As a leader, Max has an open-mind philosophy. If someone comes into his office, he asks them to share with him what they think about it. What in the industry is being done well or could be done more efficiently or effectively? "Everyone has a good idea, so I encourage them to share," he says. "I'm a hundred percent open to listening and changing direction. I've developed specific systems and processes on my own to see if they'll work, but I embrace suggestions for change, because I don't have all the answers."

In advising young people entering the working world today, Max emphasizes the importance of networking. Identifying it as one of the greatest challenges young people face today, he points out that the advent of new technologies like smart phones and social media can create a barrier to developing strong interpersonal skills. "It's crucial to know how to sell yourself," he affirms. "Start networking and learning how to talk to people. It's all about how you present yourself and communicate your vision."

This advice stems from a lifetime spent understanding the value of true communication and connection, and then bringing that value to others. Indeed, taken collectively, Max's journey is about learning new languages and mastering innovative ways of communication. It's a journey of throwing himself into new sports, new countries, new industries, and new ideas, living life not with fear, but with impassioned interest in the challenges and experiences that can make him a better person, and a better leader. It's a journey of the family that grounds him, just as it's a story of the new friends, partners, and relationships that open him to deeper connections and broader vision. It's the true journey—never easy, but always worth it.

BERNHARDT
WEALTH MANAGEMENT

Sylvia Lagerquist

Music as a Map

Sylvia Lagerquist can still remember the music wafting into her childhood bedroom as she fell asleep at night. During the day, her mother was busy taking care of her and the three siblings that came later, so the only time her mother had a moment to play the piano was in the evenings, after the children were in bed.

In a way, from those earliest memories, music became the map that would lead Sylvia to happiness and success all through her life. She asked to learn how to play piano in first grade, and even though the nuns at her parochial school did not start teaching the instrument until third grade, she was able to convince them to begin giving her lessons the next year. Music carried her through college as she studied Instrumental Music Education, and over to Salzburg, Austria, where she was invited to join one of the city's four major bands—a large wind ensemble. It was through music that she met her husband, and in music that they dreamed together, hoping to start a music school and instrument repair shop together.

Sylvia enrolled in the USDA graduate school in her late twenties and took her first accounting class so she'd have the knowledge to handle the books for their future music school. Yet in working to make one dream a reality, she unlocked another. She took to accounting immediately and later passed all four parts of the CPA exam on her first try, becoming certified in the fall of 1984. Sylvia joined Leopold & Linowes, a CPA firm that soon merged with BDO Seidman. This experience gave her the opportunity to work with solo practitioners and small firms and fueled her passion for solving the problems of small business owners. After eight years spent at various public accounting firms, she decided to set out on her own in 1993, and Lagerquist & Associates was launched in the bedroom of her home.

With several clients following her and billable time from the beginning, she was able to develop a nice practice fairly quickly. "We focus on depth over volume," she explains. "When I started, I wanted to keep the number of clients low so I could be very engaged, reviewing their books and analyzing their financial statements on a quarterly basis. I'd write lengthy memos of what I was seeing, and I made sure the client got things done. My fees reflected that depth of service."

When her daughter Kirsten graduated from high school in 2005, Sylvia was ready to grow the firm and began looking for acquisition opportunities. Through a broker, she was introduced to a tax and write-up firm in Bowie, Maryland, that had pursued quite a different modus operandi that centered on high-volume, low-fee service. "I liked that they serviced a lot of small businesses," Sylvia reflects. "The firm didn't delve very deeply in terms of services, so I was hoping that some of these clients could use the additional financial analysis services I offer."

Since acquiring the firm and assuming the role of President and sole owner of Haines & Lagerquist, Sylvia has created a business that evades the typical cyclically-driven work schedule of most accounting firms. By keeping volume down and focusing on complex clients, the work is spread more evenly throughout the year, and tax season finds her employees only working about 50 hours a week, while the hours of CPAs at other firms are often much higher.

The experience has not been without its obstacles, however. "Merging the two firms has been a challenge," she admits. "The employees at the acquired firm had to adapt to a new culture and different expectations regarding skills and professionalism, as well as gain an understanding of how to provide a deeper level of client service. In contrast, my current staff of five is highly trained and familiar with the breadth of knowledge we offer and the lengths we're willing to go to provide meaningful service. I don't want to be a commodity to our clients. At Haines & Lagerquist, we add more value."

Sylvia was always inspired to reach for more, even as a young girl growing up in Berlin, a paper mill town in the White Mountains of New Hampshire. Like many of the immigrants in the town, both sides of her family had come from Quebec, and she was raised bilingual, with half the school day taught in French and the other half in English.

Sylvia's mother, a diligent and organized homemaker,

relied on her heavily to help out with the other children. "She was always looking ahead, and I'm very much that way now," Sylvia remarks. Her father, a gentle soul, started as a truck driver for a wholesale distributorship of groceries, beer, and cigarettes, stocking the restaurants and grocery stores of half the state. When he was promoted to a salesman, he was on the road four days per week, with his workload doubling during the busy tourist season in the summer.

Sylvia, herself, was a hard worker, earning her first buck through a newspaper route and selling vegetables from her grandfather's garden in the summers for a cut of the profits. She was also a Girl Scout, and decided to enter their National Opportunities contest by writing an essay explaining why she wanted to attend an arts and crafts program in Kansas. She was accepted to the program, but it was canceled, so she was instead given the chance to attend the launching of *Apollo 12*. "We didn't have the money to send me, so we had a bake sale and other small fundraisers to make it possible," she remembers. "I was in the local paper, and I still have the picture I took of President Nixon in the bleachers at the launch."

In elementary school, Sylvia was one of the brightest kids in her class, which won the admiration of her peers. When the kids voted for someone to lead an initiative, they often voted for her. At home, she was the creative type, learning sewing techniques from her mother to make clothes for her Barbie dolls and then mastering the art of making her own clothing by high school. Though she never had any formal art training, she was always doing art projects—a character trait that balanced nicely with her tomboy leanings. She'd play street sports as a child, and a nun at school taught her how to play basketball in seventh grade. Around this time, Sylvia's mother got a job at a local retailer, and Sylvia took on the responsibility of making dinner for the family and looking after the children.

Sylvia spent her ninth grade year at a parochial boarding school, where piano lessons were too expensive. Instead, she decided to try something new and joined the debate team. The experience prepared her for participation in a three-week-long debate institute that summer, where she was taught to see both sides of an issue. "I was incredibly shy, so I kind of clung to the one other person I knew, even though we weren't friends," she recalls. "Because of that, I missed out on opportunities to meet others in the group. When it came time to leave, I decided that, in the future, I wanted to go somewhere completely foreign, where I didn't know anyone, and focus on really connecting with the new people around me."

Sylvia returned home to attend the local parochial school that fall, where she came to a fork in the road. Her youngest brother, still a toddler, would go to bed at 7:00 PM, so if she wanted to continue piano, she'd need to practice right after school instead of going to the high school basketball team's practice. Sylvia chose piano.

Though the thrill of following her passion for music was invigorating, she found herself confronted with an entirely new challenge. After being so popular in her younger years, it was daunting to enter a new environment where cliques had already formed, but the experience ultimately taught her to be bold. "If I wanted to go to a basketball or hockey game, I wasn't going to stay home just because I didn't have anyone to go with," she recalls. "In addition, I'd do crazy things the nuns didn't like, like run for Treasurer, when girls were supposed to run for Secretary. I recruited people to revive the school's debate team. That independent streak has helped me make my way in the world ever since."

Sylvia's independent nature became particularly crucial several years later, because in Berlin, New Hampshire, college was rarely discussed. Her father had mentioned offhandedly very early on that Sylvia would go to Rivier University, where she'd be taught by the same order of nuns who ran her elementary school. Somewhere along the line, however, the narrative flipped, and he asserted it wasn't worth spending the money to educate girls. "The seed was planted, but then there was no nourishment," Sylvia remarks. "But the summer before my senior year, I thought about it. I didn't have a boyfriend, so I wasn't getting married anytime soon, and I didn't want to work at the mill. I was playing the piano, taking lessons every day at school for two years, so I thought, maybe I should go to college and study music."

Her parents didn't set roadblocks, but they didn't pave her way, either. Nor did the school guidance counselor provide much assistance. On her own, Sylvia would pour through the thick book listing all the colleges and universities in the country, looking for a Bachelor of Music degree. With the help of her piano teacher, she made an audition tape. She applied to two schools and was accepted at Catholic University of America in Washington, D.C., on a half-tuition scholarship. Sylvia wasn't just going to go to college; she was going to realize her goal of going somewhere completely new, where she didn't know anyone.

Sylvia borrowed and worked to cover the rest of her costs, and as the librarian for the reading orchestra, she'd put out the music and set up the chairs in the rehearsal hall. She started as a Piano major but then switched to Instrumental Music Education when she picked up the flute. Upon graduating in 1975, she was hired as a cataloger in the music section of the Copyright Office, where she catalogued music for copyright for two years before taking a leave of absence. In the spring of 1977, she was invited to play in the D.C. Community Orchestra, where she met John Lagerquist, an accomplished flutist himself.

Then, Sylvia decided to press the limits of her boldness and independence even further by enrolling in a University of New Hampshire program that would send her to Salzburg, Austria for a year. There, she fulfilled a lifelong dream of studying German at the University of Salzburg. In the dorms, a saxophone player overheard her practicing the flute and invited her to join the prominent Railroad Employees' Wind Ensemble, which became the heart of her social life. "I learned to speak German with my friends during rehearsals and afterward at the 'Gasthaus,'" she remembers. "It was an incredible time."

Sylvia returned to Washington, D.C. to work for the summer but she set her sights on traveling back to Salzburg that fall to serve as the Fine Arts teacher at an American prep school 25 kilometers outside the city. Before flying back across the Atlantic Ocean, she stopped by Dale Music to buy some books to use in her classes. Sylvia was surprised and delighted to run into her old friend John Lagerquist, with whom she'd played flute duets and in the D.C. Community Orchestra.

Sylvia returned to Salzburg for another year, where she truly became a citizen of the world, enjoying the remarkable differences between the Austrian and American ways of life. "I think everyone should live abroad at some point in their lives," she says. "It broadens your perspective and shows you there are other ways of doing things that are just as good, if not better. Today, my diverse experience allows me to meet somebody and find common ground between us relatively quickly, which is crucial to the personal relationship philosophy I bring to public accounting. Trust is incredibly important, and the experience of living abroad has taught me diverse ways of building that trust."

When Sylvia returned to Washington for good the following year, she got a job as an administrative assistant at the East Europe desk of the organization that administers the postdoctoral Fulbright program. John crossed her mind from time to time, but it wasn't until a year later that he crossed her path, riding by one day on a bicycle as she stood on the street corner. He invited her to a party, and in no time, the two were married. That fall, Sylvia enrolled in an accounting class at the USDA graduate school, intending to pick up skills to further her career in music but falling in love with the accounting profession instead. "It's a very tactile subject, which I love," she explains. "I love geometry and algebra, and as I got into the coursework, I realized I had a real future in it. I'm a problem solver, and it's all about problem solving." The professional pivot from music to accounting was a crucial moment in her life, and both have remained central themes in her character's composition ever since.

Now, as a business owner, Sylvia strives to lead by example, always doing her best and producing the highest quality work possible. This work ethic has landed her on the SmartCEO list of top CPAs for the past three years, and she was a finalist for its Power Players Award in the fall of 2013. As a female business leader in a profession that is still predominantly male, she remains a trendsetter and is driven by the joy of making decisions and directing her business according to her vision and values. "I like that I have nobody to answer to but myself and my clients," she remarks. "I love to solve problems for the small businesses I work with. With my creative background, I can come up with creative solutions to solve the unique problems my business owners face instead of trying to box everyone in with a standard solution."

Through it all, John's support has been integral to her success. As the piccolo player for the Kennedy Center Opera House Orchestra, he also studies voice as his avocation. He has continued to pursue their dream of owning a music school and repair shop by teaching and repairing flutes at their home in Hyattsville. Over the years, his schedule has allowed him to handle meal preparation and many of the household chores so Sylvia could work and take accounting classes. Without John, Sylvia couldn't have gotten to where she is today. "He encourages and empowers me to do what I feel I need to do," she affirms. "Small accounting firms face unique challenges in attracting top talent or the right client base, but when I come home at the end of a long day and tell him about my struggles, he always says he knows I'm doing my best."

John also was supportive from the moment Sylvia expressed interest in buying a Steinway Model L piano. In 2003, when they sold Sylvia's flute and traded in their old 1920s Model M Steinway to help cover the costs of the new Model L, Steinway was celebrating its 150th anniversary, and Sylvia and her daughter were given a free trip to New York City to tour the factory and attend a gala at Carnegie Hall.

Now, the piano sits in the Lagerquist home and has allowed the family to host concert dinner parties to raise money for their church, or to bring together family and friends. With their dining room and sun porch set up to host two dozen guests, Sylvia, John, and the church pianist would select a musical program around 45 minutes in length to perform. Sylvia spent five years perfecting Beethoven's first piano trio, which she, a violinist, and a cellist from her neighborhood performed for family, friends, and business associates in 2013—a premier accomplishment that required tremendous amounts of both skill and sensitivity.

As she reflects back on the personal triumph of that performance, Sylvia is at once keenly aware of how much has changed since the days of her childhood playing duets with her mother, and all that remains timeless. Like the Beethoven trio itself, with its parts shifting between rhythmic precision and flowing, melodic lyricism, music has been the true North that has never led her astray. To young people entering the business world today, she emphasizes the importance of starting with what you love, because it will provide that map. "From there, get a broad education, and try to experience the world, because experience will both strengthen your skills and inform your ambitions," she says. "Start with what you love, and the rest will fall into place."

Rebecca Linder

Bringing It to Life

Rebecca Linder leads a dynamic group of event architects—experts who excel at choreographing all the things that leave clients and their guests clamoring for more. Her firm, Linder & Associates, is based in Washington, D.C., but it has international reach, and as she helps clients re-invent the classic conference or summit in the digital age, the risks and opportunities are greater than ever.

Rebecca's willingness to reach for those opportunities stems from a spirit emboldened by her journey to this point, and perhaps most profoundly by a decision she made when she was seven years old. Would she admit defeat and go home, or would she dive into the challenge before her and shape her future with her own hands?

The daughter of a diplomat in the Foreign Service, Rebecca was the embodiment of the diverse cultural experiences of her young life. Her mother was Jamaican, and Rebecca was born in West Africa. The family moved to Brussels, and then to Amman, Jordan in the Middle East, before coming to Washington, D.C., where she felt like an outsider for the first time in her life. "I remember walking down the street, and the other kids ran and hid behind a tree when they saw me," she recounts now. "They had all grown up there, and they were afraid of my darker skin and my accent. I was exotic."

Sadness threatened her spirits, but in that moment, she realized she had a choice. With that, she grabbed a basketball and began dribbling up and down the street until the other children came out and played with her. "That experience made me realize how important courage is," she says. "I was either going to go home and stay hidden away, or I was going to make myself fit in. It worked, and ever since then, that's been my approach to overcoming challenges. I immerse myself in the challenge. Defining moments are about the moments you create for yourself, and about the way you participate in them." Now as the founder and President of Linder & Associates, Inc., Rebecca has spent her life approaching those moments from a perspective of action, optimism, and progress.

Rebecca launched the company in 1997, and today, it specializes in planning events that span the gamut from small C-level functions up to galas, balls, parades, festivals, and conferences. Linder & Associates takes care of every aspect of the process, including conception, production, registration, website development, air and ground transportation, crowd security and management, execution, and post-production issues. It employs a team of 28, but actually invokes and coordinates hundreds of people at a time when subcontractors and vendors are factored in. "We're really a management consulting company," she says. "We don't own any of the equipment or push out our own graphic design. We live in a universe where we pick and choose the best options for each particular client."

Linder & Associates typically serves Fortune 100 companies and high-level non-profits, and they've put on events for the World Bank, USAgainst Alzheimer's Campaign, the signature events of the National Cherry Blossom Festival, and the USA Science and Engineering Festival, which has half a million attendees. "Our work is incredibly dynamic," Rebecca says. "Events are an organization's biggest marketing opportunity and brand experience. They're an opportunity to truly connect with customers, and can have real impact on a company's ROI. Recognizing this potential, our firm is about excellence and service and making the impossible possible, bringing the visions of our clients to life with clarity and purpose."

The Women Presidents' Educational Organization has named the firm a Certified Woman's Business Enterprise, and it is a Top Owned Business according to DiversityBusiness.com. Linder & Associates is a member of the Washington D.C. Convention & Tourism Corporation, Special Event Sites Marketing Alliance, and International Special Events Society. In addition, Rebecca is a member of Les Dames d'Escoffier, a worldwide philanthropic society of professional women leaders in the fields of food, fine beverage, and hospitality.

As President, Rebecca is the visionary of the company. She tangentially oversees some of the creative work from the production side, but much of that work is now driven by the firm's project managers. For the most part, her days are spent building and maintaining sales relationships while immersing herself in new ideas and concepts. As an industry leader and a top-five D.C.-based event planning firm, Linder & Associates relies on Rebecca's proven ability to gauge where the industry is headed and to position the firm ahead of the curve.

The company's approach may seem avant-garde, and is indeed defined by its innovative and holistic style, but the fuel for its fire is as simple as it is timeless. "We just love the pure joy and challenge that comes from engaging with our clients and making them happy," Rebecca says. "Our job is bringing someone's vision to life, which is a constant challenge but also a constant source of gratification for us. We love engaging in conversation with someone, trying to understand their mission and goals, and translating that vision into a lived experience that allows people to come together and connect. That's extremely powerful for us."

Joel Simon, Fundraising Director for LifeBridge Health, can offer a client's perspective. "Rebecca's team helped us put on the largest fundraising Gala in Maryland history," he reports. "Their professionalism, technical proficiency, and ability to work with professional staff, volunteer leaders, and other vendors was superlative. I cannot recommend them enough for such events."

Linder & Associates has an eye toward sustainably. It is keenly aware of the impact of its actions on future generations, as well as the wellbeing of the environment. The team is committed to sustainable practices, both internally as an organization, and in partnership with clients for their programs. In planning events, they help clients maintain their environmental standards and can even augment them through recommendations on everything from venues with sustainable practices and locally sourced food, to the use of electronic communications rather than traditional printed materials.

Linder & Associates also works for a closer community and a stronger society by supporting Horton's Kids. This worthy organization provides comprehensive services to the children of Washington, D.C.'s challenged neighborhoods, improving the quality of their daily lives and nurturing their desire and ability to succeed. With programs that include tutoring, mentoring, enrichment, advocacy, and family support, Horton's Kids is truly making a difference.

In a way, Rebecca's work is about creating the kind of collective experiences that had such a profound impact on her as she grew up. Her life has essentially been centered around the kitchen or the dinner table, and the unique exploration of taste, flavor, family, and life that occurs in these settings. "It's like its own philosophy—a way of connecting to the various places I've been and sharing them with others," she explains. "I'll never live in the Middle East again, but I can recreate it and bring it to life through the food I cook and the way I share it. To this day, my brother, mother, father, partner, and our young children come together to celebrate the moments that food nourishes and the traditions passed down from one generation to the next. It's what connects us, and it's what I want to give my kids."

As a child, Rebecca watched her parents host wonderful events that transcended cultural difference and served to strengthen connections not only between people, but between nations. Cultivating in Rebecca a zest and passion for life, they taught her that nothing was impossible, and that the choices she made in life had the power to unlock every opportunity. Along with a sense of wonder and adventure, they modeled self-reliance and kept Rebecca and her brother grounded in who they were and what they were connected too, even when the family moved to new countries. "Sometimes it was hard to move, but I wouldn't change a thing," she says. "My family is very close, and our parents were very good at getting us excited about experiencing a new culture."

Rebecca's efforts led her not only to fend, but also to flourish. Her family moved to Greece just before she started high school, and the first thing she did in her new country was run for president of the freshman class. Such boldness led her out of her comfort zone and didn't come naturally to her, but she understood it was important to insert herself in new surroundings and get to know her classmates in courageous and intentional ways.

Upon graduating, Rebecca returned to the U.S. and enrolled at Boston University because she wanted the chance to get lost in a bigger school and city. "The distinct advantage of moving is the opportunity to reinvent yourself," she remarks. "That's something I love about the work I do now. In a way, each event is an opportunity to develop an idea and an identity, with a definitive end point in mind, where you'll move on to the next one."

Though her parents would have been happy to give her money, she didn't rely on it and instead held a host of jobs through college. She worked for a stockbroker and a lawyer, hoping the experiences would help her figure out what she wanted to do in life. Through her first exposure to catering, she became familiar with the behind-the-scenes world of putting on events for thousands of people. Her most profound college experiences, however, happened not behind the closed doors of the kitchen, but instead under the open lights of the stage. After seeing a casting call poster for an Edward Albee play, she decided to step outside her comfort zone once again and audition. "I had to dig pretty deep to go out on stage in front of an audience, portraying a character that wasn't me and emotions I didn't feel," she remembers. "I realized that, if I could overcome my fear and triumph in that scenario, there wasn't much I couldn't do."

Rebecca spent the summer after her junior year at an acting school in Los Angeles and then decided she wanted to pursue a career in the field after graduation. Once she received her degree, she moved to Washington, D.C. and took a job at Arena Stage, but quickly realized her commitment to acting full-time had waned. "If you don't fit the physical profile of a part, you're out of luck," she points out. "I couldn't get behind that. But what I did love was the production—the energy, creativity, management, leadership, and level of coordination that went into it."

She had several other jobs at the time that also drew upon these interests in one way or another, but she soon decided to streamline her focus by immersing herself in the world of food and catering. With that, she accepted a job at a D.C. catering company—an experience that utilized her passion for production in an environment characterized by her first love, food. She started in sales and then took on a special project, ultimately creating for herself the role of Director of Operations. In that capacity, she handled the production aspects for the company, as well as high-end accounts for the Smithsonian and the National Gallery of Art.

Rebecca gained tremendous exposure to the business and to the culture of the city, working with inspirational mentors like Genevra Higginson, the Director of Special events at the National Gallery. A tremendously accomplished woman in everything from tennis, to writing, to cooking, to leadership, she was challenging in all the right ways, teaching Rebecca never to compromise. Thanks in part to this wisdom, Rebecca soon decided she wanted to learn and do more. "I didn't want to just produce one aspect of an event; I wanted to be in charge of the full event," she remembers. "So I decided to step out on my own. I didn't know how I'd do it, or with what, but I was committed to making it work."

Thus, Linder & Associates was born. "I remember calling my dad and saying I needed a desk," Rebecca laughs. "I had a studio, and he came and helped me buy a plank of wood where I could set up my leased computer. I got a guy to incorporate me for $500, and then I sat there in my pajamas wondering, what did I do?" Positive, upbeat, and self-assured, she immersed herself thoroughly in the production end, just as she had done in catering when she got a black suit and learned how to wait tables. Wanting to understand the whole experience, she did the same with lighting and staging companies. "I believed in myself and in the idea that, if people started hiring me, I'd get it done," she remembers. "And I did."

When she grew busier, she hired her father as the accounting and business manager, and when she outgrew the studio, she hired her mother to design and manage her new office space. As a child of the world, she has worked toward a vision with global breadth, participating at every level of her organization and leading by example. In an industry where churn-and-burn leads to high employee turnover, her team now has people with tenures up to 14 years in length. "Our success comes from constant introspection and evolution as a business, but also from the way we interact with each other," she explains. "Every day, as a leader, I show up with my fist in the air and a smile on my face, ready to go. You have to be committed to your own energy and inspiration in order for that to trickle down."

Ever since she watched her relatives start their own drapery, dress, lingerie, and hat shops, Rebecca has equated entrepreneurship with independence, freedom, and choice. It lends her a control over her own destiny, agenda, and life that fits perfectly with her personality, and while leadership can at times be stressful, the love and support of her partner, Lisa Bodager, serves as a perfect counterbalance. "She's wise counsel, and I love her willingness to engage in my ideas, because I'm always thinking about new things I might like to explore or pursue," Rebecca says.

In advising young people entering the working world today, Rebecca stresses the importance of being prepared to work hard and absorb new ideas. "Don't be afraid to interact with everybody, because that's how you learn," she says, underscoring the courage she used to dribble that basketball up and down her street all those years ago. "If you're asked to take on a new responsibility at work, relish the opportunity to make a name for yourself and play an active role in your growth. The ones that rock it are the ones that believe in themselves and just jump in." By bringing this philosophy to each project and each hard mark one aims for, every day finds new ideas and opportunities waiting to be brought to life.

BERNHARDT
WEALTH MANAGEMENT

Carol J. Loftur-Thun

The Holistic View

When the plane hit the Pentagon on September 11, 2001, the explosion could be heard at the Child Development Center in the nearby town of Alexandria, Virginia, where Carol Loftur-Thun worked. History will remember that day as an iconic tragedy and a symbolic turning point for American consciousness, but for Alexandria and other communities like it, the reverberations of the event were tangible and immediate.

Many of the town's residents worked in connection with the airport, hotel, and cab companies in the area, but with the airport shut down for an extended period of time, families that were just getting by found themselves unable to make ends meet. Carol, who was employed by Alexandrians Involved Ecumenically (ALIVE!), was deeply struck by the hardship that struck her community. And worst of all, a woman who had mentored for ALIVE! had been among the passengers who lost their lives in the crash.

In a stroke of grace, however, the husband of that woman used his allotment from the 9/11 Fund to launch the Alexandria Community Trust Fund. "The fund announced that its first round of awards would be no more than $50,000 each, but we knew we needed $100,000 to provide emergency assistance to the economic victims of the disaster in our area," Carol remembers. "So we made the case for it, and we got it."

The Presbyterian Church in the area also committed to funding ALIVE!'s efforts in several installments, and by the end of a three-year period, ALIVE! had become the country's largest private emergency financial assistance program for 9/11 economic victims, providing $480,000 to several thousand people. Through those efforts, Carol and her team were also able to connect those people to the social services they wouldn't have known about otherwise. They developed a strong relationship with the local community resilience workers employed by FEMA, who were able to speak multiple languages to reach micro-communities and cultures.

"Through partnering with the Salvation Army and the Department of Human Services, we were able to leverage a wide range of resources to get connected to people who needed help," Carol explains. "If a child was showing signs of developmental issues, we connected those parents with local programs that did free child assessments. If a diabetic person was taking half-doses of medicine because he couldn't afford it, we showed him that he was eligible for subsidized housing and ongoing assistance. In a city that didn't really have resources for how to find resources, I started to see how connecting people to the services they needed made a huge difference in their lives and couldn't ultimately save money and hardship in the future. In effect, I became the information referral for Alexandria."

Connecting people to opportunity has been the constant theme threading the diverse experiences of Carol's life into a view of humanity that is perceptively holistic, allowing her to address society's greatest challenges with uncommon potency. Indeed, her countless opportunities to explore the many facets of the human condition began from the earliest days of life. Born in the foothills of the Andes Mountains in Quito, Ecuador, Carol was the only child of two impassioned Quaker missionaries who each heralded from a rich tradition of such work. Her great-great grandparents were missionaries to the Cherokee Indians. Her grandfather, an otherwise practical man, would tell her stories so spiritual that they bordered the supernatural, recounting an experience in war-torn China where he, unarmed, was charged with protecting a house full of girls from an enemy army. A man appeared at his side as the army approached, and the pair was successful in convincing the army to leave, but when Carol's grandfather turned to thank his companion, he had disappeared.

"These kinds of stories were a part of my childhood, and they're cornerstones of my worldview today," Carol affirms. "I'm practical and rational to a fault, but I do get the feeling that I'm led through life with some kind of divine protection and purpose. I've never had any kind of grand plan, but I get the sense that I come to the right places at the right times and with the right gifts to share."

Carol's family moved to a compound in a port town soon after her birth, where her father taught Bible School. She learned Spanish before she learned English, and "Why?" was her constant refrain. When she was five, the family moved to the U.S. so she could start school, and her father enrolled at the Princeton Theological Seminary for his doctorate.

Growing up in the late 1950s and early 1960s in a small urban development off a county road, Carol would roam the woods and fields nearby or play elaborate imagination games with her friends until her interests shifted to academics. She was a voracious reader, taking a break from books long enough to secure a paper route in her father's name, as girls weren't allowed to do such work at that time. She would deliver papers on her bike after school and on weekends, saving up money that her father helped her invest in stocks. Through their work, her parents frequently escorted mission trips to other countries, and with her earnings, Carol was able to pay her own way and join them in Brazil, Argentina, Peru, and Chile. She earned the money to fund a trip to Lebanon to visit her cousins one summer, and a trip to Spain later on.

Beyond the global experiences of travel, Carol was deeply inspired by the work her parents did in their local community. They taught in prisons in Trenton, and at community colleges, where their students often came from troubling backgrounds. "They were both natural teachers, and I have always been moved by the strong tradition of mission and service in my family," Carol affirms. "Growing up in the research triangle, I became passionate about anthropology and the sciences, and because of my roots in helping others, I dreamed of becoming a doctor when I grew up."

By the time Carol enrolled at Davidson College in North Carolina as a premed student, she was accustomed to the kind of deep thought higher education aims to inspire. Through challenging high school teachers who spurred her intellectual development, and through watching her own parents struggle with questions of faith and spirituality, she started her college career with a seasoned penchant for philosophy that many of her peers were just beginning to discover. After becoming disillusioned by a particularly disengaged biology professor during her sophomore year, she dismissed her dreams of practicing medicine and instead opted to design her own major in Anthropology and the Economics of Third World Development.

Through the Fulbright Program, Carol participated in the college's first semester abroad program in India, where she had the opportunity to meet the President of the country and work with top scholars, archaeologists, and professors. As one of only 23 Americans in Madras, a city of 3 million people, Carol was struck by the intense contrast between privilege and poverty. "India is a very spiritual place, but it's also incredibly depraved," she remembers. "It's a compelling window into the competing forces of need and want. That trip changed the trajectory of our lives."

Carol traveled in Europe for six months during her junior year, living in Florence and then with the family of her boyfriend in England. Upon graduating from college, she had visions of joining the Peace Corps, but decided to postpone that dream to fulfill another. She and her boyfriend took a bus from Alabama to Mississippi and then hitchhiked to Seattle and Alaska over the span of several weeks. "It's something you could never do in this day and age, but it was one of the most incredible experiences I've ever been through," she recalls. "If we needed our faith in the Americana persona restored, that was the way to do it. People invited us into their homes, fed us dinner, and gave us their beds. Everyone had a story, and everyone was wonderful."

In Alaska, Carol worked at a salmon plant on the Kenai Peninsula, where she met young people from California, immigrants from Israel and Australia, mountain climbers from Norway, and Robert, the man who would become her husband. Once they had gotten their fill of Alaska, they made their way down to Washington, where Carol earned money picking apples and eventually bought herself a car. In that car, she drove across the country and finally arrived home in New Jersey. By that time, Robert was living in D.C., and after a period of courtship, Carol moved down to the nation's capital.

Carol and Robert got engaged with their sights set on joining the Peace Corps, just as she had dreamed about in college. But life had different plans in store for them, and while the Peace Corps ambition faded away, their marriage became the foundation of everything Carol would accomplish through her professional life. As Robert earned his CPA degree and engaged her in deep conversations about entrepreneurship, she grew intrigued by the business mindset and enrolled in MBA courses at George Washington University. Robert took the helm of Windows Catering Company, steering it from $2 million in annual sales to $5 million within three years, and Carol's love of business and marketing drove her to join the team as well. As the Director of Marketing, she helped put on events for the National Gallery of Art, Exxon Mobil, the Corcoran Gallery, Maria Shriver, and Arnold Schwarzenegger, among others. "It was a wonderful experience to be in a company as it transformed from a heavily debt-financed restaurant into a highly-successful catering company," she remembers.

When Robert and Carol moved on, he decided to launch his own business, while she decided to take a job in retail. It was a way to pay the bills and pass the time, but Carol found herself yearning for the mission and service that had meant so much to her growing up. With that, she began to get involved with ALIVE! through her daughter's preschool at the Child Development Center in Alexandria. Realizing a passion for early childhood education, she became the organization's Chair of Early Childhood Programs and found herself writing grants with her daughter asleep in her lap. "We were operating out of a church basement, and with our image as a charitable organization for low-income families, there came a scarcity mindset," Carol recalls. "We didn't have a lot of money, so there was a feeling that we simply had to sustain, rather than grow. But I felt that wasn't good enough. The building was falling apart, and even construction paper was beyond our means. Those kids deserved better, and I knew the money was out there, so we needed to go out and find it."

Thanks to Carol's perseverance and innovative approach to the nonprofit mindset, that's exactly what they did. With the funds they raised, they renovated the center, hired a new director, increased teacher salaries, and made sure they had the materials they needed. They brought in donated computers, provided mentorship opportunities for teachers, and passed their reaccreditation with flying colors. "I was surrounded by incredibly good people who gave generously of their time," she remarks. "Six of our eight major programs were run entirely by volunteers like me, and with 39 member congregations, ALIVE! was the largest private safety net in the city. I absolutely loved what I was doing."

A year after Carol had her second daughter, ALIVE! offered her a part-time job as the assistant to the president, a legend in Alexandria's nonprofit scene. Together, they orchestrated a massive fundraising event at the Torpedo Factory, raising over $40,000 with the help of the 900 attendees. "We had never seen that kind of money," she muses. A month later, ALIVE! offered Carol a full-time position. In that capacity, she spent several more years working to transform the city of Alexandria by focusing on basic human needs like food, shelter, and emergency financial assistance. She then accepted a position at CrisisLink, a nonprofit dedicated to addressing the mental health troubles that people otherwise suffer in silence, and later The Women's Center, a nonprofit whose mission is to significantly improve the psychological, career, financial and legal well-being of women, men and their families.

Through Carol's intuitive pursuit of her life's purpose, her work has always been inspired by others, and focused on others. "When I remind myself that my work is about others and not me, I'm able to forget my insecurities and ego and the other things that might otherwise trip me up," she says. "My work is about my board, my staff, my clients, my community, and my constituents. It's also very important to me to look at each person as an individual, and not a type of person, need, or issue."

After experiencing humanity from so many vantage points and in some many guises, through both her personal experiences as a young woman and her professional pursuits later on, Carol's ability to view people and situations with a holistic view has become the defining philosophy in her approach to business and life. "What I've loved most about my career is the fact that I've had experience in such a wide range of services, from childhood development programs, to homeless shelters, to domestic violence programs, to suicide prevention," she recounts. "Being a generalist has allowed me to examine the human experience across the life cycle, and across generations. I've worked with newborn children, grandparents, and everything in between."

Just as a holistic perspective is invaluable in addressing social issues, Carol incorporates it into her leadership philosophy by pushing her team to think in 360 degrees. "It's not enough to just think outside the box," she emphasizes. "We have to think all the way around a problem, seeing it from an array of perspectives to drive innovation and come up with better ways of accomplishing our goals."

With this mindset, Carol envisions a new future for the nonprofit sector—one where the intense fragmentation, dire undercapitalization, and maligned leadership practices plaguing the industry are replaced by a new model that embraces sustainability through earned income streams and other entrepreneurial principles. "We need to encourage sustainability as the motivator for both businesses and nonprofits, highlighting the opportunities for each to learn from the other in aspiring toward a new vision of a triple bottom line for people, planet, and profit," Carol avows. "If we can pursue hybrids of business principles and socially-minded goals, we can create a more efficient system to alleviate injustice and stabilize society."

In advising young people entering the business and nonprofit worlds today, Carol stresses the importance of abandoning antiquated ideas of charity that encourage a compartmentalized lifestyle. "Instead, be thinking about how you can push the changes you want to see in the world through whatever you're doing," she says. "Think more broadly than putting in an allotted number of charity hours each month. Think about what you do every day, every minute, and how it can be part of building a more sustainable or just world. I would invite everyone to become part of this conversation about how we can innovate in this way. Indeed, the progress America so dearly needs right now will be accomplished only by seeing holistically and acting collectively."

Kimberly "Kymm" McCabe

The Science of Transformation

Growing up, Kymm McCabe's parents told her bedtime stories, including Russian fairy tales from a book that had been in her family for many years. One story was the tale of a princess held captive by an evil czar in a castle high among the clouds. Her true love was told he could only rescue her by climbing the immense staircase to the castle without looking back.

The catch was each stair step was haunted by the soul of someone who had tried and failed to climb to the castle. With each step the prince took, the trapped soul exclaimed words of discouragement and whispered tales of disappointment from underneath his feet. However, his desire and faith drove him on until he ultimately persevered and rescued the princess. "My parents' point in sharing this fairy tale was to impress upon me that I could accomplish anything I set my mind and heart to, and that I needed have the confidence, tenacity, and passion to persevere through adversity," Kymm explains today. "I have grown to value this lesson so deeply that the fairy tale gave rise to my son's name."

Willing her professional journey to embody the spirit of the ascent up that staircase, Kymm is now the President and CEO of ASI Government (ASI), a company dedicated to providing the Federal Government with full spectrum acquisition and program management services and products. Founded in 1996, the company began as the vision of three former federal acquisition "revolutionaries" who believed "Big A" acquisition was key to achieving government outcomes. "I would say that's even truer now, knowing that half of the federal discretionary budget is spent on acquisitions, even during this time of budget austerity," Kymm comments. "Back then, as now, the members of Acquisition Solutions believed acquisition could be strategically positioned to take advantage of the power of this function in finding savings while driving results."

Fueled by this mission, these three visionaries set out to transform federal acquisition. Their first accomplishment was creating the "Seven Steps to Performance-Based Acquisition," which they developed through interagency collaboration and turned into government-wide guidance. They went on to crack the nut on knowledge management and created the Virtual Acquisition Office™ (VAO), which provides original research, online training, tools, and templates that help federal acquisition professionals excel in their respective roles. Today, ASI's acquisition program management products leverage leading technology, supporting more than 130 government organizations and 45,000 federal acquisition professionals. "We continue to face the market with the guiding philosophy that the workforce is the key to driving outcomes," Kymm confirms.

In addition to modernizing the world of "Big A" acquisition, ASI's founders left an important legacy in the company's values of teamwork, integrity, and excellence. "The integrity of our team, our culture, and our brand were constructed with care and intention from day one, and the spirit of teamwork and positive impact that permeates ASI is critical to maintaining it," Kymm remarks. "Even through significant transformation over the years, those values have been the common threads, and as a result, ASI has one of the healthiest cultures I've ever encountered."

Today, the company's mission has broadened to include program management. ASI's client base cuts across every cabinet-level agency, with half of the 250-person company dedicated to the intelligence space. "The entire company has reach-back to our incredible ASI Research InstituteTM. That allows us an unparalleled line of sight and depth of understanding across the federal sector, and the ability to deliver invaluable data to our clients," she says. "I believe the team is successful because, in addressing our market, we've developed this unique attitude that we are both here to deliver solutions to the country's most challenging problems and to uplift our clients. The way we see it, when it comes to serving the public and the country, ASI and the client are in this together, and we can accomplish anything as long as we are united and believe in our ability to have an impact. I'm extremely grateful to be at the helm of this company and to be part of a team who feels so passionately about acquisition, which I believe could be the most powerful and underutilized lever in the Federal Government."

While Kymm has worked at ASI for three and a half years, she worked alongside the company years prior when she headed her own business, Advanced Performance Consulting Group, Inc. ASI recognizes this is an extremely competitive, even crowded, space—a new dynamic for the company that launched the federal acquisition support market 18 years ago. As a result, corporate owners realized they needed a leader who could reshape the company to take it to the next level through strategy, innovation, and positioning, so they turned to Kymm. "I'm only good at two things: leading transformations and making a heck of a guacamole," she laughs. "I focus all of my professional energy on thinking about transformation and change as a science. I try to bring the soft sciences, like organizational and social behavior, to the hard sciences, like physics. When you integrate those fields, you start to see the commonalities and applicability of scientific theory to organizational change and development. For example, in organizations, you can observe patterns, like fractals, which you can then address to change the culture and organizational results."

A third-generation entrepreneur, Kymm has a passion and proficiency for her work that is as innate as it is seasoned. Her grandfather grew up during the Great Depression and learned at a young age how to find ways around adversity to ensure his family never went without. This determined and resourceful outlook led to his eventual ownership of several businesses. "His mindset was, if there was a road block over here, he would just find a new way around over there," she recalls. "His approach had no room for limitations, and instead focused entirely on finding new paths around obstacles."

Kymm's family was centered in Los Angeles, California. Her father, a psychologist, worked for the government during her early childhood and later practiced psychology as one of the owners of the medical facilities in which he worked. Her mother, originally a zoology major, earned a master's degree and then a PhD in public administration while working full-time and raising two children. Kymm still remembers late-night sessions at home during which her mother poured through stacks of papers with a highlighter in her hand. While both parents did very well financially, they carried on her grandfather's mentality of careful spending and determined resourcefulness. "My parents inspired me to find that thing I really loved and was passionate about," she says. "They stressed that there was a time to work, a time to learn, a time to play, and a time to give back. Because of that work ethic and focus on contributing to the community, money never had to be a major motivator for me; rather, I found my passion in public service and never looked back."

Growing up, Kymm lived within a few miles of her extended family, including her grandparents. She grew extremely close with her grandfather, spending hours sitting beside him and soaking up his stories about seeing the first airplane and the installation of electricity in his home when he was a kid. "I hold close the lessons he taught me about resilience, the importance of family, and the value of steadfast integrity in business," Kymm affirms. "He lived those things, and I hope to follow in his footsteps."

As a young girl, Kymm was unsure of what she wanted to focus on professionally. However, her parents suspected early on that she would be a leader in business. When Kymm was six years old, her mother asked her to clean her room, which Kymm did by enlisting her neighborhood friends to do the job for her. She employed these leadership skills again in elementary school, when a rainy day created chaos in her classroom. "The kids were completely out of hand and the teachers were totally overwhelmed," she recalls. "I realized what was happening and felt uneasy about the behavior, so I stood up on a chair and convinced my friends to stop and help the teachers. Amazingly, all the kids calmed down. It reinforced my belief in the importance of taking a stand when a situation seems wrong or negative."

Kymm's first job was working in the medical records department for her father's hospital during the summer. "We'd go to the doctors' offices and pick up these huge carts of records, which we would then wheel back for filing in a giant warehouse," she says. "It was tedious, but it was essential that we did everything right because each file represented a person, and if anything happened to the information, it could impact the patient's care."

While the filing was monotonous, this and other summer jobs with her father often required her to spend extended time in the hospital, which gave her a first-hand account of how a medical team comes together to save a patient's life. "One summer, I worked in urgent care and was right next to the gurney when a man underwent a massive heart attack," she recalls. "I could see how every job in the hospital aligned to reach the common goal of saving his life. It's really true that everyone from the janitor to the engineer plays an important part in helping get those astronauts to the moon."

When she was not working, her parents kept her busy with extracurricular activities, allowing her to try just about everything. "They got me into music, sailing, horseback riding—you name it, I probably tried it at one point," she says. "They taught me early on that I could do and be anything. They were always there to support me and be that net so that if I fell off the trapeze, I wouldn't crash. They allowed me to experiment, and even fail, so I could learn and grow."

Later, Kymm attended the University of California, Santa Barbara as an undergraduate, when she and a friend decided to create her first business providing home services in the area. "The university was adjacent to some of the wealthiest populations in the country," she says. "I knew they had money we didn't have, and we had time they didn't have—it was a match made in heaven. So we negotiated contracts with local vendors and hired friends at well above what they would normally earn to provide whatever services were needed, whether it was dog walking, house cleaning, or delivering fresh flowers. The business grew, and we were able to make decent money while having a good time."

Before Kymm entered her senior year in 1990, she decided to take a year off of school to work with Senator Ted Kennedy on Capitol Hill. Leaving the home services business to her co-founder and roommate, she traveled to Washington, where she had the opportunity to learn firsthand how a Senate office is run. "Regardless of your political beliefs, there is no denying that Ted Kennedy was an exceptional person to work for and learn from," she says. "He was passionate about issues, and his office was a well-oiled machine. The best of the best worked there, and I was able to learn about policy making, stewardship, being a public servant, and the business of politics."

At the end of her time on Capitol Hill, Kymm returned to Santa Barbara to finish her final year of college and met the man she would marry, Matthew McCabe. After earning her bachelor's degree, she supported the White House Advance Team while launching her first consulting firm and enrolling at the University of Southern California to earn a Masters of Public Administration with an emphasis on strategy and organizational behavior. "I wanted to pursue a unique mixture of the public and private sector, so the University worked with me to create a degree that spanned the School of Public Administration and the Business School," she explains.

In 1995, Kymm and Matt married, and the newlyweds returned to Washington, D.C., so he could earn his PhD in Philosophy from the University of Maryland, College Park. They had few friends or family in the area, no money, and no jobs, so one day, Kymm began flipping through a magazine to search for clues as to what she should do next. She scanned a list of Top 50 Women-Owned Businesses and decided to reach out to a woman who ran a marketing firm in the area, introducing herself and asking if she was looking for help. Luckily, the woman was, and Kymm was hired.

Kymm stayed at the marketing firm for several months before joining EDS, where she eventually co-managed their government performance management practice. After a few years, her entrepreneurial spirit urged her to start her own business. "I was really struggling over the decision, as I had been interviewing with another firm," she says. "I called the partner who interviewed me and shared my vision for a new company. He encouraged me to run with it, so I did. He has since become a close friend and mentor and now serves on ASI's Board of Directors, offering tremendous guidance."

With the unwavering support of her husband, family, and mentors, Kymm founded her second company with another woman from EDS. "I was a 29-year-old CEO doing federal management consulting to senior government executives and general officers," she says. "It was absolutely incredible, and I couldn't help but wonder, where but in the U.S. would this opportunity present itself?" Together, Kymm and her co-founder built the company and sold it to ICF International eight years later. "We had a great run with that company," she recalls. "I grew professionally and as a leader. It was a period of introspection during which I learned about my capabilities and gained clarity on what skills I needed to develop."

After selling her company, it took Kymm a while to adjust to the influx of capital. "We've never been big spenders in my family, so my first thought was to invest it," she says. "My husband was wonderful, though. He reminded me that I needed to acknowledge and appreciate the accomplishment and urged me to buy the concert grand piano I'd been dreaming of to mark that moment. The truth is that the piano has been a great source of joy for me, especially now as I watch my children playing it. "

Kymm continued to work with ICF until Charles Rossotti of the Carlyle Group contacted her. Kymm was humbled by an offer of employment, and also understandably hesitant, as working for the company would require a long commute at a time when she had a toddler at home, so she decided to commit to a short-term trial period.

Toward the end of that rewarding time, Kymm received a phone call from a friend and Army Senior Officer, asking her to lead their new transformation office, then called the Enterprise Task Force. Knowing the transformation was vital to supporting American soldiers suffering the stress of two long and active conflicts in Iraq and Afghanistan, she heralded it as a once-in-a-lifetime opportunity to serve and make a meaningful contribution to her country. Thus, Kymm accepted and spent the following three years leading the Army's business transformation in the Pentagon. "At the time, the Army was engaged in two active conflicts, in the midst of the largest BRAC in its history, facing an economic decline, and in the process of a political transition. The odds were stacked against us, to say the least," she explained, "When the planes hit on September 11th, our military jumped into action and did what it does best—whatever was needed to defend our country. The system and soldiers began to experience strain after a couple of years of combat, and the historical military funding declines after every major conflict dictated the need to drive a more cost-conscious and business-minded culture. Our soldiers' deployments were too long, and so we were laser focused on getting our troops what they needed and then getting them home while preparing the Army for the austerity that is now upon us. The capability and sheer will of our military is incredible, but it must be sustainable. It came down to the fact that the Army needed to change to meet current and future mission needs. Our Army is currently the most capable it has ever been, and they wanted to transform to preserve their capability and health over time."

Kymm's organization first reported to the Army Chief of Staff, and then the Undersecretary of the Army, working closely with the most senior officers across the Department of Defense. She was exhilarated by the willingness to collaborate across military services, as well as by the level of capability and dedicated focus of those with whom she worked. Her boss, LTG Robert Durbin, insisted she learn as much as she could, so she visited sites across the Army, such as the National Training Center; talked with soldiers in deploying brigades and wounded warriors in returning brigades; and witnessed the breadth of what the Army offered. "My position allowed me to see our incredible military from the inside out and to witness their amazing efforts and accomplishments in the name of our nation and soldiers," she recounts reverently. "At the end of my tenure, I felt overwhelmed by our soldiers' courage and civil servants' dedication, in awe of the Army's capabilities and leaders, and deeply grateful for our military. I truly believe that the experience working with our Army made me a better leader, citizen, and person. It was a profound experience—one of the most challenging and significant of my life."

After an impressive run at the helm of the organization, Kymm left her position as the Acting Deputy Director of the Office of Business Transformation in 2011 for ASI Government, and has spent the past three-and-a-half years transforming the company from a small team of acquisition revolutionaries into a potent and innovative professional services firm, set apart by its culture, conscience, and soul.

When she's not working, she serves on the Board of the Professional Services Council, TechAmerica, AFCEA, and NCMA, while also using her love of connecting people to organize what she calls her "Good Egg Happy Hours"—gatherings of what consistently ends up being between 50 and 90 great and trustworthy professional friends—to catch up and make meaningful connections. "I love to seek out people who not only are good at what they do, but are also good people, and to bring them all together," she says.

Kymm is also actively involved with numerous causes, including Linda's Legacy supporting the local homeless, and the ITP Program, which assisted in treating her son's speech disorder when he was young. "The government paid for his speech therapy for several years, so that today, he has all the verbal capabilities of other kids his age," she says. "We were so grateful for the assistance. It was all free, and given how small the ITP's budget is, Matt and I are honored to donate regularly so they can continue helping other families in need." She is also proud to belong to a company rooted in the principle that a good business partner also must be a good community partner. Indeed, ASI believes so strongly in community outreach that it offers employees an additional paid day off per year to volunteer. Many teams spend their day of service together, making it a team-building event as well. Additionally ASI's employee-led community relations committee, ASI Involved, sets priorities for the company's philanthropic and community outreach program, identifying opportunities to contribute to nonprofit partners like the Arlington Food Assistance Center, the Children's Inn at the National Institutes of Health, the Fisher House Foundation, Operation Jump-Start, and Toys for Tots.

While she has had many mentors and influential colleagues during her career, Kymm identifies her husband, Matt, as the single most essential person to her happiness and success. Matt, who works as a Professor of Philosophy at Washington College, is an involved father who genuinely and constantly supports her. "I literally could not have done anything that I've done without him," she says. "The most important thing that has ever happened to me is marrying him; his love, support, and partnership enable me to do anything and everything."

If her husband's support provides the foundation of her work, Kymm's deep passion and love for her country provides the framework. While she always felt grateful to live in America, her career trajectory illuminates that the American Dream is, in fact, very much alive, and that any goal is achievable with the right amount of determination and stamina. Yet as grateful as she is to be a woman in America, where she had the ability to become a CEO at a young age, she acknowledges that being a woman in the workplace still has formidable challenges. This concept was highlighted when Kymm recently served as a guest lecturer at a Gender and Work course, where a young woman from India confided that her biggest challenge was her brothers' and father's strong disapproval of her pursuit of a higher education. "All I could tell her was that she had already done it. All she had to do was keep going," Kymm says.

"If I could offer advice to young people, it would embody the moral from my childhood Russian Fairy Tale: if someone says you can't, find another way and persist. There will always be obstacles, so you have to find a way to disregard the whispers from the souls under those stairs. If you can persevere through that, you can—and will—reach your goals."

BERNHARDT
WEALTH MANAGEMENT

Sean McDermott

Now is the Time

At the bedside of his father-in-law the night before he passed away, Sean McDermott saw what it meant to live a fulfilling life. His father-in-law had been tremendously successful, selling his business at age 55 and remaining remarkably active until he fell ill with cancer. Through it all, he was a loving family man, and when Sean asked him if he had any regrets, he said he only wished that he could see his grandchildren grow up. "That was a very defining moment for me in recognizing what was important to me as a person," Sean remembers today.

The epiphany came three days after Sean had been let go from his job—a sequence of events that unlocked in him an inner resolve to say, "Now is the time." He always knew he would start his own business, but some might have argued that the wake of his father-in-law's death was not the time to do it. His wife, Susan, was working through her grief, and the family had a house and a mortgage to pay off. But when he told Susan he thought he should take the leap, she saw the tremendous potential in her husband's will and supported the idea. "Seeing how much my father-in-law had accomplished and how content he was on his deathbed really gave me new confidence," he says. "I decided to follow this path where I could control my own destiny, make my own decisions, and ultimately be able to say, I did everything I wanted to do."

With that, Sean founded Windward IT Solutions, a hundred-employee-strong consulting firm that specializes in helping Fortune 500 companies and the DoD manage complex, global networks and data centers, making their businesses leaner and more competitive. The firm has evolved greatly since its inception in 1997, and so has Sean's outlook on leadership.

"I've learned along the way that companies, like their founders, go through a maturation process," he reflects today. "After the excitement of the initial building process, with lots of risks and unknowns but free reign to do what needs to be done, founders can fall into the rut of the day-to-day grind. As it becomes more stable, a company acquires more bureaucracy and processes. That's important for the long-term growth of the company, but it can also be stifling. That's why it's so important for the CEO to continue to create."

Sean took a hiatus from Windward in 2004 to launch another business, RealOps—an avenue by which he could enter another major phase of personal creativity that he craved. RealOps was a true startup in every sense of the word. There, he built software from scratch, raised venture capital, and took the product to market. The RealOps software, incubated within Windward, was a set of predesigned code that could increase efficiency in implementing and automating IT processes. "For three years, I was running around, raising money, talking to investors, and building customers in New York and California," Sean recounts. "It was an exciting time, and the team was really energized." When he sold RealOps in 2007 to BMC, a multi-million dollar management software company, he stayed on for a year and learned how to survive and thrive in that new large company environment.

When Sean returned to the helm of Windward in 2009, he struggled at first, missing the thrill of building something new. But he soon realized that Windward would need to evolve to meet the challenges it faced in the marketplace, and that his creative energies could be used to formulate and implement strategies to make those changes. "I started looking at the services we were taking to market, how people perceived us, what markets we could go after, what our messaging and marketing platform should be, and how we could restructure the organization accordingly," Sean says. "It got me into creative mode—the mode I find most fulfilling."

Now, Sean strikes a balance between growing the company and keeping his creative currents flowing by envisioning what Windward needs to look like in three years, and what needs to be done now in order to get there. Keeping the company at the industry's forefront while also keeping Sean engaged takes innovative efforts today, even if they may not come to fruition until months down the road. Bringing strategic thinkers onboard has helped advance the dialogue within the company, and Sean is always looking at how new markets, capabilities, and investments can advance the company's goals.

This focused approach is built on the belief that success is garnered from stepping beyond one's comfort zone—a philosophy Sean embraced as a young boy growing up in Ankara, Turkey. He was born in Washington, D.C., but his father was a cryptologist for the National Security Agency, prompting the family to move overseas when he was nine. "Every year, at the end of Ramadan, the residents in Ankara would slaughter sheep in the courtyards," he says. "It's one of my most vivid memories. There was a lot of poverty, and life was lived very differently. My time there changed the way I saw the world. I came to understand that opportunity isn't a given, and that it's incredibly important to get out of your comfort zone and experience other ways of life."

The McDermotts returned to the D.C. area when Sean was twelve. The youngest of four children, he was always considered a responsible child. His mother, a homemaker, was a skilled painter and sculptor who started her own interior design business. She inspired Sean's lifelong penchant for creativity, to the point that he worked one-on-one with his art teacher in high school, won creative awards, and considered pursuing art in college. That creative leaning, paired with the intelligence cultivated in him by his father, made for an unusually effective mind for business.

Sean earned his first wages when he took over his brother's paper route. He got a job at a pizza place by the age of fifteen and has worked every day since then. When he was laid off from that job, he was hired at an even better pizza restaurant—his first lesson that seemingly bad situations can lead to far better outcomes. Whether he was roofing houses or working at gas stations, Sean was always working multiple jobs at once.

Through high school, Sean watched his father buy and run a woodworking business in Annapolis, which he eventually sold. He risked a lot and lost a lot, but he went back to work after his entrepreneurial venture, built back up his wealth, and ultimately retired well. "His example showed me that it's possible to rebuild your life after adversity," Sean remembers. "The stress was hard on him, but I have a lot of good memories of how my parents got through that hard time. I saw him get knocked down and get back up, never giving up or feeling sorry for himself. I also saw him run his own business and be his own boss, and I wanted to be like that."

Sean's father had picked himself back up by working as a program manager at General Electric's Valley Forge Space Center in Philadelphia, where he built satellites for government agencies. When Sean began college at Villanova University, he was inspired to study mechanical engineering in part by his father's work, and in part by the drafting and design that the field entailed. He soon realized, however, that the theories and minutiae of the work didn't interest him, so he switched to electrical engineering instead, which Sean saw as more versatile.

Though he made Deans List both semesters of his senior year, he struggled substantially with the dense material and stiff teaching style. "Looking back, I think that a lot of the challenges I faced revolved around how I was being taught," he recounts. "I don't do well with lecturing; I'm a hands-on learner, but there wasn't much of that back then. My father had every opportunity to come down on me hard for my performance, but instead he was very supportive, and that's stuck with me. He tried to understand the issues and challenges before he reacted, and I try to act with that level of patience now."

Sean worked for a small company during his first year out of college and was then hired by the telecommunications division of the Department of Justice. "I didn't even know what telecommunications was, but accepting that job was one of the best decisions of my life," he recalls. It was the early 1990s, and with the explosion of the internet on its horizon, telecom became the fastest growing industry in the last hundred years. "That job landed me in the field that defines my success today," he says. "It was pure luck."

After four years of working with various telecom networks in that capacity, Sean decided he wanted to start his own consulting company, but his specialized expertise caught the eye of the consulting firm Booz Allen Hamilton. He accepted a job with the large firm because he knew it would better prepare him to pursue his entrepreneurial ambitions. The job entailed an education all its own, and Sean mastered the craft of proposal writing and deliverables. He learned how to run teams more effectively, how to build companies, and how to close new business. "They gave me world-class training, and I would not be where I am today if it weren't for that experience," he affirms. "They gave me opportunities and held me to an incredibly high standard. If you're up for it, you can use that kind of experience and come out a totally different person."

When Sean decided to resign in 1996, his boss was not surprised. At Booz Allen, employees of Sean's caliber either become partner or leave to start their own successful companies. Before starting his own business, however, Sean made a pit stop at a small company that was thrilled about the processes and skills he brought from his previous work experience. But the company's culture was marred by power brokering and positioning that ultimately led to his termination—the humbling experience that prompted him to hop in the car and drive to his ailing father-in-law. Several years later, the company's senior leadership pitched the idea of a merger, which would make Sean CEO of the new company. However, by then he had already brought Windward to stable ground and was poised to launch RealOps.

When Sean and Susan agreed that starting Windward was a good idea, they said "yes" to entrepreneurship with no idea of what that agreement entailed. He started the business at the beginning of the internet boom and grew it to 125 employees in four years. "I tell my kids that it takes a lot of hard work to put yourself in a position where you can have good luck," he explains. "You make these decisions about the unknown with no clue about what the future holds for you, and it definitely hasn't been roses all along. Though the company went through several very hard times, once you make your bed, you're in it for the long haul, unless you say you're done. But I'm not one to give up. So much of business is about working hard to put yourself in a position where, if something good happens, you can take advantage of it."

Over the years, Sean has come to find that the most important challenge of leadership is communicating a vision that compels a team to go all-in on that organization's mission. This he accomplishes in part by making prompt decisions and trusting his instincts. "The biggest thing I've learned about leadership is that, sometimes, you just have to follow your gut and do what you know is right," he says. "My family's health and our unity are very important to me, but most business aspects are fluid. You need to get over them and move on, so take action and don't agonize too long."

In advising young people entering the working world today, Sean emphasizes the importance of being a sponge and absorbing as much as possible. "To this day, I ask people for their opinions because I know I don't know everything," he explains. "I'm still learning. There are so many opportunities to learn from people, experiences, and most of all, mistakes. Fail, learn from it, and move on. As long as you take the time to really reflect, you learn more from failing than you do from winning."

Sean's own commitment to learn from mistakes and engage in a lifelong pursuit of success landed him the 2009 Professional Achievement Award from his alma mater, Villanova. And now, to connect more deeply with the local community, he is one of the founding members of the board of the Medical Children's Charitable Partnership Foundation, which provides medical care to underprivileged children in Fairfax County, Virginia. He is also on the Board of Advisors at Villanova's College of Engineering, helping to build entrepreneurial skills and business acumen within the organizations. As a company, Windward participates in an array of volunteer work with the Ronald McDonald House, Habitat for Humanity, soup kitchens, and Toys for Tots. It is in the process of pivoting to a single, more unified focus.

This demonstrates a company culture that embraces hard work while prioritizing the things in life that are most important, like community and family—values that are evident in Sean's own life as well. In times past, he traveled frequently for work because very few of Windward's customers are local. Then, while working for BMC, he ran a $200 million unit and flew around the world, frequenting locations like London, Amsterdam, Singapore, and Australia. When he resigned to return to Windward, the CEO offered him a worldwide senior leadership position, but Sean wanted to watch his three daughters grow up. "My perspective has really changed over the years," he remarks. "I still love to travel, but now, I focus on doing that with my family. Susan and I both grew up with rich memories of traveling with our families, and we want our kids to have that. It's those memories and photographs that I cherish most. I think success is measured not just in business, but in life, and Susan and I have a great family."

Whether in building a family or building a company, Sean is most at home and most alive when he's in creation mode, and his success is about channeling that creativity even amidst stabilization and security. It takes real courage and creativity to take that first entrepreneurial leap and make something out of nothing, but it takes commitment and even more creativity to make that something into something better. "It's important for entrepreneurs to transition their companies from the beginning startup phase into a more operational phase, without losing that excitement and creative spark," he says. "It's easy to fall into a rut, but it's also easy to get out of one. Because we're creating again, I'm more excited about Windward than I have been in years." Indeed, if we are to find ourselves at the end of our lives with no regrets, we must continue to see fresh starts with each turn, and continue to say, "Now is the time."

BERNHARDT
WEALTH MANAGEMENT

Brendan McGinnis

Thinking Big

Even when new opportunities for success come into his life, Brendan McGinnis has a track record of staying true to the things that have shaped him. When he was working toward his MBA at Southern Illinois University-Edwardsville, he took classes during the day and would then hop in his car to drive back to his hometown of Alton, Illinois, where he managed the Post 126 Junior American Legion baseball team. Through his youth, he had been an American Legion player himself, and with his father and brother also deeply involved in the sport, it became a strong bond shared between the whole family.

"Being involved in American Legion Baseball takes strong character and discipline," he affirms today. "It's challenging, but you get a real satisfaction from succeeding, and from working in a team setting." Brendan learned about passion for the game from Dennis Sharp, Post 126 American Legion General Manager, who coached him, and he was committed to teaching that same passion to other young players. Baseball was a fundamental element of his character, and even as other areas of life demanded time and energy, he made sure to keep that element a vibrant part of his story.

That level of passion and commitment is mirrored in his involvement today with the Water Resources Action Project (WRAP). In 2009, he helped establish WRAP as a nonprofit organization that improves the public health of underserved communities in the Middle East through greater water stewardship. Now the Executive Director of the organization, Brendan also serves as a Founder and Managing Partner of a for-profit environmental and business development consulting firm called The Horinko Group, and while the two remain completely separate entities, each enables his involvement in the other, creating a symbiotic relationship that garners success for both.

To maintain the energy and motivation to work what essentially amounts to a second full-time job that provides no monetary compensation, Brendan thinks big. WRAP's overarching goal is to build peace in the Middle East by easing the strain on the region's scarce water resources and promoting cultural exchange. As water is dwindling in the arid lands of Israel, Palestine, and Jordan, exacerbating the tensions within the area, the organization is working to install rainwater harvesting systems in schools in each of the three areas. Water is diverted from the roofs of buildings into storage barrels or underground cement tanks, and can then be used for sanitation, community gardening, and other needs of the school.

The project also has a strong educational component, teaching conservation and the shared responsibility in caring for the environment. What's more, the water and educational programs serve as platforms for students from diverse backgrounds to begin communicating and building trust. "In the beginning, it could be as basic as, 'How much rainwater did your school save through the harvesting system?'" Brendan explains. "WRAP can provide common ground that leads to video chats, field trips, and pen pals. That very basic communication builds, leading to relationships over time. Stereotypes, hatred, and prejudice begin to break down, leaving room for understanding and peace."

WRAP is a nonprofit in the purest sense of the word. It is run entirely on volunteer efforts, and all of its funding goes toward its mission—something Brendan wouldn't be able to guarantee if not for the security he earns through The Horinko Group. "Certainly, I would be unable to pursue WRAP's mission without earning enough to make a living," he points out. "But I've seen a lot of nonprofits that spend well over 17 percent of their funding on overhead costs, and then spend even more on extravagant things that are far from necessary. With WRAP, that's what we set out *not* to do. I've seen projects very similar to ours done at three times the cost. We're proof that you don't need to throw gobs of money around to make a real difference. What keeps me going is the challenge to be able to do more with less."

Brendan observed a similar drive modeled in his father, who grew up in a low-income, rural household. Few thought he'd attend college, but he took matters into his own hands and defined his own future by landing a football scholarship. With raw honesty and transparency, he raised his sons to have the same sense of control over their destinies, demanding perfection in everything from grades to batting averages. From his mother, Brendan learned compassion and understanding, as well as a regimented work ethic that left no task undone at the end of the day. The support of his parents meant the world to him, and his determination to make them proud is a cornerstone of his success today.

After graduating from high school and spending two years playing ball and taking classes at a junior college, Brendan's priorities began to shift away from playing baseball. "I was good at the sport, but not at the level where I would be drafted," he reflects. "I worked my ass off to get to the point where I could compete with others who were. I began to envision a different future for myself, and in the end, I decided to commit to a Business major because I knew it would provide me with a good base to build upon."

Even before he had officially earned his bachelor's degree with honors, he began to take courses toward his MBA. Though he was taking classes, managing an American Legion team, and conducting baseball camps and private instruction to help pay his way, he was able to finish the degree in nine months. "I made enough money to pay some bills while still saving for my next step," he recalls. "My agenda at the time was to move from the Midwest. Having gone to school so close to where I grew up, I didn't really get away from home enough, so I was still yearning for that sense of freedom, independence, and adventure. I had an internship lined up at an international environmental group in Arlington, Virginia, so two weeks after I graduated, once the baseball season was finished, I packed my car and drove to the East Coast."

Thanks to a passion for environmental conservation handed down to him from his father, Brendan proved a good fit for the organization, and the six-month internship yielded a full-time position near the end of 2005. He hadn't traveled much in his life up to that point, but when his job warranted his first international trip, he was hooked. "They sent me to Cape Town, South Africa, and there was no turning back," he remarks. "I wanted to see as much as possible."

At the firm, Brendan and several of his colleagues provided project support for Marianne Horinko, a former U.S. EPA Acting Administrator. Brendan gravitated toward working on additional projects with Marianne, as she always treated the staff with respect and interest. She had helped launch a consulting firm earlier in her career, so one day, Brendan suggested she try it again. "I felt I had grown all I could at the organization and was ready to try something new," he remembers. "I told her that, if she had any interest in running a consulting firm again, I'd definitely be onboard." Justin Oberst, who had started as an intern just before Brendan, was also interested in taking that risk. After several strategy sessions, the group resigned from the firm, and shortly thereafter, The Horinko Group was born in 2008.

While exhilarating, transitioning from a secure work environment with a steady paycheck to a situation of endless possibility but no guarantees was among the most challenging experiences of Brendan's life. "When you're an entrepreneur, success is completely dependent upon yourself," he says, reminiscent of the pressures of playing baseball. "What you get is what you put in, and in many cases, the payoffs aren't immediate."

In the beginning, each step was trial by fire. Whether it was securing office space, conceptualizing the firm's website, establishing a benefits package, or drawing in business, Brendan was at once an entry-level employee and a business partner. Initially, he wondered if he had made the right choice. "Now, looking back, I don't regret the decision one bit," he says. "I have an understanding now that would have taken me much longer to acquire otherwise. I love the work I'm able to do, and the people I'm able to do it with."

With Marianne widely known as a leading expert in finite waste and contamination issues, the boutique consulting firm now consists of seven full-time employees and a handful of specialized advisors focused on domestic water and waste issues. From remediation selection, to transfer liability, to achieving productive reuse, to community development assistance, the group advises on a range of issues and opportunities, while looking at how high-level policymaking effects the concerns of it clients. "We do something different for each client we serve because each has unique needs and interests," Brendan affirms. "Through our core group and senior advisors, we have the expertise to address virtually any domestic water and waste issue."

At the same time, Brendan joined a mentor and colleague, Bob Cole, in helping to launch WRAP. Bob shouldered much of the minutiae of getting the organization up and running, even though he was an internationally recognized tax lawyer and could have easily passed the work on to a staff person. Once the project was on stable ground, Bob asked Brendan to assume full leadership responsibilities of WRAP. Bob passed away suddenly in 2013 of cancer, and WRAP dedicated its first project in the West Bank to him. "A lot of my passion for WRAP comes from the promise I made to him to continue the work we started," Brendan affirms. "From the groundwork he helped to lay, we have five projects currently underway, and we hope to eventually have an interconnected network of around thirty project schools. From there, our model could be replicated elsewhere."

Through The Horinko Group and WRAP, Brendan promotes work environments that thrive on the energy of independence and new ideas. As long as the work gets done, he encourages employees and volunteers to do their jobs on their own schedules, and he looks to fresh ideas to keep his process evolving. "I certainly don't have all the answers when it comes to managing WRAP," he affirms. "I have a growing understanding of running a nonprofit. It's an ongoing challenge to get various groups of people motivated about the latest effort, or to drum up grassroots support. I look to our volunteers to be active participants in growing the group's impact."

In advising young people entering the working world today, Brendan stresses the importance of shouldering responsibility and being proactive about identifying the additional value one can contribute. "There are countless people ready to fill a position," he points out. "What value will you add to make yourself stand out? Work to make yourself invaluable." Beyond that, Brendan emphasizes the importance of networking. "A lunch at your desk is a missed opportunity," he says. "Take that opportunity to establish a relationship with someone you find of interest. Build your network by looking for ways to help and connect other people."

One's network, however, is nothing without the unparalleled inspiration and support structure that comes from family. In 2013, Brendan married Jennifer, a hardworking first grade teacher who invests in the future each day by passionately guiding and expanding the young minds entrusted to her. Both Brendan and Jen have always worked to advance society, but now that they're expecting their first child, the stakes are even higher.

"When we pass this planet on to our kids, and they ask what we did to make it better for them, we'll have something to say," he affirms. "That's why we're passionate about education, about the environment, about peacebuilding." By thinking big and acting globally, Brendan is redefining what it means to provide for one's family. He's not only providing a safe, secure life—he's providing solutions today for some of the toughest problems his children's generation will soon face.

BERNHARDT
WEALTH MANAGEMENT

Carolyn Merek

A Flash of Opportunity

In the winter of Carolyn Merek's freshman year at Montgomery College, she found fortune at a pick-up game of basketball. "Usually it was just me and a bunch of guys," she recalls. "One day a girl I'd never seen showed up to play. Naturally, the guys paired us together."

An immediate connection blossomed between the two basketball enthusiasts. Carolyn soon learned her new friend played basketball for Fordham University, and she suggested Carolyn try out for the team. At the time, Carolyn lived at home and held a half-hearted plan to matriculate to the University of Delaware. The opportunity to play basketball at Fordham was the sea change she needed—a flash of opportunity, and a chance to alter the tide of her life.

A phone call and a meeting try out later, Carolyn was awarded a basketball scholarship, and without the pressure of tuition payments, she was able to take full advantage of an education in the classroom and on the court. Fordham was where Carolyn established a community of lifelong friends and where she experienced the benefits of teamwork first hand. Thus, what started as a chance encounter in an informal setting eventually became the foundation for Carolyn's future as a leader. "I believe in divine intervention because my fortuitous meeting set me on a defining path," she says. "I think everything happens for a reason, and I believe you should always do the right thing, because being a good person is a reason in itself. I believe good things happen to good people."

While luck has played a hand in Carolyn's success as a businesswoman, her commitment to do the right thing is why she's now the founder and CEO of eMentum, a management and information technology consultancy. Founded in 1999, eMentum's mission is to help business owners break down complex technological challenges in an ever-evolving world. Whether the client's aim is to save money, receive information faster, or improve security, eMentum provides a soup-to-nuts service. Carolyn's team will even go as far as to assist with custom coding to achieve exactly what the client wants, and the company's willingness to go the extra mile for its clients derives from Carolyn's allegiance to fairness in an otherwise cutthroat climate. "A lot of business owners are at a disadvantage because technology is difficult to keep up with," she explains. "People who don't know what to look for can easily be taken advantage of, and I don't think that's fair, so we're staunchly against that kind of practice at eMentum."

Today, eMentum mainly focuses on two things – complex/ high impact management consulting service and security solutions for the federal government. The company has maintained a fourteen-year history of uninterrupted service to the large Federal Agency focused on Law Enforcement, a relationship Carolyn takes very seriously due to the sensitive information entrusted to eMentum. Carolyn and her team work hard to bring commercial best practices to the government, which can be heavily outdated. eMentum recently launched a small and medium sized business offering and expanded service into another large Federal Agency focused on securing our Country. Typical projects include overseeing enterprise transformation initiatives, like moving applications to the cloud or consolidating many applications or datacenters down to an ideal number, as well as securing buildings with newer technologies, perfecting cyber security, and ensuring the right employees have access to confidential or sensitive information. "It helps to have a relatable mission," Carolyn reasons. "And the fact that we work to protect the country we live in is the icing on the cake."

Most recently, eMentum signed a five-year contract with the same large Federal Agency's Identity Management Services Program. Under the $62 million agreement, eMentum will be responsible for the security of the people, information, systems and facilities. eMentum will also work to implement government-issued biometric smart cards designed to access buildings, networks, machines of all types, and a variety of databases. The move will help federal agencies reduce spending costs and merge redundant solutions, and it will allow employees access to work from home. With a team of 35 information technology experts and strategic thinkers by her side, Carolyn continues to deftly solve the critical issues her clients face. And while the company's client base is impressive, Carolyn treats her customers as friends and isn't afraid to tell the truth. "It's important to call a spade a spade," she says. "If your customers are doing something foolish, don't tell them what they're doing wrong, but what they could do better." Carolyn's straightforward and constructive attitude with her clients perfectly sums up eMentum's simple motto, "Do good, have fun, and add value."

eMentum's good will, however, isn't limited to the corporate world. The company's philanthropic roots have extended across the Maryland and D.C. communities for years, and while its laundry list of charities is striking, what's even more admirable is the hands-on nature of its involvement. eMentum employees personally buy fixings for the Thanksgiving baskets they dole out each year, and it's common practice for employees to donate their own coats for the company's annual coat drive. Carolyn's parents, people she describes as common day working folks, were just as giving as she was growing up. "My parents were good neighbors and a constant for those who needed help," she remembers.

While Carolyn credits her strength and business acumen to the women in her family, she attributes her passion for technology to her father. A member of the United States Air Force, he worked for one of the armed force's first TV stations. Eventually, he earned the title of Chief Technology Officer for Montgomery County before landing a job at the Library of Congress. "My dad had a simple yet effective philosophy," Carolyn recalls. "Be honest, work hard, and enjoy your life." The combination of his fascination with technology and his Protestant-like work ethic propelled him into a rewarding career Carolyn yearned to replicate.

High school was where Carolyn first put her parents' wisdoms to practice, taking on many responsibilities and making use of her natural talents. Over the course of the four years, she played three different sports, held a few odd jobs, and maintained a decent grade point average. After high school, she became the first person in her family to pursue higher education and used the money she had saved up in a pickle jar to pay for Montgomery College. Montgomery College wasn't Carolyn's first choice, but she realized the economic value of the two-year school. "It's important to be smart about where you spend your money," she advises.

Carolyn's early economic smarts paid off in spades. On her first day at Montgomery College, she met the father of her children, Blake and Brittany. It was also where Carolyn met the woman who urged her to try out for Fordham's basketball team, the chance encounter that irrevocably altered the stars of her universe. "I always seem to be in the right place at the right time," she jokes. Coincidence, however, didn't play a role in her decision to pursue an MBA in Management Information Systems from the University of Maryland. Once she graduated from Fordham, Carolyn worked as a bank teller before landing an office manager position at her now ex-husband's family business. The experiences she garnered post-college paid the bills, but they lacked the electricity of "a Calling"—a deficit which inspired Carolyn to secure an MBA. While her graduate career was difficult to balance amidst a sea other responsibilities, including marriage, she persevered thanks to her family. "I was really lucky to have a support system during that time," she acknowledges. "Now kids are pressured to be independent, but they often lack the resources."

Once armed with an MBA, Carolyn secured a job at Andersen Consulting, which eventually became Accenture. At Anderson, a major information technology consulting firm, Carolyn oversaw the optimization of multi-million dollar businesses and led teams with as many as two hundred people. After Andersen was absolved by Accenture, Carolyn's technical and leadership responsibilities soared. As associate partner, she spearheaded crucial enterprise resources planning implementation projects and other high-risk ventures when she was re-hired as an independent subcontractor.

Accenture is also where Carolyn discovered her strength as a woman, as she was the first woman in her telecom group to return as a mother to the main consulting office. Most female colleagues Carolyn knew traded high-power positions for HR or recruiting, but she committed herself to a different path. Her higher-ups even started a women's mentoring program due to concerns over an unbalanced gender ratio, and while Carolyn was lucky enough to choose a female mentor, most of her female co-workers were assigned to men because there weren't enough women to go around. "It was the norm for me to be the only woman in a conference room," she affirms. "The top is mostly dominated by men."

During her fourteen-year tenure at Andersen Consulting, Carolyn took part in an abundance of professional development opportunities that provided her the education to eventually found eMentum. Drawing on her "do good" philosophy, she now tries to make similar opportunities available to her employees. "It's important for me to invest in my people," Carolyn says. "I want my employees to leave eMentum as even better people than they were when they came."

Carolyn's commitment to investing in people is why she ultimately left Andersen Consulting to become an independent contractor. Not only was she motivated to pursue electronic e-Commerce, but she also realized she didn't want to work with people who held dissimilar core values. Over time, she came to view herself as an honest broker and as someone who didn't place an emphasis on money. Branching out on her own was a decision ripe with uncertainty, but Carolyn forsook security for happiness. "Success is being true to yourself and knowing who you're willing follow as a leader," she says. When she founded eMentum, her resolve to stay true to herself and her values proved beneficial as she drew clients from past projects. In fact, her ability to garner trust from her customers is why eMentum survived its first years. "eMentum was born from a desire to do what I wanted and how I wanted for the right reasons," she emphasizes. "People can see that kind of honesty in the work we do, and it resonates with them."

A strong moral compass is a big piece of Carolyn's advice to young people looking to strike gold in today's turbulent market. "It's important to do good," she says. "Be true to yourself and do the best you can with your God-given talents."

Carolyn tries to impress these same values on her son and daughter, both young adults now, and while she finds the prospects for her children's generation scary, she reminds her kids not to sweat the small stuff. "Worry about the big things," she advises. "Don't be afraid to try, and don't feel like you have to sacrifice your own self-fulfillment." Not afraid to take her own advice, Carolyn was the assistant coach for her daughter's basketball and softball teams. While her schedule couldn't accommodate a head coach position, she found the experience extremely rewarding, and it taught her a valuable lesson. "You have to make concessions in life and be realistic about your time," she says. "Otherwise you'll make yourself sick."

Carolyn's quest for self-fulfillment and truth lies at the heart of her philosophy as a CEO, which stands in stark contrast to the approaches of many she's come in contact with over her long career who are solely after power and affiliation. "I'd rather just achieve," Carolyn says. "I'm fine with having power, but I won't play the CEO card unless it's necessary." To help her avoid the pitfalls of power struggles, Carolyn draws from her experience as a basketball player. After countless hours on the court, it was only natural for Carolyn to internalize the collaborative spirit of teamwork so crucial to the game. "I like criticism and bad feedback," she says. "It's the only way you grow."

Today, Carolyn focuses on the professional growth of eMentum. Now a small company, she aims to recruit more talented employees in the near future. In her grand plan, she foresees eMentum expanding to a team of fifty or even a hundred. The expansion, Carolyn hopes, will give both her clients and employees more opportunities to be better. "I take my stewardship responsibilities for my employees very seriously," she says. "We're a small community here."

Luckily for her employees and clients, community has always been the brightest point in the constellation of Carolyn's life. While some mystics believe our stars are fixed, Carolyn's dedication to do right by her clients is why eMentum continues to yield fortune, and though financial success is important to her, the well-being of her customers will always come first. "We're our clients' right hand, if they'll let us be," Carolyn reaffirms. "eMentum is there for companies who need help." Acting as a lighthouse, eMentum provides a sense of direction and comfort, and this kindness, a deceivingly simple gesture, is why Carolyn will continue to lead the company to success in a world where nothing is ever certain but flashes of opportunity are all you really need to redefine your path and realize a better future.

BERNHARDT
WEALTH MANAGEMENT

Sarah E. Nutter

Faraway Places

Faraway places
With strange-sounding names
Far away over the sea—
Those faraway places
With strange-sounding names
Are calling, calling me.

– *"Far Away Places"* Lyrics by Joan Whitney and Alex Kramer

When man first set foot on the moon on July 20, 1969, the whole world was watching. The whole world, that is, except for nine-year-old Sarah Nutter. As Neil Armstrong took one giant leap for mankind, the young girl was busy taking a giant leap of her own.

Her parents had taken her overseas for the first time to stay at the house of a family friend in Scotland, and there, she found a new world with its own culture and way of life. "It forever changed the way I interacted with the world," she recalls now. "Taking that trip at that particular moment in my life was a tremendous gift, permanently changing my perspective. Like the rest of humanity at the time, I was learning in my own way that you can't restrict your thinking to your own small sphere and geographical location. There are faraway places, and we're meant to find more of ourselves in them."

Now, as the Dean of George Mason University's School of Business, Sarah's mission is to empower people every day, one person at a time. More than 168 countries are represented on George Mason's campus, and 40 percent of the 2014 freshman class is first generation American. "These students coming from all over the world tend to have a tilt toward entrepreneurialism and innovation," she explains. "They see the world through different eyes, so they bring a new perspective to solving the world's problems. Indeed, they bring just as much to the vibrancy and diversity of the campus as the campus brings to them. And while other institutions measure their success in taking certain people certain places, George Mason is about taking as many students as possible from wherever they are to wherever they want to go. In truth, the magic of George Mason is about making those faraway places and achievements attainable."

Having served in the School of Business since 1995, Sarah was asked to join the University's Senior Executive team starting in 2012 to prepare for then-President Alan Merten's transition from leading George Mason. When Angel Cabrera assumed the Presidency, she was tapped to run the University visioning process. "It was humbling and inspiring to lead that effort, wherein we sought the input of 4,000 voices to set the course for the next forty years of the university's growth," she recalls. "It was a time when we recognized that we had grown from nothing to 34,000 students since we started awarding degrees in 1972. Our task was to capture the essence of the university's identity in a new mission statement, painting a picture that would allow us to forge a future based on our accomplishments, strengths, and vision."

From this process, the George Mason IDEA emerged. IDEA, or Innovative, Diverse, Entrepreneurial, and Accessible, marks the four components that thread through the DNA of the university. "We're an inclusive and innovative academic community committed to creating a more just, free, and prosperous world," Sarah avows, reciting Mason's mission statement. "This fits in perfectly with my own mission statement, which is to empower people every day, and is reflected in the work and fabric of the business school."

What truly sets George Mason apart as an institution of higher learning is the way it measures success, judging itself not based on how many people it turns away, but on how many people with talent it can educate. The Business School alone has an enrollment of 3,200 undergraduate and 550 graduate students, and is home to the Mason Innovation Lab, a center where any student can come in and turn an idea into an action plan. Currently number 62 in the *US News and World Report* rankings of the nation's top undergraduate business schools, it attracts high-caliber faculty who are equally engaged in innovative research and in the surrounding community. Among the top 200 research universities in the world, two of its faculty members have received the Nobel Prize, and it is often recognized as a top up-and-coming school. "Mason is a place where magic happens," Sarah affirms. "It's a place where we're deeply committed to giving equal opportunities to those who might not otherwise have them, allowing them to take their lives to great lengths."

In many ways, George Mason feels like home to Sarah because she could have easily been one of the students she now works so hard to serve. A native of Big Rapids, Michigan, growing up on a fourth-generation family farm, she always knew she'd have to pay her own way through school. Still, her parents equipped her with a thoughtful, engaged, impassioned approach to life that would allow her to forge her own path forward and seize the opportunities that would come her way. "The only thing that was off-limits was the dairy when the milk inspector was around," Sarah laughs, remembering a time when, at three years old, she rammed her tricycle against the door of the processing plant and ran into the unsuspecting inspector. "Other than that, we were taught to have a big worldview."

This worldview was explored and expanded over family meals at the kitchen table, where the Emmons family kept two books—a Bible and a dictionary. "My parents were very politically aware and engaged in the world around them," she recalls. "Our conversations were animated and in-depth, and before the end of any meal, one or both books would be out on the table."

Emmons Dairy had graduated from raising cows by the time Sarah came along. Essentially born into business, she would ride on the bulk milk truck with her father to pick up milk from the area farmers. Her first official job came at age five, when she would pick up the small empty half-pint containers and burn them behind the dairy for a penny a case. At the same time, she helped to support her parents' burgeoning political careers. Each took a turn serving as Township Treasurer, so she would help stuff envelopes with tax bills. Her father went on to become County Commissioner, while her mother eventually served in the state legislature.

"Today, my husband, David, says I got the best of both of my parents," Sarah relays. Her father, an incredibly smart and passionate person, taught her that whenever you put your mind to something, you should also put your heart to it. This created a symmetry between his mind, heart, and actions that served as an important model for Sarah and her younger sister, and became particularly important later on when the dairy was driven out of business by large farm cooperatives.

Rather than give up in defeat, her father launched a new career at age fifty, becoming an insurance salesman for the Aid Association for Lutherans. "It was an incredible demonstration of how resilient our family is, and how powerful that can be," Sarah reflects. "Now, I keep the glass bottles and bottle tops that display our dairy's emblem, reminding me of the importance of the small businessman. Large corporations may dominate the landscape in terms of dollar revenue generated and number of jobs, but it's the small entrepreneur that uses their own personal ingenuity to make the world a better place. They do it day after day in tough conditions, and I'm dedicated to honoring and supporting the individual amidst the large institutional structures." Having missed out on the opportunity to go to college in his younger years because he was running the farm, Sarah's father never gave up on his goal of higher education, and finally completed his undergraduate degree at age 75.

Sarah's mother, as well, was a remarkable role model. She earned a Home Economics degree from Michigan State University and taught school for a few years before Sarah was born, giving that up to focus on managing the books for the family business and volunteering as she raised her children. Later, she decided to start a political career at age 52 when a seat opened up in the state legislature. By the time she retired as the Floor Leader of the Michigan State Senate, she had made her mark as a woman of strong capabilities, political prowess, and constructive communication skills that allowed her to connect, marshal, and move forward on important initiatives. "She really knew how to find common ground and help people move from total disagreement to agreement," Sarah remembers. "Her great gift was building consensus and moving things forward. What's more, she knew how to separate position from person. If you're in a high-profile role, you get a lot of attention, but it has nothing to do with who you are as a person. Coming from a long line of strong women, my mother was able to stay grounded even as she served in office—something I have always strived to do in the various roles I've served."

More than anything else, her parents instilled in her a curiosity about the world that led to a lifetime love of learning and education. She can still vividly remember coming home from her first day of kindergarten, upset that she hadn't learned a single thing that day. But the one-room schoolhouse taught kindergarten up through eighth grade, and the small girl quickly found opportunities to absorb the lessons of the older students. Before long, she mastered all the seventh-grade spelling words, developing flexibility in her approach to life and learning. "The school was like an incubator that encouraged curiosity and allowed me to develop in a very unconstrained environment," she recalls. "It was a very free place for learning and growing."

When the school closed down after her second grade year, Sarah switched to a parochial Lutheran school. It soon became clear that she was well ahead of her third-grade peers, and at the end of that year, she tested out of fourth grade and was sent directly to fifth. In high school, Sarah got a job working twenty hours a week at a keypunch operation, entering in the property tax information for the county. It never occurred to her not to go to college, so she knew she had to start saving up money early. She graduated first in her class of 180 students, with teachers trying to persuade her to go get her next degree and then return to teach alongside them.

Sarah enrolled at Ferris State University at age 17 because it was local and affordable, and it turned out to be a perfect environment for her. She was able to continue working for the family business, delivering milk to the entire Chippewa Lake School District while maintaining her studies. On top of these obligations, the school had a program that allowed students to spend alternate quarters either taking classes or working, and the Department Chair of Accounting sought her out to offer her an opportunity to spend a work quarter at the Pontiac Motor Division of General Motors.

After spending two quarters working in that capacity, Sarah decided it wasn't for her, so the Department Chair found her an opportunity to try out a CPA firm. "I did that for a cycle, and I learned something else really valuable: I didn't want to do that for the rest of my life, either," she remembers. "The Ferris State faculty taught me the 'give it a whirl' philosophy, wherein you aren't afraid to try and fail, or try and change. I came to understand that you should take advantage of every opportunity that's given to you, because not every choice is a permanent choice. If you go down a path that's not right for you, you can just chart another course."

As she was working through these questions during her senior year of college, she met David Nutter, the son of a Ferris State professor of geology. He had an expansive worldview that had been forged through three years in the military as a trumpet player in Heidelberg, Germany. Sarah happened to come across an ad in the university's newspaper for a hiking trip to the Grand Canyon being led by David's father, and it turned out they had room for one more.

Both artistic, adventurous, musical people, Sarah and David had a lot to talk about as they traversed one of the seven natural wonders of the world. But when he told her he wasn't interested in dating anyone, and was instead hoping to find a wife, twenty-year-old Sarah quickly cut off the conversation by wishing him luck. When he called her up that January, however, to invite her to a hockey game, she decided to listen to her gut over her nerves. In February, he proposed. Shortly thereafter, Sarah took him to meet her great Aunt Julia, the first of the family to earn a master's degree. A true trailblazer, she had pursued a career in school social work, counseling the most troubled children from the most difficult backgrounds. A woman of remarkable courage, fortitude, and character, Julia recognized David's integrity and granted her seal of approval, and the couple married that September. "David is awesome," Sarah says today. "Through everything, he has always let me be who I am. And our worldviews fit together perfectly, leading us to travel around the globe, driven by the prospect of empowering others."

Their journey together started at Michigan State, where David finished his undergraduate degree and Sarah worked toward her MBA in accounting and finance at the suggestion of her Ferris State mentors. Her MBA professors began urging her to get her PhD and then come back to teach with them, but she had never tried teaching, so they gave her a class to lead. Then, the Nutters were given an opportunity to go to Germany together, where David would pursue a Masters of German and Sarah would teach for the University of Maryland University College. Their first son was born there, and the passion Sarah felt for far-away places grew deeper.

While there, Sarah also developed an interest in the taxation of expatriates. When they returned to the U.S., they continued their studies at Michigan State—David, a Masters of Medical Geography, and Sarah, a PhD—until David landed a job in defense mapping at Intergraph Corporation in Washington, D.C.. Fueled by her interest in expatriate taxation, and needing to finish her PhD, she approached the IRS with a modest request for data. "They told me that, as I had requested the data, it wouldn't be useful for my proposal at all," she recalls. "They needed someone to help train their young economists on tax accounting and policy, so they offered me a job which would allow me to come and go as I pleased while I worked on my dissertation. The experience was fascinating, and once I finished my PhD, I stayed on to look at international tax issues, exploring ideas for creating a system that puts U.S. businesses on level playing field globally."

After five years at the IRS, Sarah was hired by the School of Business at George Mason University. She taught tax and accounting for several years, later becoming the Director of the Executive MBA Program and then the Department Chair of Accounting. Then Tom Hennessy, then Chief of Staff, urged her to come over and help with the transition in the President's office. After leading the charge to develop the university vision, she was asked to step in as the Acting Dean of the School of Business. After a national search, she was formally named Dean—the most recent in a string of leadership positions she's been tapped for since grade school. An institution-builder with a mind for strategy and politics like her mother, she realized that her added capacity for administration meant that she could reach her mission more effectively in a leadership role rather than a teaching role. "Also, people often view these types of roles as stepping stones," she points out. "I don't. They're opportunities to make a real difference by building an institution that's sustainable long after you've moved on."

Through her various leadership positions, and especially now at the George Mason School of Business, Sarah has focused on the little things that add up to make a big difference. As a *Washington Business Journal* "Women Who Mean Business" award recipient for 2014, she seeks opportunities for small innovations and contributions that can redefine a community or professional culture, allowing for greater collaboration and fuller thinking. "Leadership is modeling the actions, attitudes, behavior, and perspective you hope will inspire others to want to do the same," she says. "Leadership is about being who you are, setting the tone, and creating an environment where people can thrive. As my mother would say, if you don't care who gets the credit, you can get a lot done."

In advising young people entering the working world today, Sarah stresses the importance of knowing yourself and focusing on your strengths. "I've seen so many people who feel like they need to shore up their weaknesses, or work toward something that just isn't a good fit," she remarks. "Don't live by other peoples' expectations of you, and don't waste your time working against yourself. Lean into your strengths." Beyond that, Sarah underscores the importance of the curiosity that has driven her professional development.

More than anything, however, her success is founded on commitments made to empower people every day. Just as others saw gifts in her she didn't see in herself as she worked through school, Sarah makes a point to invest in individuals to help their gifts come forth. "I'm a big believer in the micro—in helping others be the best they can be," she affirms. "My work has always been about changing lives, one person at a time."

Sarah and David's work with Empower International Ministries, a small nonprofit, is no different. The organization is committed to healing families, restoring communities, and transforming cultures through combating the root cause and lethal effects of abuse, abandonment, and injustice. As board members since 2009, Sarah and David have traveled to developing countries around the world in support of egalitarianism and equality of all people in the eyes of God. "We help people understand that relationships between people can be so much more than transactional," she explains. "So much of the brokenness people experience is based on cultural expectations imposed on them by the world around them. We work to free people through education so they can be the men and women God called them to be."

Across all the places she's gone and the people she's helped, the mission statements of the various spheres of Sarah's life coalesce into a song of opportunity and change. It's heard by the people of Rwanda, Uganda, Kenya, Burundi, and other developing countries. It's heard by the students of George Mason University, whose education is guided by the vision she helped lay out. It's heard by her three children and four grandchildren, who bring joy to her life every day. It's a song about empowering people, one person at a time, to reach their own faraway places and realize their own distant dreams.

Bill Ploskina

True Accomplishment

As 17-year-old Bill Ploskina walked the dark floors of the copper factory where his father worked as a crane operator, he watched with fascination as the glowing metal rods sped along a series of rollers. Having grown up in a middleclass household in McKeesport, Pennsylvania, he was anxious to start earning money and building a life for himself. There, amongst the machinery, he imagined his future, finally able to truly earn his own way by working in the mill like his father. With his high school career coming to a close, he was faced with the decision of what to do next, and the reality of entering the workforce was so close, he could almost feel the weight of a hard day's wages in his pocket already.

When Bill's father heard his son might opt to head directly into the workforce instead of pursuing a college degree, he had asked Bill to accompany him to the factory. They wouldn't be making the trip during the day, though—his father wanted to take him at night. Bill had been perplexed at first, but he was excited for the excursion nonetheless. And now, touring the factory with his father by his side, his excitement only grew—until they came to a pit.

As the large copper rods came flying off a set of rollers into the pit, they were caught by a man. He swung them around his body and landed them on another set of rollers, one by one, in continuous mechanical rhythm. As Bill squinted at the figure, he recognized the face of his Uncle Pete. "This is where you'll be if you don't go to college," his father said softly.

It was as if, for a moment, Bill himself was one of those glowing copper rods, and his father was the man in the pit, working diligently to swing him from one trajectory to an entirely new one. The scope of his horizon magnified exponentially as his sights went from short-term to long-term success. Now, after pursuing higher education and spending several key years at General Electric (GE), Bill is the owner and President of Bill's Hardware and Home Center, voted the best hardware store in Arlington by *Arlington Magazine* time and again. "I've spent a lifetime pursuing a sense of true accomplishment," he affirms today. "And I've come to find that it comes from seeing the world differently. It's about seeing the opportunities around you, and then taking action."

Bill bought the hardware store in March of 1979—a 3,800-square-foot building with four studio apartments on the second floor. The owner, Mr. Reed, had been trying to sell for years, but hadn't been able to find anyone who met his rigid qualifications. The buyer had to be a nonsmoker, and had to have a mechanical background. Much to his relief, Bill—a former GE employee who stayed away from cigarettes—was an ideal candidate. Mr. Reed also had an instant connection with Bill's father, who was excited about coming down to help his son with the business. Tragically, on the very day Bill signed the contract to rent the property and assume leadership of the store, his father passed away from a heart attack. Though he never got the chance to see his son's full-fledged entrepreneurial skills in action, he had nurtured them throughout Bill's life, and his legacy echoes in the footsteps of each satisfied customer that leaves the store.

Mr. Reed generously financed Bill's transition into ownership of the business and property, and Bill was committed to doing things right. He interviewed several product distribution centers to make sure he was getting the best merchandise, opting to stay with True Value. He visited all the hardware stores in the region to see what he could do differently, deciding that service would be the key to setting his business apart. Thanks to his team's mastery of customer service, the store did exceptionally well, to the point that he was able to rent out the Five and Dime store across the street to expand the business. Five years later, he bought the property, bringing his total square footage to 10,000.

In the 35 years since he took over the hardware store, its annual revenues went from $350,000 to $1.8 million, and though growth has been limited in the years since the Great Recession, the company exceeds every industry marker of success. An average store purchase is around $25 per customer, and the store's success rests on the personal experience of each person who walks through the doors. "There have been highs and lows through the years," Bill says, noting a recent incident where the local residents barred the development of a Home Depot in the area because the increased traffic flow would tear up the streets of the community. "But our enduring focus is helping every single customer find something helpful, whether it's one of our products, or the address of another store that has what they're looking for. I believe the phrase 'How may I help you?' is more powerful than 'May I help you?' For us it's not a question of if we can provide service, but how best to serve. That's the heart of our culture."

This spirit of service is genuinely homespun, sprung from his days as a young boy helping his father sell bacon and eggs door-to-door. He was ten when his father taught him how to candle an egg, holding it up to the light to check for blood spots that devalued the product. "We'd arrive at the farmer's door at 4:00 AM to pick up the eggs," Bill recalls. "Then we'd go to the slaughterhouse, where my father would get a side of pork to sell."

Bill's grandfather immigrated to the U.S. from Yugoslavia. He bought a farm in Liberty Borough, Pennsylvania, had eleven children, and became the night watchman at a candy factory when he could no longer perform the backbreaking work of a farmer. He would rotate between different areas of the factory according to a pocket watch, which was passed down to Bill's father, and then to Bill. "I remember going up to the farm for celebrations with the family, and there'd be tons of candy," Bill says. "He spoke only broken English, but we understood each other just fine."

As a young child, Bill struggled in math—a tide that would turn dramatically when his parents moved to a new home in a new school district just before his fifth grade year. When he started school and was given his math textbook for the year, he noticed that he had somehow gotten a book with all the answers printed in the back. While many boys that age might have used the answers for cheating, Bill instead used them to check his work, allowing him to reason through problems and find his way to the correct solution. Once he had the tools to gauge his logic, he was able to guide his own path toward success, excelling in math from that day forward.

Bill was twelve when his father tried to pursue entrepreneurship in earnest, building a dance hall where people could enjoy a band and the open air. The venture went well, until neighbors began to complain about the new traffic on the dirt road leading up to the venue. Influential figures who had pledged their consent later retracted their support, so the venture had to shut down. Still, the two performed handyman services around town—a pastime Bill had helped with since he was a small boy. "My dad was simply not willing to give up," he remembers. "If he ran into a roadblock, he figured out a way around it. I learned perseverance, resourcefulness, and dedication from him." Thanks to his father's strong influence, Bill was comfortable in hardware stores from an early age, picking up valuable skills whose worth would magnify later in life when he took over his own store.

As Bill got older, his father purchased a home, which he converted into multi-dwelling units. Along with a partial scholarship, the money from the venture helped to fund Bill's college education at Penn State University. The institution had a branch campus across the street from his high school, so he lived at home the first two years to save money, using an old Hudson Hornet gifted to him by his father to get to campus. After earning strong grades in aerospace engineering, he received job offers from GE, Boeing, and McDonnell Douglas upon graduating. "They offered comparable salaries around $9,000, which was a lot of money back in 1968, but I felt like I couldn't sit behind a desk all day looking at drafting paper," he recalls. "I wanted to be working in a factory, using my hands to make things. GE offered that opportunity in Allentown, Pennsylvania, as part of its Manufacturing Management Program, so I chose that."

The program was divided into six experiences over three years, each lasting six months, so participants could evaluate their interests. Bill had the opportunity to work in quality control, manufacturing, and purchasing, as well as maintenance. He got to try out an engineering department, and he spent time working on the floor. His big break, however, came when the company needed to send someone to Singapore to recreate an Allentown manufacturing facility overseas. "I was single and extremely low-maintenance compared to the more senior candidates, who would have expected chauffeurs and larger homes for their families," Bill laughs. "I was there for two separate six-month assignments, and I loved that contact with another part of the world. I remember it now when I look at the cedar storage chest I brought home for my mother, which was passed back to me when she died. The deep carvings of battle scenes and gardens are reminiscent of the culture and life I discovered there."

Bill spent five years with GE, deciding to try something else after being passed over for a promotion because the company decided to hire externally instead. With that, he began looking for jobs in New York City, where he was dating the woman that would become his wife. An opportunity came up with Rockwell International, where he joined a team of four internal consultants within the company's Meter and Valve Division. If a problem arose at a particular factory that couldn't be handled by the individuals on-site, his team was brought in to solve the issue. After three years in that capacity, he was offered a position as the assistant manufacturing manager in one of the factories he had assisted. He enjoyed the work until he set his sights on new horizons, eventually moving to Chicago Heights, Illinois, to serve as the manager of quality control for GE once again. "At that point, I was making more money than if I had stayed with GE from the beginning," he remarks.

The money was good, but the stress of the position began to get to Bill after a year on the job. As the first child in the family to go to college, he put significant pressure on himself to live up to his own expectations, but the job didn't feel like a fit. "After ten years of climbing the corporate ladder in the engineering business, I realized I had to get out," he says. "I was working six days a week but never feeling truly accomplished and appreciated. I wanted to be my own boss, and I was drawn to the idea of helping homeowners solve the problems that arise. Because of the work I had done with my father as a kid, it felt natural."

Many entrepreneurs find running a business to be a 24/7, 100 percent commitment of time and self, but Bill found himself relaxed and into the rhythm and responsibilities of being self-employed and leading a team. This was particularly crucial when, at age 40, divorce dealt a devastating blow that almost knocked him out for the count. Thankfully, with community support, thoughts of his three sons, and the fulfillment of his commitment to the store's customers and employees, Bill pulled through the hardest time in his life to achieve new independence and focus in life.

Now, as a business owner, Bill leads by the power of listening. As a low-key, even-keel manager, he minimizes worry and focuses on turning problems into opportunities. "I really hear my employees," he explains. "I let them talk. Everyone wants to be listened to. Even the customer coming through the door has a story to tell, and a need. It's our job to listen and solve."

In advising young people entering the working world today, Bill lays out a path to success that starts with the identification of a person's passion. "Don't go looking for the big buck off the bat, or you'll get eaten alive," he says. "Find something you love, and then see if you can become an intern to get a foot in the door. Get experience under your belt, and get your mistakes out of the way while you're young. It's really tough for kids right now, but don't get negative. The opportunities are there—you just have to learn to see them. I'm where I am today because I'm one of the lucky ones. I saw opportunities and made the decision to move forward, basing my measure of true accomplishment not on the amount of money I could make, but on the service I could provide to my community, face-to-face, every day."

BERNHARDT
WEALTH MANAGEMENT

Dan Regard

Why Not Start With Yes?

It was springtime when eight-year-old Dan Regard got the phone call he had been waiting for. A beehive had just split, and a swarm had taken flight. He and his father wasted no time hitting the road, successfully capturing the bees to bring them home to the new apiary they had set up. As a young beekeeper raising his hive and harvesting honey, Dan had assumed his first profession.

But Dan wouldn't just work the job—he was to become a young entrepreneur. His parents equipped him with bottles, labels, and a red wagon to cart the honey door-to-door. "Thanks to that experience, I've always felt like work was a very natural and seamless part of life," he explains today. "There was no abrupt transition into working life, and work never felt like a burden. That perspective was one of the greatest gifts my father gave me, because it paved the way for a lot of success that was driven by a commitment to a strong work ethic, rather than financial success." Now the cofounder and CEO of iDiscovery Solutions (IDS), a consulting firm operating on the cutting edge at the intersection of law and technology, Dan brings that same seamless joy in life and work to his clients and employees alike, thanks to his unfailing willingness to embrace the unknown and simply try.

As technology continues to transform the ground upon which whole sectors and industries are built, IDS is closing the gap between existing business practices and the ways of the future. Focusing on the discovery process in law, wherein the two sides of a case provide answers to questions and relevant documents, the firm recognizes that an increasing amount of information is created and stored in computers, never to be printed on paper. Dan and his team help lawyers locate, gather, analyze, transform, exchange, review, filter, and interpret that electronic information. "We might be asked to interpret information on a micro scale, like figuring out if individual documents or emails have been tampered with," Dan explains. "Or we might be tasked with working on a macro scale, like identifying trends in millions of records. Based on our work, we then help our clients do the analysis, and then write up reports, opinions, testimony, or depositions."

Among the most gratifying aspects of Dan's work lies in the many smart and talented clients he serves, and the wide array of problems he has the opportunity to solve. He might find himself helping with a document retention program for a global pharmaceutical company one day, and sending a team to China the next day to investigate allegations of counterfeit goods sales. The day after that, he might find himself assisting with the investigation of the kidnapping of the Honduran president. "Our team works on widely divergent issues, each one fascinating and giving us the opportunity to work with different skill sets and people," Dan says. "It's a thrill to work in an environment like this, where there's never a dull moment."

This fast-paced, lively, and diverse work environment resonates so deeply with Dan because it echoes the colorful, nuanced upbringing he experienced as a boy growing up in Louisiana. The rich culture of the State, permeated by a sense of community, adventure, and friendliness, became the very foundation of Dan's approach to life. "To me, my Louisiana heritage is as tangible as any object," he affirms. "The music, the food, the family—things other people celebrate, we take as a way of life."

Dan's mother was a schoolteacher, but she retired to become a homemaker once his younger siblings were born. His father, an attorney, had his own practice, which allowed him ample free time to pursue entrepreneurial endeavors. "My dad had a diverse set of interests," he explains, reminiscent of his own multifaceted pursuits. "Thanks to him, I grew up in a world that begged to know, 'Why start with no? Why not try? Why not start with yes?' I helped him clear land for developing residential neighborhoods, clean laundry machines at the Laundromat he bought, and work his pecan farm, where we also spent a lot of time hunting, fishing, and camping."

Along with outdoor activities with his father, books and education were Dan's passion. As a teenager, he developed an interest in personal computers, which were just becoming a household word. His father shelled out $2,000 for a Tandy Model 3 in the 1980s, and hired a young man to give Dan lessons on how the machine worked and how to store information on an external cassette tape recorder. "He taught me how to program, and I was hooked," he remembers. "While I was still in high school, I took summer classes at the university. Another summer, I started setting up the books and records of a local clothing company on computer. And one summer, my father arranged for me to intern at a local, but cutting-edge, computer graphics company. I was a young kid who had a lot to learn, but they were extremely supportive as I learned the ropes."

When Dan enrolled in college at the University of Southwestern Louisiana in Lafayette, he began pursuing computer engineering but couldn't deny that his true passion lay with programming. "At the time, nobody knew what computers would become capable of, and nobody imagined how integrated they would be in our lives," he remembers. "The personal computer was still an experiment. There was a lot of potential, and it was a great time to be in college, on the precipice of this big technological transformation."

His education in computers was further enriched when he took a year off from college to participate in a year-long Congressional exchange program. After several trips to France growing up and a summer spent in Germany studying language, he applied for the program despite feeling unqualified. He wasn't admitted at first, but when a participating student pulled out two days before the program's commencement, he was the only person willing to drop everything at the last minute and jump on a transatlantic flight.

In Germany, Dan underwent intense language training for two months and was placed with a host family for a year. That family helped him trade out his pre-arranged banking internship for an internship at a computer company, where he became an instructor, teaching business executives how to use Lotus 123 and Lotus Symphony. "It was an interesting time, and I absolutely loved it," he recalls. "I came back empowered, and a little older. I didn't want to build computers—I wanted to apply them. I changed my major to computer science and began consulting for a variety of small businesses doing point-of-sale accounting systems and custom inventory tracking systems. I was helping petroleum engineers use their computers to do financial forecasts of oil reserves, and helping geologists develop computerized graphics to reflect their opinions for legal trials. So I was doing litigation support and technology before I understood that that was an industry."

Upon finishing his undergraduate degree, he spent two years in Lafayette dong freelance consulting, managing to secure clients, track his time, send out invoices, and keep his head above water. He started taking night courses for an MBA, but soon realized it was worthy of full time attention. He moved to New Orleans and enrolled in Tulane University's joint degree program toward an MBA/JD. A friend introduced him to a lawyer who struck out on his own and hired Dan as a law clerk even before he began his first year of law school. Though first year students technically weren't allowed to hold jobs, and though his class schedule was initially too spread-out to permit time to work, he spoke with the administration and befriended the secretary of scheduling. "I was able to keep that job, where I learned just as much as I did in the classroom," he says. "The experience really confirmed for me that there are often alternatives to the established way of doing things, if you're willing to put in the time and energy to bring them to fruition. Engaging with your environment, asking questions, being creative, and having a friendly attitude can really open a lot of doors."

Thanks to a heavy course load and summer classes, Dan completed a JD, a MBA, and a certificate in international law in four years. In that time, he also clerked for the law firm, held several other jobs, briefed on law cases for his father, became a martial arts instructor, and cofounded a company that converted paper documents to electronic images for law firms and law departments preparing for trial. He got a job building computers for a mail order computer supplier, and another teaching students how to prepare for the LSAT and the GMAT. "That was a time in my life to gather a lot of experiences and be exposed to a lot of different industries," he remembers.

Upon graduation, Dan spent two more years working in the legal technology industry. Then he moved to Phoenix and, unexpectedly, was offered a job with Deloitte in Los Angeles. He accepted, commuting between the cities for a year with client trips to San Francisco, Boston, Israel, New York, and other places. He was then reassigned to the New York office, where he later transitioned over to FTI Consulting. That prompted a move to New York, NY, and then another to Washington, D.C., where he later took a job with LECG. In that capacity, he opened offices all over the U.S. and in London.

In D.C., Dan met Elizabeth, an attorney who shares his passion for leading an adventurous life. They met in 2006, married in 2009, and now have a daughter, Amelia. "Liz has been the light of my life," Dan says. "She's always been a huge source of support for what I do."

That support became crucial on January 1, 2008, when Dan launched IDS with his partner, Neal Lawson. The two had met in the early 1990s when Neal was sent over to install some software Dan's company had purchased. The two became friends, and in 2002, when Dan was working for FTI Consulting and looking to expand his team, he brought Neal onboard. They built out a robust capacity of around forty people before leaving FTI for LECG, another consulting company that tasked them with building a division to work on electronic discovery. From scratch, they built the division to 120 people in less than four yours.

By the end of 2007, Dan and Neal decided to branch out on their own and set to work on formation planning. Discussing their prospects with a banker and a CPA around their kitchen table, they set up a bank account and rented executive office space in a pay-by-the-month office. IDS grew to four people, and then to six. By the end of the first year, they had grown into a team of eight.

In the years that ensued, Dan and Neal focused on building up the infrastructure they had taken for granted while working within larger companies, while relishing the opportunity to direct the company according to their own strategic vision and ethics. "We've built up the clientele and the processes, and I couldn't be more proud of the team we have today," Dan affirms. "In 2013, we were named one of the top 50 companies in the D.C. area by *SmartCEO Magazine*. But more than that, we've really come together to form a cohesive entity with its own brand and character. There's a great energy within our culture, with everyone bringing the best they have to offer to the office each day as we work toward a common focus and vision for our clients."

The company also extends that common focus to giving back, having adopted Bread for the City as the main recipient of their charitable giving. IDS has a pro bono program as well, and matches the charity work of its clients as long as its budget allows. "Giving back to society is the best thing we can do," Dan recognizes, having recently set up a charitable trust for his own family.

For all its technical expertise and range of aptitude, IDS's greatest accomplishment perhaps lies in the promise it makes to its employees, who count on the company to support a good living for their families. "We've had the chance to build a place where people can create careers, and that remains a true focus point for me," Dan remarks. "I never forget that IDS pays 43 mortgages every month. We have 43 families relying on us, and 43 people who deserve a chance to grow professionally. Of all the reasons we keep on doing what we're doing, this is among the greatest."

In advising young people entering the working world today, Dan stresses the importance of focusing on your passion. This means developing an expertise around something one enjoys, which magnifies one's chances of success. He also highlights technology as tool to increase competitiveness. "Technology will play a role in everyone's future, so try to tie it into your passion somehow," he says. "But don't get so engrossed in technology that you disconnect from the other experiences in life. It should be an enabling force."

Beyond that, Dan's success has been about breaking down every psychological barrier that stood in his path, in much the same way he broke through wooden boards with martial arts. Indeed, something changes in the brain chemistry when the foot of an introductory student connects with the plank for the first time, striking at just the right angle to make a clean break. "That's a key moment of transition," he affirms. "You've always believed it can't be done, but then you realize you can do it. You did do it. When you repeat that experience again and again, you realize that maybe you should question what can and cannot be done. You begin to ask, 'why not start with yes?'"

BERNHARDT
WEALTH MANAGEMENT

Carlos Rivera

The Plan

Carlos Rivera had been an enlisted man in the United States Navy for nine years, nine months before he completed his bachelor's degree and was poised to become an officer. But when he was told he would be commissioned in July, he had to insist that the date be postponed to the first of October. His superior officers were baffled. They explained that Carlos would begin receiving higher pay and his new career would begin a full three months ahead of schedule, but Carlos was adamant. This was how it had to be. It was all part of the plan.

"Three decades ago," Carlos recalls today, "or two years before I would become an officer, I was at a picnic. When a colleague asked me what my plans were for the future, I was not sure what he meant." At the time, Carlos and his colleague were Navy Hospital Corpsmen attached to the Marines. Carlos had two years of college under his belt already, but beyond finishing his degree, he had no plans for his future in the Navy. "This fellow corpsman said that I needed a plan," he continues. "He talked me into it, and in broad strokes, I put one together for the first time. I would finish my degree, get a commission in the Navy, and then become an Information Systems Officer. I planned it out, to the day, when each stage would come, giving my life a structure and purpose I had not experienced before."

In this sense, the overarching plan of Carlos's life has been augmented throughout its development by a myriad of small plans—solutions and reactions to life's unexpected obstacles and opportunities that together create a rich pattern of success. But long before he had any sort of plan for himself, his father had an idea of one for him. Both of Carlos's parents were attorneys, as well as their siblings and parents, so Carlos's father decided his son would attend law school.

Born in San Juan, Puerto Rico, Carlos is the eldest of six siblings. His childhood was largely carefree and enjoyable, guided by incredibly busy parents that nevertheless instilled in him strong family values and a sense of social responsibility through their example, working as attorneys for the Puerto Rican government. His father worked for the equivalent of the U.S.'s Department of Housing and Urban Development, and his mother worked for the Department of Education.

"Both of them were brilliantly focused attorneys, but perplexing," Carlos says. "For example my mother had a PhD in law and helped craft some of the laws still in place today dealing with kids with disabilities in the school system. And yet, in comparison, she never learned how to drive a car." On summer days, Carlos would drive his mother to work and then head to the beach to hang out with friends before picking her up again at the end of the day.

Becoming old enough to drive also allowed Carlos to work for his father's law office, where he became acquainted with the fundamentals of law and negotiation. "I learned a lot from him," Carlos says. "I came to understand what is important in a negotiation, and how you find that red line in a negotiation that you can't cross. This informal education has served me all my life."

Working for his father engendered a fondness for law in Carlos, and in a family full of lawyers, he could see himself becoming one as well. But after heading to college and completing one perfect semester, an unexpected detour would change their plans.

"After my first semester, I moved into my own apartment with some friends," Carlos says. "I spent less time studying and more time partying. And partying, and partying." At first, Carlos told himself that he just needed to put his head down and get through it, and then he'd go to law school. "Then I had what I thought was this moment of brilliance," he recalls. "I said I wasn't going to do the next semester and decided to drop out." Carlos believed this plan would prevent him from receiving bad grades for the semester and any corresponding disciplinary action, but unfortunately, he soon ran straight into a brick wall of adult reality.

"I was eighteen," Carlos says, "and I thought I could tell the school what to do. I told them they couldn't suspend me because I had dropped out and I was no longer a student. But they had a rule that they could suspend you even if you weren't a student. They took my I.D., escorted me off the campus, and that was the last time I stepped foot there."

Equipped with a more mature understanding of how the world works, Carlos set about pursuing a new path. His father urged him to apply to Boston College, but he didn't know anything about the U.S. north of Florida. "I knew Boston was cold, and that's really all I needed to know," he laughs. "I wanted to find my own way, so I decided to look into joining the military." After Carlos was turned away by a U.S. Army recruiter who had already met his quota, Carlos went next door to the U.S. Navy recruiter. After signing the paperwork, he had to take it home to have his parents co-sign. "Even to this day, my parents say that signing those papers was one of the hardest things they had to do in their lives," he remarks. "But it led me where I needed to go, and seven years later, at the urging of my fellow seaman, I made a new plan—the first of many."

One of those plans involved completing his degree, but the key element that would allow that to happen—his wife, Irene—had been an unexpected miracle. The two met shortly after he joined the Navy and returned from a NATO deployment. Six months after they started dating, Carlos was sent on a Mediterranean deployment for another six months, and shortly after he returned, they found themselves with a weekend for which they had made no plans. "I just said, let's go get married," he remembers fondly. "We were wed by the Justice of the Peace on a Saturday. That was it. Then I installed a radio in her car later that day. It was perfect in its modesty and beautiful in its simplicity, and we've been married for over three decades. She is the counter-balance I need. She focuses me when I need focusing."

As Carlos worked to implement the plan he put together at the urging of his fellow Navy corpsman, Irene's role proved crucial. First, he planned to finish his degree within three years, but by the time he was a mere three credits from achieving his goal, he was exhausted. Three years of evening classes, four days per week, plus attending class eight hours a day on the weekends and homework, had taken their toll. He was mentally exhausted, and as the start date of his final semester rapidly approached, he still hadn't registered. That's when Irene stepped in. "She just looked at me," Carlos says. "She asked me what I was doing. I tried to tell her how tired I was, but she just said 'Not on your life! You are registering today. You are going to finish what you started.' She's the reason I got my degree and my commission. She's the reason my plans translate into reality."

Carlos's adherence to the plan didn't end with the date of his commission. When he began negotiating his first set of orders in the Navy as an officer, he immediately declared his desire to become an Information Systems Officer. "The Navy Captain on the other end of the phone said to me, 'Well, young man, that's not the way we do things. We'll get you in a training program at a hospital and see how it goes,'" Carlos remembers. After that call, Carlos called the Chief Information Officer (CIO) for the entire Navy Medical Department. When he answered, Carlos introduced himself, voiced his desire to become an Information Systems Officer, and outlined every reason why he should work for the CIO. By the end of the call, the CIO was convinced. He called the Headquarters of Naval Personnel and informed them that Carlos would be working for him.

Despite Carlos' strict adherence to the timeline he laid out as a young man, however, it would ultimately be his flexibility that would enable him to overcome his most unexpected and challenging obstacles in life. "A plan is not necessarily rigid," he says. "Like life, it's a work in progress. You can't fixate on something if it's not working. You need to be able to adapt."

Today, three decades after becoming an officer, Carlos will be the first to tell you that things didn't always go as planned. But the methodical determination and tenacity originating from his first plan, tempered by his levelheadedness under pressure and ability to adapt as needed, have proved to be the yin and yang of his success story.

Considering the transformative experience Carlos had when he put a plan in place in his own life, it is fitting that the very nature of his business today is about making and executing plans that help government and commercial clients achieve their goals. Today, at the helm of his second successful professional services business, Vysnova Partners (Vysnova), Carlos and his team focus on four key areas: 1) management consulting; 2) public health, including veterans' health; 3) improving government operations through training and acquisition support; and 4) information technology. Founded by Carlos in April of 2012, Vysnova was formed with a contract base brought over from his first company, CAMRIS International. In its first nine months, Vysnova saw over $2 million in revenue. For 2013, revenues reached almost $4 million, and that figure is set to double in 2014.

"At my previous company," Carlos says, "we grew to more than 150 employees and consultants doing over $30 million a year in revenue. But I discovered I wasn't a fan of the bureaucratic necessities of a larger, more established company. Personally, I like the entrepreneur stage, where I'm working directly with the clients. I also like working with our people and brainstorming how to solve someone's problem." Indeed, Vysnova's work with information systems and project management is about drawing on experience and resources to create systems that direct a staff and prepare them for all possible outcomes, but the leadership aspects of Carlos's work are what truly drive him.

"As a leader, your primary role is not to tell your folks what to do on a daily basis, but to support them," he points out. "If you have to tell them what to do, then you hired the wrong people. I know there's a theorem that claims all companies are really a set of policies and procedures that get executed every day with a focus on the client and on quality, but I don't think that's leadership. Rather, I think leadership is expressed in a number of different ways. For example, I want to hire staff members that feel empowered to approach every client engagement without preconceived notions or having to agree with me. Conversely, if we have to let someone go, I want them to come out of it saying we were fair. That doesn't mean softening it up, but it does mean helping the employee understand why they are not a good fit. Leading means that you don't stop until the job is finished, and there's no job beneath you. If we're getting a proposal out, I'm the guy out there formatting documents or manning the three-hole punch."

Carlos's tenure in the Navy was essential in defining the nuance of his leadership style, especially one experience he had while responsible for directly overseeing the ordering of tens of millions of dollars in medical supplies every year. At the end of one government fiscal year, after reviewing data reports on his purchases, he suddenly realized that several orders that had failed to go through the first time had in fact been duplicated. The original orders eventually processed, resulting in overspending by over $11 million. "After sitting there for some time and getting past that moment of, 'Oh my god, what did we do,' I asked myself what I could do to fix it," he remembers. Carlos went back through the system and identified every unnecessary duplicate that hadn't shipped yet, which would clear $8 million of the total $11 million. Then he looked at the orders that were still on backlog. Once he determined how to even out the entire overage, only then did he go to his superior officer to report everything and lay out his plan for moving forward.

"What happened next was a remarkable lesson in leadership," Carlos says. "I told our Commanding Officer exactly what happened. He was very calm. When I was done, he asked me what we were going to do about it. I told him what I had worked out and proposed the solution, including what we would do to make sure that the problem would not happen again, and he told me to go ahead and do it. Within 24 hours, I had completed the plan as laid out for him, and was certain that, at that point, he would fire me. I went back to provide him a status report, expecting the worst. I even came out and asked him if he was upset. But he told me that he wasn't. He said it was a mistake, and that I had identified it and figured out a short-term—and, more importantly, a long-term—solution. He said that it was good work. That was leadership in action."

Today, Carlos painstakingly plans ventures long before he decides whether to execute them or not. "For instance, I looked into buying a vineyard," he says. "I can tell you the operating costs, the management costs, the land costs, and the tax and liability issues. How many grapes would I need to be profitable? I go through the whole iteration and develop the concept of operations, and then I reach a point where I can just say no, take it all off the table, and start with something else. I do all that work to determine if the investment is correct. If it's not, I have no problem saying no." Along with this clear-eyed, pragmatic ability to turn down unpromising ideas, however, is an equally clear-eyed and almost noble ability to know the right moment to say yes.

In advising young people entering the working world today, Carlos could offer any number of advice points, but the ideas he chooses to hit home are the importance of planning, and putting character over pure monetary achievement. "Just remember this," he says, referring to one of his favorite motivational sayings. "Nothing we do is measured by the amounts in our bank accounts. It's about making a difference in someone's life. Of course I pursue my business goals, but I like to help people too. So I try to do the best I can toward those two goals every day." Indeed, when you plan to be the best you can and leave room enough to be flexible for the unexpected people or situations that come into your life, you turn out even better in the end.

BERNHARDT
WEALTH MANAGEMENT

Brian Roberts

The Five People You Meet in Business Heaven

In the spirit of Mitch Albom's *The Five People You Meet in Heaven,* Brian Roberts has conceived of the professional world's analogue, outlining the five people you meet in Heaven based on the impact they have on your professional life. This host of game-changers might include the stranger whose advice came at the perfect place and time, so serendipitous as to seem divinely inspired. It might include the superiors whose encouragement led to higher aim and higher achievement. It might include the individual who offered you that incredible opportunity or solution you had hoped for. And it should certainly include the people who connected you to that individual.

Now the founder and CEO of Croix Connect, Inc., a management and technology consulting firm with both commercial and government clients, Brian has dedicated his life to being that connecting force. Thanks to the eloquent sequence of people, ideas, and experiences that make up his own life, he's developed a skill set and network ideal for the solutions-driven work he does today, but he couldn't have gotten here without confronting the very questions he helps his clients face now.

After working for a telecom company at the center of the internet explosion and witnessing the rise and burst of the dotcom bubble, Brian felt the urge to start his own business, but fear of the unknown and contentment with the status quo kept him from action. All that changed, however, when he was outside walking in downtown D.C. on the morning of September 11, 2001. Seeing the smoke from the Pentagon curling toward the sky, he knew inaction was no longer an option. "As a former service member, it really hit home, and I realized I wasn't doing what I wanted to do in my life," he remembers. "I wasn't seeing the Golden Rule followed in the way we treated clients, and that's just not me. I had some ownership and was making six figures, but I wasn't happy. I stopped to think, what do I want to do? Who do I want to be?"

A month later, Brian and his wife, Donna, found themselves chatting in a swimming pool on vacation in St. Croix, when the epiphany was realized in full. Brian had always been a connector—the person others came to when they needed a particular company or person to help them with a given problem. He would make the introduction, step aside, and watch the new combination of skill sets create powerful solutions. He envisioned a company that formalized this service and embraced a culture of ultimate integrity. And though Donna, an entrepreneur herself who had just experienced a 75 percent decline in business, was hesitant at first to encourage Brian to give up a steady income amidst a recession, the couple realized it was worth the risk.

With that, Brian hung the shingle and launched Croix Connect. Originally intending to put his service experience and security clearances to good use, he focused on government work despite the heavy saturation of the market. After securing a steady stream of revenue, he began shifting his sights to the commercial realm and interviewed friends in various companies about the problems they faced related to people, processes, and technology. He readily identified individuals and companies that could help with those problems, but he quickly found that people were more interested in putting their trust in him. He would then subcontract out the work and manage the projects, handling any issues that arose.

Croix Connect's first big client was AOL, and their work began trending toward technology, picking up big data analytics solutions projects for Comcast and Time Warner Cable. After determining that his time was better spent in the private sector, which boasted quicker sales and higher margins than his government work, Brian began focusing wholly on commercial business starting in 2007. Then the Great Recession hit, drying up the majority of his large commercial technology deals and driving him back into problem solving mode.

Around that time, he got a call from Vistage International, a professional development organization for CEOs and executives, asking if he would chair and head one of their executive peer groups. "Croix Connect had already made the leap from government contracting to big technology solutions," Brian points out. "I wondered, could we make that leap to becoming an executive facilitator, coach, and advisor? Aside from my enthusiasm and appreciation for the Vistage program itself, I saw it as an opportunity to develop my focus and branding message."

Thus, in 2010, Croix Connect evolved into professional development services for interim executives, and Brian became known for the advisor and coaching program he designed, Executive Whisperer. In that capacity, he focuses on being the "angel" on the shoulder of his clients, whispering advice, vetting ideas, and helping them build the courage to take action. On the side, he leads Vistage groups at the CEO and Key Executive levels. "Right now, my work primarily revolves around coaching and advising the CEOs of small and medium-sized businesses," he says. "It's some of the most powerful, exciting, fun, and rewarding work I've ever done. I work with hard-charging executives who are putting the livelihoods of their families on the line to do what they believe is right, making tough business decisions on a daily basis and always pursuing betterment. To help them on that journey, connecting them to insight and solutions, is an incredible experience, and seeing the changes in people is truly powerful."

Today, Brian is working with eight companies through his Executive Whisperer program, touching around 400 employees. Including the companies touched through his Vistage groups, hundreds of additional families are impacted. "I've always loved the proverb, 'He who influences few influences the many,'" Brian affirms. "Helping people solve their problems, achieve their dreams, and help others do the same is why I do what I do."

Having this impact on business leaders and the families their companies touch mirrors the opportunities he would have wanted for his own family when he was a kid. Brian grew up in a blue-collar, hard-working, values-driven Midwestern family in a town 15 miles west of Detroit, Michigan. His father, a heavy equipment operator for a construction company, and his mother, a homemaker during Brian's childhood, raised their children believing in the power of an unyielding work ethic and the Golden Rule. Doing unto others as he'd have others do unto him became the litmus test for every decision he made, and would become the cornerstone of his business philosophy later on.

As a child, Brian earned strong grades and loved sports of all kinds. Demonstrating an early aptitude for numbers and memorization, he bought the record books for basketball, baseball, hockey, and football, memorizing countless bits of trivia. He thought he might become an accountant or a sportscaster, though he hadn't yet come out of his shell and expressed the off-the-charts extroversion that would characterize his personality later on.

At his parents' suggestion, Brian began mowing his neighbors' lawns when he was 12. He charged only $3 per lawn, so he was shocked into silence one day when a neighbor gave him a $7 tip. "I was so dumbfounded I couldn't speak," he recalls. "Later, my father took me aside and said, 'You know, son, when someone does something really nice for you, it's important to say thank you in a big way.' I remember that as a trigger point in life. I really understood the value of taking other peoples' feelings into consideration and always doing the right thing. Now, I go above and beyond in saying thank you to people, and I appreciate anything anyone does for me."

No one in Brian's family had gone to college. They didn't have money set aside for higher education, and they didn't know about grants or scholarships. Brian had worked at the corner donut shop since eighth grade, but hadn't saved up enough to cover the cost of tuition. Despite the odds, he became the first Roberts to set his sights on advanced education, gaining admission to both the University of Michigan and Michigan State. For cost reasons, when he received an Air Force recruiting card in the mail, he decided to relieve the pressure put on his parents to help pay for school by enlisting.

When Brian took the Armed Services Vocational Aptitude and Battery test, computers were just hitting the market, and though he had no idea what the phenomenon was all about, his scores indicated a proclivity for the new technology. Thus, when he entered the Air Force on July 11th, 1977 he quickly became immersed in tech. Based in Northern Michigan, he worked on computers manufactured by Burroughs Corporation, a competitor of IBM, and planned to leave the military and enter the field after his four years were up. In anticipation of his discharge, Brian called the Burroughs headquarters in Detroit to discuss his impending job options.

The year was 1980, and the voice on the other end of the line mentioned that the job market was competitive and he'd do well to take another hitch. "I didn't know the guy on the phone, but I took his advice, and it had a huge impact on my life," Brian recounts. "Because of him, I chose to stay in the military and relocate to Colorado, where I diversified my skills through working on IBM equipment." In that capacity, Brian found himself working on Space Command, tracking missile launches and global events. As he got to know the officers he worked with, he began to see that there was nothing holding him back from becoming an officer himself. "They pushed me to pursue an officer program," he says. "I had to take algebra, trigonometry, and calculus before I could even apply, but with their urging, I did it. If they weren't there encouraging me, I'm not sure it would have happened."

With one course left in the program, Brian was burned out, so he took a 30-day vacation to road trip to California and back. If he hadn't gotten bored early and returned to Colorado on the 27th day, he would have missed the White House Communications Agency (WHCA), which happened to be in town conducting interviews for one of their esteemed slots. Brian had perfect performance records, a clean background, and the specialized skill set they were looking for, landing him the opportunity of a lifetime. "I packed my bags, moved to D.C., and spent two years working on the Presidential Advance Team," he says. "We traveled ahead of President Reagan everywhere he went to set up communication centers for his time away from the White House. I worked with top-notch people in a perfect team dynamic, and in a climate where the job had to be done without ifs, ands, or buts. I traveled to Geneva and Reykjavik for the Reagan-Gorbachev summits and took great honor in the significance of what we were doing."

At the end of the two-year WHCA appointment, Brian finished his officer program. Three years later, in 1992, a wave of base closures and a climate of general military drawdown left him faced with a decision: he could end his military career and accept a nice volunteer package, or stay and face possible termination without the benefits. He had been in the Air Force for 15 years, but planned to stay 25 or 30 and return to the White House Communications Agency as an officer. "I had to take all the emotion out of the decision and do a pros-and-cons list," he remembers. "In the end, it just didn't make sense to stay, but I treasure my time in the military. On so many levels, joining the service was one of the best things to that ever happened to me. It exposed me to tremendous diversity and incredible people. Also, seeing that even the military can lay you off, I realized I never wanted to work for a large company where I didn't have control over my destiny. It lit an entrepreneurial flame in me, though I didn't realize it at the time."

That flame was cultivated in the commercial technology sphere, when he landed in a data communications startup called MFS Datanet. The company was operating at ground zero for the internet, and was the first to offer high-speed connections to major companies like Merrill Lynch, JP Morgan, and Goldman Sachs. Brian worked on the team that facilitated the first big interconnection point that connected the various internet providers to one another, creating the Metropolitan Area Ethernet (MAE). "For the first time, the world's top six or seven internet providers were connected," he remembers. "We were working until all hours of the night, but we were having a lot of fun doing something no one else had done."

As the company grew, however, Brian realized he was much more interested in being a starter and a builder. As it plateaued, the daily grind began to set in, and he grew less satisfied. When the company was bought by WorlD.C.om, he knew it was time to leave. Brian landed at another telecom company and then transitioned over to a professional services company, learning the right ways and the wrong ways to do business and treat people.

Those lessons continued after he launched Croix Connect, augmented when he launched a radio show in 2004 called "Taking Care of Business with Brian Roberts." An acquaintance, David Bird, had a weekend morning slot, and when Brian asked to be on his program, he told Brian he should consider hosting his OWN weekly show where he interviewed government and business leaders. "Business is all about relationships, and that show afforded me incredible access and solid relationships," he says. "I could write a book about the stories from the studio and the advice I got from those leaders. It was a great way to connect with people and to then connect them to opportunities, so it was perfectly aligned with the mission of Croix Connect."

In advising young people entering the working world today, Brian highlights the importance of networking and the dangers of living in the past. "I can't stand it when people dwell on 'shoulda, coulda, woulda,'" he says. "You can't drive forward with your eyes stuck on the rearview mirror. Things happen for good reasons, so be content in that knowledge and focus on the opportunities of today with optimism and enthusiasm."

Though Brian never adopted the risk-averse, often pessimistic attitudes of his parents, who, like many people disliked change and often forecasted worst-case scenarios, his worldview has certainly been advanced by the risk-taking and optimistic nature of his wife, Donna. Married almost thirty years now, she's been with him every step of the way, a perfect partner in making choices and living life. "I'm so fortunate to have met someone as special as Donna," he remarks. "She's amazing. Everything I do now comes through and out of that, including my faith as a Catholic. We were married in 1986 at Bolling Air Force Base by their auxiliary priest, and the same priest presided over the ceremony initiating me into the faith in 1991."

As the Vice Chairman of the Board of Catholic Charities for the Arlington Diocese, and as a member of its Executive and Advancement & Communications Committees, Brian focuses his volunteer efforts on growing that agency. He and Donna also work monthly shifts at the United Service Organization's (USO) lounge at Dulles Airport, where military personnel and their families find a home away from home. They've recently become Eucharist Ministers, and in the past, Brian worked with inmates at the Fairfax County Jail, giving spiritual and community support through the transition back to society. "I've always wanted to be a helper," he says. "It's important to me to have a positive impact on everyone I touch, whether it's on the personal side or the business side."

And, in reflecting back over his personal and professional journeys, the division between the two grows less defined. The compassion and care he exudes as an advisor and coach today, for instance, is in part an echo of the kindness showed to him by a student teacher many years ago. "I was being picked on during a middle school softball game, so Mr. Kobelars threw me two of the fattest pitches," he recalls. "I slugged the heck out of both of them, winning the admiration of my peers. That's something I'll never forget. Don't underestimate the impact you have on people. Help others along the way, because you can't imagine what it might mean to them. Look for ways to be the reason they hit it out of the park. You never know—maybe you'll become one of the five people they meet in Heaven, in the end."

Anita Samarth

MAKING HISTORY

Anita Samarth was raised thinking she had three options for her career: become a doctor, a lawyer, or an engineer like her father. While she never felt particularly drawn to any of those professions, her traditional Indian upbringing had influenced her to believe that the best career was one she could count on for stability. "As the only child of immigrant parents, I believed the route to success was only down a tried and true path," she recalls. "Choosing a career in the healthcare, technology, or engineering space felt like a safe choice, since you can assume you will always be employed. It wasn't until later, however, that I realized how much of a people person I am. I had never been exposed to someone in a successful leadership role in business, so I shied away from that notion until well after college because I didn't know much else."

Anita stayed true to the suggestions of her culture by earning degrees in biomedical engineering and electrical engineering, but realized as soon as she was in the field just how successful she could be as a businesswoman. She currently serves as CEO and co-founder of Clinovations Government Solutions (CGS), a company dedicated to bridging the gap between the delivery of health care and other sectors through strategic consulting on the use of technology. With twenty employees serving predominantly government or publicly funded clients, their engagements are centered on policy, implementation, and practice.

Most recently, the CGS team has worked on implementation of the Recovery Act, which gives hospitals incentives to use electronic medical records. "We're interested in making sure doctors get compensated for sharing relevant clinical information electronically," she explains. "For example, let's say you're in a medical office building on one side of town and you have a practice on the other side of town. You're told as a doctor that you don't get incentive dollars unless you get your radiology results electronically. Your medical office building may have a radiologist with an ultrasound, but that radiologist can't afford all the electronic pieces yet, which means you're going to send your patient across town to get the radiology tests done so they can get a result sent back electronically. Now you're creating the unintended consequence of patient routing. You're making it unnecessarily difficult, not to mention possibly putting the other radiology place out of business, even though your intention was good. We are here to help that problem with programs that support effective use of technology."

Anita started Clinovations in 2007 with the intention of looking closer at policy and national agenda. "There was a lot of strange policy being enacted, and people had no idea what it was like being in the field in the healthcare system," she says. "When we work with the government, we have to simplify everything since there is a certain way it has to be implemented. On the flip side, when regulatory conditions are pushed to the marketplace, there's a demand for flexibility. Most people didn't know where the line between these two considerations falls, since they don't hang out in Washington. I saw an opportunity to inform federally-funded initiatives nationwide through practice, and to educate the practice about the policy."

Anita was born in Toronto, Canada and grew up in Texas, where her father, a civil structural engineer, worked at the nuclear power plant near Fort Worth. Her mother worked in accounting and was an exceptionally strong woman after losing her father at the age of twelve. Anita's parents had met through an arranged marriage in India and immigrated to the United States for their respective careers, where they raised Anita with a strong traditional Indian influence.

Anita attended a Southern Baptist private school for her first two years of grade school, but transferred to a public school in third grade, where she found her studies extremely easy. "I already knew my times tables from the private school, so I was ahead of everyone else," she comments. "I'm sure I was an average student at the private school, but because of the timing of my transfer, I did very well in public school."

Anita was able to maintain good grades despite undergoing a series of reconstructive surgeries for a cleft palate—the first at only six months of age. The surgeries continued throughout her adolescence, and she had her last just before leaving for college. In elementary school, it had been an even playing field, since her classmates were constantly getting new teeth, but by middle school, she had to have a bone graft that required metal implants and screws that were harder to camouflage. "It was hard to go through that in my early teens," she says. "I would tag along with my parents and their friends' kids on weekends, and I could feel them looking at me. In the long run, I can see how it taught me strategy and how to manage difficult people around me, but at the time, it was very hard."

Anita did exceptionally well in her schoolwork and took extra classes during the summer, so by ninth grade, she was invited to apply to a program at the University of North Texas to work through her final years of high school while concurrently starting her college coursework. "My parents and I went to visit, and I thought it was awful," she laughs. "The students weren't as well rounded as I wanted to be, and they still had curfews. It was college with the shackles of high school, so I turned it down and elected to graduate early instead." At sixteen years old, she moved across the country to Baltimore, Maryland, where she started at Johns Hopkins University and got her first true taste of freedom. "People would say, 'Oh you poor thing, you didn't get to enjoy yourself in high school,' and I thought, are you kidding me?" she laughs. "I was sixteen and living on my own. I loved the freedom!"

Having grown up with the understanding that Indians only became doctors, lawyers, or engineers, Anita thought long and hard about what career she wanted to pursue during her time at Johns Hopkins. She knew she didn't want to be a civil engineer since she had seen how her father's job had frequently uprooted the family, so she earned two degrees in biomedical and electrical engineering to keep her options open.

Despite her diligent focus on the career paths her family had envisioned for her, Anita's natural tendencies conflicted every so often with her intended professional aspirations. Whereas most of the libraries on campus were "quiet", there was one that was known as the "social" library, where students could talk and collaborate as they worked. Anita always chose the social option and frequently found herself abandoning her biomedical engineering work to network from table to table, catching up with old friends and making new ones as she went. She had never once considered a business major, mainly because she had never been formally introduced to the field. "My friends used to tease me in college for only going to the library to socialize," she says. "That's when I started to really notice that maybe I was in the wrong field, since I was at my best when I was able to surround myself with people and bring together their ideas. If I had been exposed to the business or information technology worlds earlier, I think I would have found them to be my forte since they are so much more focused on relationships and collaboration."

After finishing her majors and graduating a semester early, Anita received several acceptances into biomedical engineering master's programs, but after visiting the campuses, she realized the career did not feel like a good match after all. With that, she deferred her acceptances and started working as a consultant at Accenture, a management consulting and technology services company. After a year there, she realized she wanted to shift her orientation to business, so she forewent her deferrals and spent another three years with the company.

In 1998, Anita left Accenture to manage consulting and patient safety at First Consulting Group, a midsized consulting firm (now Computer Sciences Corporation) where she worked for five years before it was acquired. During the company's transition, she left to join GE Healthcare as a National Practice Manager. In her third year with GE, she attended a large conference for IT and healthcare, where she was introduced to Trenor Williams. "I always say, 'Those who can't do, manage.' In this field, that translates to, although I'm not a clinician, I manage clinicians," she says. "Trenor gave me his resume, so we called him in, and immediately, we hit it off." At the time, GE was paying physicians extremely low salaries, so Anita used Trenor as her case study to get the salaries realigned and further evolve the profile of physician consultants at GE.

Shortly after Anita met Trenor in 2005, she decided to venture out on her own for the first time by starting ASTECH Consulting. "When I started that company, my notion was that I had a unique set of skills living in D.C., in the fields of healthcare, technology, and policy, and I wanted to see what I could do with that," she says. "My initial goal was having my own freedom and independence, and just to be able to take care of myself. Eventually, however, I wanted more. I still had that fire in my belly to find out what we could change and what we were capable of, so we decided to push the limits."

Anita and Trenor ended up reconnecting in Washington, D.C. a few years into founding ASTECH Consulting. A year and a half into their professional relationship, they decided to start a new company together, fueled by their mutual affinity for connecting people. "We started "geeking out" over Health IT, building our networks and discussing why healthcare is broken and how we can fix it" she says. "Healthcare costs are bankrupting our nation, and we saw a way to make a difference—and, in that sense, to make history. I decided I wanted to get off the road and learn a little about the policy space, so we started asking people who they knew like it was an extracurricular activity." In a natural effort, Anita was able to roll the work she had accrued at ASTECH Consulting over to her new company with Trenor, thus creating Clinovations in 2007 as a collaborative and consulting firm in 2008.

Looking back, Anita credits her success as an entrepreneur to having always had a strategic plan in place, even when she craved the freedom to explore her options. "I don't think my gut has ever been wrong," she says. "I let the lessons I've learned and the challenges I've faced define me. In earlier days, when I encountered things, I would persevere and move on. Today, when I see a red flag, I deal with it sooner. That kind of foresight is what really gives you freedom in whatever career you choose."

When she's not focused on the company, Anita spends time with her husband, Bob Filley, whom she married in 2003. Like his father and grandfather, Bob works in commercial real estate, where he earns 100 percent commission. "I am type A, and he is type B, so his commission always drove me crazy," she says. "He's very mellow, and I think that's good for me. He's extremely supportive, but we are very independent. We very rarely ask each other for advice—instead, we say, 'Go find your peers and I'll find mine.'"

While she may not have chosen the exact path her parents laid out for her, Anita maintained the values they instilled in her and opened new avenues of progress for future generations to come. "I'm kind of in the none-of-the-above category," she says. "I'm not a doctor. I'm not a lawyer. And even though I have two engineering degrees, I've lost my ability to do any actual engineering. What I really am is a culmination of the things I have learned and the things I have worked for. You are a factor of your surroundings, so you take a piece of it all with you as you build who you are." By trusting her instincts and letting her natural abilities lead her away from a prescribed path and into a life where her interests and passions are redefining an industry and helping to solve one of the biggest problems our nation faces, Anita is not only happier and more successful—she's reshaping tradition and making history.

BERNHARDT
WEALTH MANAGEMENT

Karin Schwartz

The Fixer

Every Friday, Karin Schwartz's grandmother would buy a small toy or piece of candy for each of her grandchildren. To an outsider, this ritual might not seem exceptional, but to young Karin, it was nothing short of rebellious. "My grandmother was expected to cash out her weekly paycheck and then bring all of the money home to my grandfather," she explains. "Even though she was told not to, she continued to buy us gifts, and no one ever knew."

Born in the 1920s, during a time when women's rights were at the forefront of our nation's political stage, Karin's grandmother possessed a natural inclination to go against the grain, and Karin herself inherited this defiant spirit as well. While her grandmother passed away when she was just three, she can easily relate to the independent attitude she observed in those very earliest years in the woman she so admired. "I'm not much of a conformist, and I often tend to buck the system," she says today. "The last thing I want to hear from a company is, 'This is the way we've always done it.' If you think that way, how are you going to improve as a business?"

Karin's knack for shaking things up is why she's now the CEO and founder of Springboard, a business development consulting firm. Founded in July of 2008, Springboard aims to create sales opportunities for government contractors and professional services firms that lack the time, resources, or ideas to increase their sales value. Whether it's a company that's growing rapidly or a business looking to enter new markets without committing the full resources business development typically requires, Springboard allows its clients the freedom to improve without expending the full resources or overhead to hire a full-time salesperson. Its unique business model affords clients the opportunity to lease consultants, which ultimately translates into more freedom and flexibility when companies need it most.

While freedom and flexibility aren't often associated with the world of sales, Karin hopes Springboard will challenge and overcome negative preconceptions of the industry. "There's still a lot of animosity around sales," Karin says. "Of course there are people who still treat sales like transactions, but for our company, those transactions are born from trust and genuine relationships." Karin's personal commitment to transparency translates to a company culture of openness, and as a result, Springboard's salespeople are extremely forthcoming with their clients. In initial meetings with clients, Karin sets realistic expectations, and she's honest about what her team can deliver. "Our justice streak and desire for honesty is what makes Springboard different from what you see in other organizations," she affirms. "We only succeed if we help our clients to succeed."

Springboard's innovative approach to sales has allowed it to grow in both size and reputation since its inception in 2008. Karin originally came up with the idea for the company after she came into contact with business owners who showed opportunities for growth but who lacked the funds to hire experienced people, and as someone who was experienced with forging connections and executing a process, she attracted many clients who craved sales opportunities but who were too busy to manifest growth on their own.

Most of the overwhelmed small businesses owners who became her earliest clients had companies earning $3 million or less in revenue. Today, armed with twelve experienced consultants, Springboard now serves companies earning as much as $30 million annually. This dramatic shift in its client base occurred after Karin went on maternity leave following the birth of her son, Kyle. The extra time afforded her an opportunity to reconsider the future of Springboard and the ultimate goals she had for the company, and always itching to reinvent the wheel, Karin decided to focus her hiring energies on people who did business development on an outsourced basis and had experience serving a number of different industries. Thanks to that time of reflection and reinvention, Springboard now works with the U.S. Department of Defense and the Intelligence Community, as well as the commercial market. It has a strong focus on finding good fits for their services, utilizing a Client Acceptance Protocol to ensure a successful relationship. "Companies that make decisions solely based on money are not good fits for us," Karin affirms. A strong corporate culture, goals, and purpose are what drive Springboard clients.

This focus on increasing the diversity of Springboard's team has not only set it apart from competitors, but has also resulted in savings for clients and expanded opportunities for the company. "Our clients like the team approach because, in business development, it's all about the people you know and the relationships you have," Karin explains. "In our industry, success depends on the conversations you have." With this in mind, her continued goal as CEO is to make sure her team has the support and resources to get the job done. In the past, Karin worked for employers who focused too much on vanity or wealth—empty values which she refuses to bring to Springboard. "As an entrepreneur, your goal should be to create the business you love and do it with the people you care about," she affirms.

Karin embraced this "do what you love with who you love" philosophy watching her grandfather, who was one of the founding members of the Baltimore Colts marching band. Two of his sons, including Karin's father, also played in the band. The three men were extremely passionate about music, and they loved to play together even more. "It was a different time, when the guys who played football worked at Sparrow's Point, had regular jobs, and didn't have multimillion-dollar contracts," Karin reminisces. "Everyone hung out together."

Through those precious years together, Karin's family acquired a collection of memorabilia that now commemorates those close ties and good times. The collection includes part of the goal post from the 1959 championship game, a ticket book from that season, and two footballs signed by the entire championship team. "Those relics are kind of like the ties that bind my family together," she says fondly. "My siblings and I grew up on football. We have a really close family, and a lot of that closeness comes from sports."

Indeed, athletics dominated Karin's childhood growing up in Fallston, a Maryland suburb just outside of Bel Air. From soccer to softball, she played just about everything. "Our family had the flattest yard and longest driveway in the neighborhood, so if you wanted to play sports, you came to our house," she recalls. "As long as it wasn't raining, there was a game in our yard."

In addition to recreational sports, Karin also took an interest in gymnastics, and through this passion she was able to land her first job. Between the ages of thirteen and 26, she coached girls' gymnastics, while also working some retail jobs and taking on the occasional babysitting gig. The work ethic she developed as a teenager was necessary to fund anything outside of basic necessities. "A lot of people thought my siblings and I were spoiled because every Christmas there was a lot to go around," she says. "If we needed anything for the rest of the year, however, we had to buy it ourselves. Our parents wanted us to learn the value of a dollar."

While work played a formative role in Karin's life, education played an even bigger part. Her father, a hardworking man who spent his life in telecommunications, didn't attend college. In fact, he missed 47 days of school in the second grade, preferring to play Cowboys and Indians in the woods.

Karin's parents decided a college education was non-negotiable for their children. Her mother, a homemaker who later took a job in retail, stressed the importance of a college degree—a piece of paper which began to carry more weight for Karin's generation. Given the choice between Towson University and Essex Community College, she chose Towson, where she pursued a degree in finance with a minor in economics. Her choice to pursue finance was influenced by her high school accounting teacher, a man who often talked about his mutual funds and money with extreme openness. "In the 1970s and 80s, you didn't talk to your parents about money," Karin describes. "As someone who loved numbers, it was really intriguing to hear my accounting teacher talk about where and how he invested."

After Karin graduated from Towson, she worked as a financial advisor for several large institutions, and during that time, she learned a lot about herself as an employee and as a woman. Her experience with one client in particular, a large physicians group, stands out in her memory with particular color. "The planners for the group made no bones about the fact that they wanted a young and good looking woman at the front of the room when we gave presentations to the doctors," Karin remembers. "I was used to attract the specialists with the larger paychecks. But in the end, I was placed with the researchers who made a lot less, and barely a few years out of medical school all their disposable income went to pay their student loans." Karin soon realized she landed the position with the physicians group because she was female—a reality that compelled her to set the bar high for herself. Never one to adhere to stereotypes, she chose to prove her worth through hard work and business acumen instead of just skating by. "It was important for me to make my mark where I went," she stresses. "No matter what path I take, I don't ever want to be the person who was handed something; I want it to be earned."

By April of 2000, Karin had accrued years of invaluable experience as a financial advisor and reached a point where she felt she was treading water. While exciting, the stress of those years had also taken a heavy toll on her health, but actually enacting a change would take an extra push. Karin continued to advise business owners in the construction industry until that push came. "I ended up in the hospital with an asthma attack, and then my dog passed away unexpectedly," she explains. "Ultimately, those experiences led to me leave the industry after years of having stomach ulcers and being sick all the time. That series of unfortunate events enlightened me to other opportunities where I could gain more independence and change my life for the better."

Ready to create a new life, Karin was offered a position with Syndicated Research Group, which provided human resources and financial consulting for Fortune 500 companies. When the company went under after the events of 9/11, Karin went to work for Gevity, a national human resources consulting firm. Too independent to follow the traditional path of a standard employee, Karin then went on to start ImpactHR, a human resources consulting firm, with a retired executive and another consultant from Gevity. At ImpactHR, Karin cultivated new skills and gained the knowledge necessary to found Springboard. "I learned a lot about marketing from my time at Gevity and ImpactHR," she says. "It's really important to understand who your client is, who you're targeting, and what you're saying."

While ImpactHR was a successful business, Karin still craved more autonomy—a desire that ultimately gave her the courage to strike out on her own. And now that she's a mother of one with another on the way, the flexibility and freedom of entrepreneurship is even more important. "From a mom perspective, owning your own business allows you to take on multiple roles," Karin says. "There are days when I work fourteen hours, and then there are days when I can take my son to the zoo."

Today, Karin plans to buck her own system and change the direction of Springboard once again, keeping things growing, transforming, and relevant. In its next iteration, the company will take a special interest in helping small businesses build structure around business development. "I've had a lot of small companies who've said to me, 'I don't know where to start,'" she explains. "We want to answer that question for them."

While the reinvention of Springboard will require a lot of work, Karin is confident she'll be able to pull it off. "Every time I've stepped away from the business, I've come up with a crazy new idea to change things for the better," she says. "And I do think those changes have been key in our success and relevance to markets, both old and new." Karin also knows her husband, Matt, will be a great support as Springboard enters its next phase. "If I'm getting in the way of my business, Matt will call me on it," she explains. "It has been extremely helpful for me to have someone who can see how my patterns can affect my company, and how to safeguard against that."

While Karin's trajectory to success and freedom has required her to buck the system from time to time, her advice to young college graduates is more timeless. "Do your homework," she says simply. "I can't tell you how many interviews I've had where a young person didn't know a thing about our company." Karin urges young people to take advantage of all the resources available to them, most notably the internet, and to come prepared. "You need to be able to say why you think you'd fit in at company, what skills you bring to the table, and how you see your role evolving over the next couple of years," she affirms. "You also need to have a thick skin in a culture where everyone doesn't get a trophy. I look for self-starters who take initiative and don't need babysitting—people who are willing to be mentored, attend training courses, and read everything on business, leadership and mindset."

As CEO of Springboard, Karin always strives to be better, even if that means taking a risk or challenging the status quo. To reach great heights, one must be confident enough to go against what's comfortable or expected, just as Karin herself has time and time again. "My ideas don't always fit the norm. They aren't always welcomed with open arms, but it's important to think outside the box and buck the system every once in a while," Karin says, reminiscent not only of those secret Friday afternoon gifts from her grandmother, but also what they stood for. Karin, like all good rebels and like her grandmother before her, is led by her ideas rather than her fears, and has been able to lead others to success because of it.

BERNHARDT
WEALTH MANAGEMENT

Les Smolin

SUCCESS AS SONG

The lens through which we view life is the hand that guides the development of our relationships with others. This lens is forged moment by moment, experience by experience, and most dramatically when we connect with an idea or skill that redefines the optics of our worldview. Les Smolin happened to find his lens when he was a young child and first picked up an accordion—the defining moment that led him to experience life as music. "Music is about a story being told, and about communication," he explains today. "Life is full of experiences that are both harmonious and discordant, and I see the arc of those experiences joined by the melody that arises from them."

Today, Les's life motif is one of intentioned crescendos and rests that have led him to launch the Executive Leadership Forum consulting practice, which specializes in providing executive development, leadership, and strategic services to primarily middle market companies. He also leads two CEO groups and one Key group as part of Vistage International, an executive coaching and peer advisory network. As a Group Chairman in the Washington, D.C. metro area, his business acumen brings new meaning to the work of his clients, thanks to his ability to identify the thematic elements of their stories and the subtle innuendos that can make or break success. "By connecting events over time into a story that makes sense, I'm able to pick up on the trends and underlying currents of my clients' situations," he says. "This imparts a nuanced understanding that I can really work with to make a difference in those situations and in their lives."

Making a difference, after all, is the *why* behind all he's ever done. It's the time signature in which each movement of his life has been written, though he didn't always know it. "I've always been most motivated by opportunities to engage with business executives and make a difference in their lives for the better," he remarks. The building blocks for this proclivity were first evident back in grade school, when Les would turn around in his seat in study hall to chat quietly with the girl who sat behind him.

"I remember distinctly the time a friend told me I was a really good listener," he says. "My listening skills were one manifestation of my desire to understand and help others—something that pronounced itself again when I decided to major in Psychology in college. Now I have the opportunity to help and coach business and other leaders and executives—people with the ability to shape the direction of a business or organization and have a huge impact on the lives of their employees. Helping people make the most of their impact is my calling in life, and always has been, even as a kid growing up in Long Island."

A baby boomer born in 1953 in New York City, Les and his family were part of the burgeoning middle class that moved to the newly forming Long Island suburbs in post-World War II America. It was a time of growing prosperity, and a building boom was underway. The emerging middle class in New York, seeking a better environment to raise their children and escape from the challenges of urban life, pushed out into the suburbs to become the first generation of suburbanites. Towns like North Bellmore, where Les grew up, with split-level homes, a garage, a green lawn, excellent public schools, and a promise of a better life beckoned them. "It was a special place and a special time in America," Les recalls. "I look back on life in that community fondly and am still friends with the people I grew up with."

The middle child of three, Les's character was forged in a home where the phone never stopped ringing. His mother, a homemaker, was the glue that kept the family connected, while his father worked as an accountant. He also dabbled in entrepreneurship, but real financial success eluded him. "I had a sense that I wanted a different kind of future," Les says. "I knew that somehow I needed to strike out on my own. Independence and hard work became very important to me in that regard."

Cultivating that go-getter attitude in himself, however, entailed several roadblocks that he'd have to clear first. "I was an awkward, short kid who really internalized the mantra that children should be seen and not heard," he recalls. "I avoided conflict and was often too intimidated to speak my mind, but I think this helped hone my skills as a thoughtful listener that would become so important later on."

Learning how to make independent decisions was a big step in his development, but his grade school years were spent mastering the strength of mind needed to make choices and accept responsibility for their outcomes, whatever they might be. His decision-making skills and his independence were put to the ultimate test in high school, when he decided to quit wrestling. Though he was small and lacked the talent in the sport to truly excel, Les had played for six years. "There wasn't a time when I didn't have to work harder than everyone else to even get a spot on the team," he remembers. "Coach Hunt was this mythological figure at my school, and I really feared him. I was petrified of disappointing him. He would stand against the wall by the doorway to the school entrance where we'd enter from the parking lot and stare us down. I died a thousand deaths before telling him I was quitting, but the whole experience served to toughen me up and give me the kind of self-confidence it takes to assess your life and make the changes you, yourself, feel you need to make."

Les's paternal grandmother always seemed to symbolize this kind of independent thinking and strength of character. She and his grandfather lived in the Rockaways in Queens and owned several properties, along with a grocery store his grandfather ran. "My grandmother was an independent person who did things her own way and accepted the consequences," he reflects. "She had this spirit about her. She'd sit in the chair in her apartment by the beach, smoking a Parliament cigarette with a drink by her side and a glint in her eyes. I felt very comfortable with her." To Les, she was someone who lived a life true to herself, and to this day, one of his most valued possessions is a nondescript jar that belonged to her and now sits in his kitchen cabinet. "Every time I see that jar, I remember her independent spirit and how I continue to nurture that quality in myself," he says.

Les grew up in an atmosphere where young people were expected to pursue careers as doctors, lawyers, or accountants. "Those were the choices, and there was really nothing outside of those professions presented as a viable option," he explains. "It was assumed you would do something safe, so I spent my childhood ruling things out, like baseball, that weren't safe." When it came time to go to college, he packed his bags for the University of Maryland. Life in the Long Island suburbs had grown small and stifling, and he wanted a place where he could get lost and find himself.

The day Les's parents dropped him off at college for the first time, he stood on campus and realized he was going to have to make his success happen on his own. His parents had done all they could for him, and like the melody that connects isolated notes into a coherent song, it was his responsibility to fill in the gaps. With that, he found jobs to make the extra money he needed and spent Saturday nights in the library studying because he felt an obligation to work harder than everyone else.

Moment by moment, experience by experience, this sense of responsibility and determination was incorporated into the tonal quality of his motif, and Les became an extremely self-disciplined person. To this day, once he sets a goal, he immediately begins planning its execution and then sets his course to its methodical accomplishment. For Les, college was about learning how to master things both academic and personal. In addition to his psychology major, he minored in accounting as a foundation for success in business. "My liberal arts degree and business background provided a very concrete foundation for me to acknowledge both the humanistic and business orientation I needed to enter the workforce," he says. "I invested a lot in school, and I got a lot out of it."

Les was one of the few young men who wasn't drafted in the Vietnam War as it was winding down. After graduating, he went to work for the U.S. General Accounting Office as a GS-7 Civil Servant on Capitol Hill. "I was looking for meaningful work and a way to make a difference in people's lives, and the agency was looking for people with liberal arts degrees," he recounts. "I had an unconscious competency for the work and stayed for four years."

The federal government offered tuition reimbursement for graduate school at that time, so Les went to school at night to earn his MBA. He was always taking classes to satisfy his intellectual curiosity, setting him up to pioneer work in a number of today's leading industries. "I never fit into a mold," he says. "I was always kind of doing my own thing."

Les went on to work for Booz Allen Hamilton for eight years, gaining valuable experience on projects for the Department of Energy and Environmental Protection Agency at the forefront of some of the most pressing societal issues. From behind the scenes, he played a defining role and had some of his most formative work experiences, but eventually interested in pressing beyond the firm's typical mold for a consultant, Les decided to strike out on his own.

Several years later, Les was invited to run a division of an IT company based in the Baltimore, Maryland suburbs. He was leading work efforts at the forefront of what became windows-based software applications for major corporations and industrial clients. After several years running companies in the IT world, Les got a call from

Booz Allen, asking him to help with a startup they were launching to enable health care systems become more patient focused. The company and its strategic partner were building a prototype device to better manage patient care at the bedside. "My background was in management, IT, and healthcare, and in building things and finding ways to monetize them, so I said yes," he says. "We had brilliant minds and great ideas, but the dynamics among all team partners were not enough to make the business work."

Around the same time the business came undone, Les's marriage fell apart. His wife had come from a troubled background and taught Les that the resilience of the human spirit knows no bounds. "I learned from her that you can endure hard circumstances but still find the strength and courage to carry on," he affirms. "She taught me that it's in the ordinary moments that extraordinary things happen. It's the small, simple things we take for granted every day that are so special."

In the throes of the career crisis and the divorce, the power of this idea really hit home when Les found himself standing outside his house one day as a young girl rode up on her tricycle. She was carrying some drawings she had created, and she wanted to give one to Les. "My heart just opened up right there," he remembers. "Here was this little girl teaching me a very powerful lesson about giving something without expecting anything in return. I wished I had something to give her. This five year old was teaching me a lesson to keep your heart open and give, because in the act of giving there is so much fulfillment."

That's when Les remembered the glass prism. He and his ex-wife had acquired it in Harper's Ferry, West Virginia, and used to enjoy watching the light beams refract through the glass into rainbows on the wall. "I didn't have much left after the divorce that reminded me of her," Les remembers. "The prism was a symbol of our relationship. I kept it in a drawer, but that's not where it belonged. What five-year-old doesn't like rainbows? And what was I going to do with it? No one else would appreciate it the way a child would. I wanted to give that little girl something that meant as much to me as those drawings meant to her."

Les knew life through the act of giving, and his independent spirit, intellectual curiosity, and deep need to challenge himself personally continued to forge a trail that led off the beaten path and into a number of emerging industries. He found his next big opportunity at the National Academy of Public Administration, working on managing the transition of the Global Positioning System into the commercial and international markets. Once again, he was on the cutting edge of technology and leading the way from behind. "We were basically defining an industry that didn't yet exist," he affirms. "Being a part of something bigger than myself was really important to me, and working in pioneering fields gave me the opportunity to do that."

Eventually Les wanted to do something different, and that's when he crossed paths with Vistage. Now, as an executive coach and consultant, he approaches each client's unique situation by asking himself, "What can I contribute to this executive and organization?" "I could never work at something that wasn't purposeful or meaningful to me," he affirms. "To me, working with and being a leader means being connected to your passion."

Motivated by intellectual curiosity and making connections with people drives Les in both his personal and professional life. "People wear a lot of different masks and can lose themselves and their passion in the day-to-day grind," he explains. "When my life hit a crisis, I realized I needed to reconnect with myself in order to be able to help other people do the same thing, and I am the coach I am today because I went through that process myself. A person must be truly in tune with who they are and what's happening in their lives, or at least working toward that self-awareness, if they want to be really effective as leaders. I help them achieve that."

The importance of self-awareness struck Les again and most profoundly about 15 years ago when he was sitting in a diner in Tyson's Corner with a Vistage colleague, discussing the challenges he was facing in his work. Les had proposed a solution involving a merger of two groups, but was experiencing considerable resistance to the possibility. Sitting in the booth, his colleague asked him who would benefit from the idea. Les paused and then he heard himself say, "I think that merging is in the best interest of both groups, the parent company, and me, too."

At that moment, he found a voice in himself that he didn't know was there. It wasn't a quick transition, taking nine months of planning and positioning, but he realized the power in the act of declaration. "When you declare what you want, you garner the strength and self-respect to set the direction needed to impart real momentum," he remarks. "You're able to forge ahead and accomplish things you didn't know were possible."

For the last 20 years, these accomplishments form a collective impact that has touched hundreds of businesses, helping to garner several billion dollars in revenue and transforming the lives of almost 20,000 employees. A natural bridge builder, he uses his ability to connect the dots to jump into any industry and spin success out of sink-or-swim situations. Yet this legacy of professional success is built, more than anything, on the strong fiber of his character and the ideals affirmed through both hard times and good. "Every experience is a gift," he affirms.

In advising young people entering the working

world today, Les reminds us that when we give of ourselves, we get so much more in return, and we never know how our actions will affect another. "Everyone is living a story that is at once deeply personal and deeply universal," he says. "The true successes, the true turning points in life, the true masterpieces, come when those stories intersect in brilliant bursts of giving and learning, and that's what I strive to achieve in my work each day."

Hildegarde M. Sylla

To Challenge and Be Challenged

The day Hildegarde Sylla's brother told her she could choose one of his oil paintings to keep, she wasted no time and immediately claimed the large canvas with the beautiful rendering of a country minister. "But it's not finished yet!" her brother laughed. Hilda, however knew that it was painting she wanted, and she wasn't going to leave without it, even though the minister's hands were not quite finished and her brother hadn't even had time to write *Holy Bible* on the spine of the book he held.

Though her brother has since passed, the painting hangs in her home, a profound symbol not of any one concrete thing, but rather of Hilda's character and values. The product of her brother's self-taught talent, it is a piece wrought from will, determination, and self-sufficiency. It speaks of a close-knit family, a respect for morality, and a clear sense of knowing exactly what one wants in life and pursuing it without distraction. And above all, the piece is elegant in its incompleteness—a reminder that no matter how much one accomplishes in life, there is still more that can be done.

Hilda has always wanted to do more, rising to the next challenge as she challenges society to both expect more and deliver more. Like many D.C. natives, she did her time working for the Federal government. For 16 years, she rose along the GS ranks—first in the Department of Transportation, and later in various parts of the Department of Agriculture—all the while observing frustrating inefficiencies. Those inefficiencies arose, in large part, from structural problems and a widespread aversion to change. "I was encouraged to attend trainings and conferences, but when I attempted to bring what I learned back to the office, no one was interested," she recalls. "They wanted to continue doing things the way they had always been done."

This status-quo approach didn't sit well with Hilda. Her entire career was built on constant self-evolution, seeking new challenges rather than simply collecting a paycheck. Determined to make the most of her talents and interests, she can now say what few can: when she decided what she might like to do, she went out and did it. When she decided it was time to move on, she did so quickly, wisely, and with her eye on the next bend in the road. Secure though she was after nearly two decades in government, Hilda knew she could do more at a company that matched her spirit: self-sufficient, streamlined, ambitious, and adaptive. It was this spirit that, in 1994, drove Hilda and her husband Abe to launch AIS Engineering, Inc., the company they would build themselves from the ground up.

AIS Engineering (AIS) is a global provider of telecommunications, satellite communications, and information technology. Working primarily with the Department of Defense and large commercial communications firm, it boasts remarkable accomplishments despite its small size. Today the business employs 28 people at offices in Silver Spring, Maryland, and Melbourne, Florida. "I think we provide superior service at low costs," she remarks. "There are a lot of large businesses doing what we do, but we've streamlined our processes and have top-notch, carefully selected employees who truly excel in the satellite and IT arenas. We can move faster, and we're not bureaucratic. We know what we're doing, and we give the government a big bang for their buck, which is a win for taxpayers."

To preserve the company's nimble efficiency, Hilda has no immediate plans to grow the business significantly larger and instead relies on hard working employees, efficient structure, and careful budgeting to keep her projects rolling. "Both at home and in the work place, it's important to live within one's means," she stresses. "Poor financial decisions affect everyone. At AIS, employees are carefully chosen and are the best at what they do so that we can truly make the most of what we have. I learned from my parents growing up that success is based in large part on the company you keep, and we keep visionary, enthusiastic, success-oriented company with our employees."

Hilda is also adamant that layoffs are not an option at AIS because of the ripple effect they have on employees, families, and communities. This attitude and commitment to the company's employees, clients, and overall quality has kept her business growing slowly, steadily, and smartly for almost 20 years.

Hilda's decision to go into telecommunications rested on two main factors. Having worked closely with other contractors to gain familiarity with the types of technology that were just beginning to catch on, she could see that telecommunications would gain incredible traction in the coming years. In the early 1990s, engineering was revolutionizing business practices, and Hilda knew expertise in the field would be in high demand. Beyond this motivation, her husband, Abe, had an engineering and telecommunications background, working for GE and then Voice of America. He had been offering his services as a consultant, and Hilda was unhappy with the irregular pay, long hours, and travel. "He was on a trip, and I decided to start the business," she laughs. "I set everything up, so that when he came back, we had a company!"

From their home office in Maryland, Hilda and Abe received their first contract from Marathon Oil, who hired them to handle their new communications systems. Soon after, Hilda took a buyout from her government job, and AIS landed the State Department contract that has gone down in the books as their big break. "They needed to have better communications capabilities with different embassies all over the world," she recalls. "Their calls were all routed through the U.S. embassy, and the embassies didn't have direct communication with each other."

After that first contract, the company's positive past performance reports enabled them to bid on, and win, similar jobs. It was also able to move into its first office, in Silver Spring, Maryland. Soon after, they received a major 7-year contract with the Department of Defense at Patrick Air Force Base—a win that really put AIS on the map. Today, AIS partners with many of the major telecommunication companies on projects under various task orders and GSA Schedules. Along with their partners, AIS handles global telecommunication and IT projects. Abe, the Senior Executive Vice President, handles the technical side of the operation, while Hilda continues to serve as the major strategist and is more hands-on with the business's paperwork, staffing, and structure.

Although geographically close to her childhood home in Washington, D.C., Hilda's success as an executive is a million miles away from anything she imagined while living there. Growing up as the youngest of five children, she learned firsthand how to stretch a dollar from her frugal, responsible parents. Her mother was a homemaker and part-time domestic worker, and her father worked at the Navy Yard. "Both of my parents always worked," she remembers. "They didn't believe in any kind of credit, so if we couldn't pay cash for something, we weren't getting it. They believed strongly in saving and did very well for the income they had."

Her parents' advice carried over into Hilda's adult life, where her cautious financial planning has served her well in the business world. And during childhood, when her future career as an executive wasn't even on her radar yet, her parents' emphasis on self-sufficiency and education spurred Hilda to seek out part-time jobs from a young age. They stressed the importance of college, and Hilda was eager to contribute to what she knew would be a difficult expense. Her first job, working at a small costume jewelry shop on 14th Street, was also her first introduction to inefficiencies in the professional world. The store was understaffed, rife with shoplifters, and poorly managed. The following summer, she landed her first office job, doing clerical work at the United States Information Agency, compelling her to save money for college and begin considering her future career.

Hilda at first wanted to focus on music, but her practical parents asked, "What will you do with it?" She opened herself to the idea of something more stable, and the attentions of a tough teacher soon piqued an interest in English. In the beginning, Hilda found the class too difficult and asked to be transferred, but the teacher wouldn't hear of it. "She told my mother that they wouldn't have placed me in the class if I didn't belong there," she remembers. "She told me to come back and work with her after class."

Hilda took on the challenge and studied harder, and today, she's grateful the teacher never gave her a break or lowered her expectations. Her hard-won success in the English course stayed with her, factoring strongly into her decision to major in English in college. After her freshman year at Saint Paul's College in Virginia, Hilda transferred to the District of Columbia Teacher's College—an attempt to save tuition costs by living at home—and earned a double major, a Bachelor of Science in English and Secondary Education, as planned. While at D.C. Teachers, she worked part-time during the academic year and then began working full time for the government in the summers. She became focused on teaching as a potential career path, and immediately moved on to a two-year master's program at Howard University the semester after completing her bachelor's degree.

For the next two years, Hilda continued to work and study. As she earned her master's degree, she thought about teaching on the college level, but that would require a doctorate. She had had enough of sitting in classrooms for a while, so when she earned her degree, she accepted a position as an English teacher at Roosevelt High School in northwest D.C.. "The experience was very rewarding and instructive," she remembers. "I bonded with my students and was able to tailor subjects like Shakespeare and current events to their academic level, personalizing the subject matter so they could relate to typically unappealing subjects. I will always look back at that time in my life as a period where I was both a teacher and a student, because the students taught me as well." Then, after two years, Hilda began to look for a new challenge. Her many summers of experience working with the government made it easy for her to find work in the Department of Transportation, and in 1978, she began a long tenure of federal employment.

Over the following years, Hilda held a variety of positions, learning much along the way. "I started out in human resources management," she recalls. "I had to analyze jobs, write, interview people, manage programs, and put together organizational charts. It was a behind-the-scenes thing." Hilda built these crucial skills working for the National Highway and Traffic Safety Administration, a regulatory agency responsible for testing cars and tires for safety and issuing highway safety regulations. As an HR Manager, she acquired a good sense of the government's inner workings while also developing her own analytical skills and mastering the art of translating them to paper. She then went on to the Department of Naval Warfare.

After several years of strategic job changes within the government, collecting skills and information that she'd use for years to come, Hilda once again decided it might be time for a new challenge and enrolled in law school. But a year and a half into her studies at Catholic University School of Law, tragedy struck. Hilda's mother passed away, and the ensuing chaos and emotional trauma left her unable to complete her degree. "I wanted to go back and finish, but I just didn't have it in me," she says. Instead, she was offered a position in the Department of Agriculture and returned to the government.

Once again, Hilda found herself working in personnel, but she was determined to find something more fulfilling—and determined not to let her law experience go to waste. She asked questions around the department and did her research, and before long, she found what she'd been looking for. "They had a Civil Rights Division with an Equal Employment Opportunity section, and I knew that was what I wanted to do," she remembers. "I took Equal Opportunity Law for a semester at Antioch Law School nearby, and then someone transferred out of the Civil Rights Division, so I got in there and immediately developed the skills of writing employment decisions and adjudicating discrimination complaints." After so many years of looking, she'd found something close to her ideal job. Over time, however, the inefficiencies of government began to weigh on her mind. By the end of the 1980s, the idea of owning her own business was a seed waiting to germinate, and Hilda was ready to be challenged again.

When the time came to make that decision, she willingly took the reins, and today, she and Abe couldn't be happier with that decision—or the business that sprung from it. Of course, the lifestyle is not without its challenges. "I wish I'd known how easily it becomes a part of you," Hilda reflects. "I have some other things I'd like to do recreationally, but running the company is all-consuming. It's almost like a child—you just want to do all you can to make it better and grow. But ultimately, these challenges are what make it the rewarding, fulfilling profession I've always been looking for."

In advising young people entering the working world today, Hilda encourages others to value their own fulfillment above all else. "I would tell them not to guide their success by how much money they're making," she says. "Do some research. Look at what the Peace Corps and similar internationally focused organizations do and see if it's something you'd like to do to give back. Or maybe you'd rather do something on your own. Don't guide your young life by how much money you're making."

Giving back is also a priority for Hilda herself, who four years ago launched a foundation and built a school in Guinea, in West Africa. Today the foundation is working to build an additional wing for older children, and she's asked her engineers to devise a solar solution for the lack of electricity in the village. "I want to continue doing that," she affirms. "I didn't want to teach school, but it's important to me to further the cause of education." Years ago as a teacher, Hilda found meaningful contribution difficult within the rigid structure of a suffering educational system, but today she's found a better way to share her talents while challenging the world to improve, just as she does each day with AIS. Her career demonstrates that rejecting systemic inefficiencies and embracing challenge will always lead to something better—even if you have to build it yourself.

BERNHARDT
WEALTH MANAGEMENT

Trenor Williams

Betting On Yourself

By the time Trenor Williams graduated from high school, he knew he wanted to be a doctor. Having watched his entrepreneurial father do well but then suddenly lose the family's home and cars in the wake of a bad real estate market when Trenor was 13, he had resolved not to touch entrepreneurship with a ten foot pole. "I wanted stability and a steady paycheck," he remembers. "I had a natural affinity for the sciences, and thanks to my mother's influence, I liked the idea of being able to give back to the community as a physician."

One can only run from one's genetic makeup for so long, however. An animated extrovert with high risk tolerance and a natural ability to capitalize on ideas of real value, Trenor couldn't snuff his own entrepreneurial spirit, which went from a quiet inkling to a steady flame, and from a steady flame to the calling that has come to define his professional legacy. "Stability is certainly important, but as I grew up, I came to learn that I was willing to bet on myself," he says. "And it wasn't only that I was willing to do it—I *needed* to do it." Now the cofounder and CEO of Clinovations, LLC, a consulting company providing game-changing clinical and operational expertise in the healthcare sector, Trenor's willingness to bet on himself and win has repeatedly surprised people over the years. "Though I've made some untraditional moves along the way, my family has had an unwavering belief in me," he affirms. "Still, I don't think any of us expected what we've achieved today."

Most of the work Clinovations does centers around care delivery health systems, including both inpatient and ambulatory outpatient services. As technology has become such a huge component of how care is delivered, patients are managed, and information is shared, the company has also built out its IT expertise. "Essentially, our model bundles highly experienced management and operational consultants together with clinical acumen and expertise, creating a dyad that lends unbelievable value to our clients," Trenor affirms. "We bring a nuanced understanding of the clinical, operational, technical, and financial impacts of the decisions our clients face, which allows us to be real change agents for these organizations and health systems around the country."

Trenor had extensive experience in the commercial business environment and co-founded the Clinovations Collaborative in 2007. He enlisted a team of clinical leaders from around the Baltimore Washington area to gather for dinners, breakfasts, meetings, and other events. And in the fall of 2008, Clinovations LLC was founded as a clinically-focused strategic consulting firm.

By September of 2009, Trenor had set enough groundwork to hire a 23-year-old part-time analyst. By January of 2010, he hired their first full-time employee. When October rolled around, that number had jumped to six, and the growth continued at a steady pace so that, today, Clinovations employs a team of around 300 full-time employees and contractors. One hundred forty of those are physicians engaged in full or part-time work in clinical settings, highlighting the strong physician focus and influence that makes Clinovations so unique in the consulting sphere.

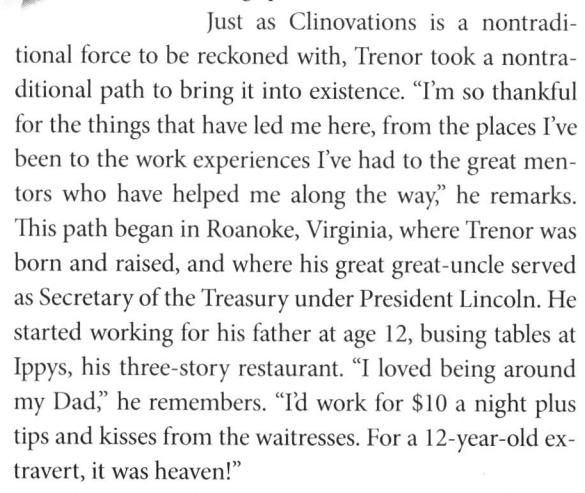

Just as Clinovations is a nontraditional force to be reckoned with, Trenor took a nontraditional path to bring it into existence. "I'm so thankful for the things that have led me here, from the places I've been to the work experiences I've had to the great mentors who have helped me along the way," he remarks. This path began in Roanoke, Virginia, where Trenor was born and raised, and where his great great-uncle served as Secretary of the Treasury under President Lincoln. He started working for his father at age 12, busing tables at Ippys, his three-story restaurant. "I loved being around my Dad," he remembers. "I'd work for $10 a night plus tips and kisses from the waitresses. For a 12-year-old extravert, it was heaven!"

Trenor saved up his earnings, and when he had earned enough money, he made his first big purchase—sending his father to a hypnotist to help him quit smoking. "The treatment proved successful—though his conviction may have had more to do with my dedication to the cause than with the actual hypnotism," Trenor laughs. The following year, at age 13, he had earned enough money to send himself to Duke basketball camp. Between soccer, basketball, baseball, and volleyball, he was always playing at least one sport each season, developing a resilient and determined work ethic in the process.

While his father instilled in him a drive toward risk and reward and a penchant for incredible generosity, his mother was the rock of the family. With a Masters of Social Work, she spent time employed with United Way and is now the Director for Southwestern Virginia for the League of Older Americans. "From a work ethic and stability standpoint, my mom is the yin to my Dad's yang," says Trenor. "I am very much their child and have the utmost respect for what they taught me—perhaps the most important of which is how easy it is to tell someone you love them. That openness and love is the foundation of my family today, and it manifests as transparency and an enthusiastic open-door policy in our company."

Though he participated in student government and clubs and was a member of the Young Entrepreneur Council in high school, Trenor didn't have much formal leadership experience until college. After graduating in the top 15 of his class, he first enrolled at the University of Virginia, where he became the manager for the women's soccer team. He then transferred to Virginia Tech after three semesters, taking a semester off in between to launch and coach the girls soccer team at his old high school. That paved the way for an invitation by Virginia Tech to coach their women's intramural team, which played a full varsity schedule and beat a number of prominent D1 teams. Virginia all-state players who could have earned scholarships for other schools instead opted for Trenor's team at Tech, and thanks to his leadership, the team went D1 the year after he graduated.

In college, Trenor would bartend to earn money and focus on mastering his premed courses, already feeling an affinity for family medicine due to the diversity it afforded and the stable career it would engender. Upon graduating, he opted to attend the Joan C. Edwards School of Medicine at Marshall University in Huntington, West Virginia. With only 47 classmates, it was the second smallest medical school in the country at the time, and Trenor focused on delivering care for West Virginians. He also got involved with Planet Hope, an LA-based charity delivering healthcare for homeless women and children that led him to spend summers on the West Coast, providing immunizations and physicals for families from nine different shelters.

Most medical students go straight from med school to residency, but Trenor felt driven to do something a bit different, and as always, he was willing to bet on himself.

With that, he took a year off, which began with him sleeping on the couch of a good friend in Richmond while waiting tables and saving up money. Another friend was coaching a club soccer team at the time, and once Trenor had saved enough, they took the team over to Europe and spent several weeks touring Germany, Amsterdam, and Denmark. Trenor then spent six more weeks traveling through 13 European countries before coming back to the U.S. with a more concrete vision for what he wanted out of medicine.

Knowing he wanted to do his residency in Los Angeles but would need to build up his Spanish language abilities, he then saved up enough money to spend two months in Guatemala, where he did a four-week immersion class for eight hours a day, volunteered at a Catholic hospital, and spent some time exploring the rest of Central America. "My poor mother thought I was crazy for taking that year off, but I was confident I'd get into a great residency program regardless," he affirms. "Taking the time to go out and have those experiences allowed me to really solidify the story of why that exposure would make me a better physician, especially in family medicine. I focused on expanding myself as a person so I could better understand other cultures and backgrounds." True to his vision, Trenor landed a Kaiser Permanente residency in LA and made the move shortly after returning to the U.S.

During his three years in residency, he took up a side project with some friends from college who had left Napster, a music sharing company, to launch a music technology business. They needed a contact in LA to work the music industry there, so they equipped Trenor with talking points and sent him into meetings to do business development. Later, he got involved with a project to launch a healthcare dotcom, which inspired him to start one of his own. "The idea was to provide an informative resource supporting medical students and residents, building brand loyalty so that, when their salary quadrupled upon graduating, they would utilize the platform to make bigger purchases," he explains. "At that time, I was a second- and third-year resident, moonlighting and stretched thin as the dotcom bubble was bursting, so it didn't work out, but it was a great learning experience."

Indeed, it was clear that Trenor felt pulled toward a world beyond medicine, but it wasn't until one fateful day in 2001 that the contour of this world began to take shape. His dotcom work had fueled an interest in the burgeoning field of healthcare informatics, so in his third year of residency, he decided to look up healthcare IT conferences going on in the area. The Gartner Group, an analyst company, was holding one in San Diego the following week, but the attendance fee was $1,700—far too steep for a penniless resident. Undeterred, however, Trenor drove down on the day of the conference, donned a shirt and tie, and walked in. "I told them I was a family practice resident and would love to get on the show floor," Trenor recalls. "They let me in for $150, and I walked through the doors and into my future."

As Trenor took in the universe of health IT and got a feel for its terrain, a young woman named Sara came up to him. She worked for the Vice President Trenor had haggled with to gain entry to the conference, and said, "I don't know who you are, but that kind of thing doesn't happen!" The chemistry between the two was instantaneous, such that when she accompanied him to dinner five hours later and slid comfortably into the restaurant booth with him, the married couple across the table from them asked how long they had known each other. The pair dated long distance for two years and have now been married for almost a decade. "Sara has been unbelievably critical to the success of my company and the success of my family," he avows today. "She is a perfect partner for me in every way, and has been more supportive than I ever thought possible. She has astounding emotional intelligence, and we work incredibly well together."

As his Family Medicine residency concluded in the summer of 2001, Trenor decided to use his medical education as a vehicle to explore the U.S. Through a Locum Tenens staffing agency he did some traveling medicine work for the Sioux in South Dakota and the Navajo in New Mexico. He then received a call for a medical director position at a ski resort at Mammoth Lakes, high up in the Sierra Nevada Mountains of Northern California. There, Trenor managed an ambulatory family practice of three doctors and two nurse practitioners, responsible for both outpatient and inpatient services.

Then, in January of 2003, Trenor bet on himself again, enacting a pivotal life transition by deciding to leave not only Mammoth Lakes, but active practice all together. He returned to Northern Virginia to wait tables and plan his next move, which involved attending a San Diego conference of the Healthcare Information and Management Systems Society in March of 2003. As luck would have it, he passed a table for a consulting firm called HealthLink, where he recognized a man playing guitar as the guy who used to lead Gartner Group's healthcare IT conference. The two had met back at the conference in 2001, and though Trenor interviewed with five places that day which all offered him jobs, he ultimately decided to enter the world of consulting via HealthLink. "I had no experience in consulting, but they took a chance on me, which was powerful," he remembers. "It was an opportunity to start brand new, and that was very defining."

Poised at the intersection of consulting and medicine, Trenor gained a nuanced understanding of the personality characteristics that make physicians good consultants. It takes natural humility and the kind of 360-degree perspective that has become rare in today's siloed medical scene. It's about mentality over specialty. It's about emotional intelligence as much as it's about specialized training and core skills in specialized technology. It's about acute problem solving, facilitating meetings, and working with executives and broad community stakeholders alike to achieve a healthcare goal. "Being a good consultant is about helping clients see all the solutions," he affirms. "It's about painting the entire picture."

After HealthLink, Trenor worked as a consultant for Deloitte for several years and refined his perspective on physician development. "What we're trying to do now is develop a curriculum and support structure that helps our physicians and consultants develop skills on an ongoing basis, creating an institution of learning and knowledge," Trenor affirms.

In advising young people entering the working world today, Trenor, who was named by *Modern Healthcare* as one of the top 100 most influential people in healthcare, stresses the importance of remaining open to opportunities. "I'm living proof that, as long as you're delivering and working hard and learning, veering off the traditional path will create even more opportunities for you," he says. "The path to success doesn't have to be linear. I believe the people who are open to broader opportunities can reach even greater heights, so don't limit yourself to preconceived notions of what you think you should do."

Today, Clinovations works with some of the top pharmaceutical companies in the world, as well as with the Department of Defense and the VA, as they develop cutting edge informatics plans. They work with payers and provide clinical services around Accountable Care Organizations, and with big technology companies who have the tools and solutions but need that extra push to deliver their strategies effectively in a health system. Thanks to this success, which all ties back to the company's core strength of care delivery, *Washington Business Journal* named Clinovations one of the fastest growing companies in the D.C. area, and Inc. 500 put them at number 175. "To me, these recognitions are a testament to what we've built and what our people deliver every day," says Trenor. "To be effective in the future with the expansion of healthcare, you have to get out of your comfort zone in terms of who you partner with and what you do, and I think our company has really excelled at that."

Effectiveness in this arena also entails thinking outside the box, and even outside the business—something

Trenor, Sara, and the Clinovations team do through their philanthropic support of organizations like D.C. Greens and Share Our Strength, which expand access to fresh food, food education, and school meals. "We make the effort to give back through our intellectual capital as well as through fiscal support to create scalable solutions across the country," he explains. "It's just another way to bet on ourselves and our ability to effect far-reaching change in the future, and that's what drives us." Indeed, by betting on himself and always walking confidently along the path he felt was right, Trenor has magnified his impact a hundred fold, changing the way care is delivered in America and changing lives now just as his legacy promises to do years into the future.

Pvt. Jonathan Lee Gifford was the first U.S. soldier killed in Iraq. He was killed just two days into the war on March 23, 2003. Spc. David Emanuel Hickman was killed by a roadside bomb in Iraq on November 14, 2011. The Washington Post on December 17, 2011, said Hickman "may have been the last" U.S. soldier killed in Iraq. After reading an article about Gifford and Hickman my sister, Gloria, was inspired to write the following poem.

From Gifford to Hickman

By Gloria J. Bernhardt

From Gifford to Hickman…and all those in between,
You fought bravely amid chaos and dangers unforeseen.
Twenty-one guns have sounded, the rider less horse walks on.
Fond memories are remaining. A nation's child is gone.

Sons and daughters; fathers, mothers -- broken hearts intertwined.
Hugs and kisses; their successes – major milestones left behind.
Your selfless gift -- a life laid down; for fellow soldier, family, land.
Duty called -- call was answered -- no greater love hath man.

"I'm getting taller. I lost a tooth. I got 100 on my test!
Miss your pancakes and your tickles, goodnight kisses were the best.
Who will answer all my questions now? I've important stuff to learn!
You said you had a big surprise on the day that you'd return."

"I talk to you at bedtime -- after lights go out at night.
I told Jesus that I miss you…sure wish you could hug me tight.
When Grandpa says I look like you, Grandma starts to cry.
I'm mad that you're not coming home…I need to say goodbye!"

From Gifford, to Hickman, through every soldier who has served,
Liberty's fruits are savored and freedom is preserved.
We live freely due to soldiers, willing to support and defend
Our Constitution, our country -- against enemies 'til the end.

Sons and daughters; fathers, mothers -- broken hearts intertwined.
Hugs and kisses; their successes – major milestones left behind.
Your selfless gift -- a life laid down; for fellow soldier, family, land.
Duty called -- call was answered -- no greater love hath man.

"I had a dream the night before…you smiled and walked on by.
When I awoke, I thought it odd…it seemed like a 'good-bye'.
I couldn't put my finger on the dark cloud that remained,
When the phone began to ring…I knew my life had changed."

"I questioned God, 'Why MY child? Why do I have to lose?'
I imagined His response would be 'If not your child, then whose?'

Your bright life flashed too briefly… seems He only takes the best.
I'm thankful for the time I had. For that I'm truly blessed."

From Gifford to Hickman and every warrior who has passed,
The price you've paid bought freedom, but will we make it last?
Your last breath drawn for citizens in this country and abroad
Are we worthy of such gifts is known only but to God.

Sons and daughters; fathers, mothers -- broken hearts intertwined.
Hugs and kisses; their successes – major milestones left behind.
Your selfless gift -- a life laid down; for fellow soldier, family, land.
Duty called -- call was answered -- no greater love hath man.

"My world stopped spinning…I couldn't breathe! Lord, how can I go on?
My days are all one midnight…but they say it's darkest 'fore the dawn.
I can hear you say, 'I'm proud of you! I know that this is hard.'
What do I do without you here? What dreams do I discard?"

"I miss your laugh. I miss your smell. I even miss our fights.
No more messes. No embraces. It's more 'real' late at night.
I saw you in a crowd today; but you vanished in the throng.
Wishful thinking changes nothing! I know my "rock" is gone."

FOR Gifford, FOR Hickman…FOR all the fallen in between,
You've trudged through shadowed valley and joined heroes' ranks unseen.
Upon freedom's altar, we sacrificed our daughters and our sons.
Empty boots stand at attention. The flag is folded. Your mission's done.

© 2015 Gloria J. Bernhardt. All Rights Reserved.
Reprinted by permission.